David Rudes

Paul M. Barrett, for eighteen years a reporter and editor at *The Wall Street Journal,* where this book originated, currently directs the investigative reporting team at *BusinessWeek.* He is the author of *The Good Black: A True Story of Race in America* (1999).

Additional Praise for *American Islam*

"[*American Islam*] fills a real need and does so remarkably well. . . . It delivers a set of powerful insights about Muslim life in the United States and the tensions that are shaping the community. . . . Paul M. Barrett's carefully crafted approach is a smart one."

—*Slate.com*

"Throws much light on the murky mysteries of the Middle East as they are revealed right here in America. . . . This is a book every American should read."

—*Contra Costa Times*

"Eye-opening, penetrating, and unfailingly honest, *American Islam* brings us deep into the lives of influential doers and thinkers across the spectrum of Muslim diversity. Paul Barrett's intelligence and keen eye for detail make the book a pleasure to read; his admirable balance in writing about controversial figures makes it a major contribution to the continuing debate about the future of Islam in the United Sates."

—Noah Feldman, author of *After Jihad* and *Divided by God*

"Offer[s] valuable insights into the Muslim-American experience."

—*The Christian Science Monitor*

"What sets apart this new work from Barrett is that he provides portraits of individual Muslims living in the United States. By focusing on the personal experiences of these individuals, Barrett is able to offer a distinctive view of Islam in America."

—*Library Journal*

"Balanced and insightful, this grassroots journalistic account mines the complexity and depth of American Islam."

—*Publishers Weekly* (starred review)

"Engaging and clearly written, *American Islam* offers a valuable snapshot of the dynamism and controversies that characterize Muslim communities in the United States today."

—*America*

AMERICAN

islam

The Struggle for the Soul
of a Religion

PAUL M. BARRETT

PICADOR

FARRAR, STRAUS AND GIROUX

NEW YORK

for Julie

www.picadorusa.com

Picador® is a U.S. registered trademark and is used by Farrar, Straus and Giroux under license from Pan Books Limited.

For information on Picador Reading Group Guides, please contact Picador. E-mail: readinggroupguides@picadorusa.com

Some of the material in this book first appeared in slightly different form in *The Wall Street Journal.*

Grateful acknowledgment is made for permission to print excerpts from the following material: "What Became of Tolerance in Islam?" by Khaled Abou El Fadl, reprinted by permission of the author; "Among the Midianites" and "Khadija Gets Her Groove Back," unpublished poems from the manuscript *The Hagar Poems* by Mohja Kahf, reprinted by permission of the author.

Designed by Cassandra J. Pappas

Library of Congress Cataloging-in-Publication Data
Barrett, Paul (Paul M.)
    American Islam : the struggle for the soul of a religion / Paul M. Barrett.
        p.   cm.
    Includes bibliographical references and index.
    ISBN-13: 978-0-312-42745-0
    ISBN-10: 0-312-42745-X
     1. Muslims—United States.   2. Islam—United States.   3. Muslims—United States—
Social conditions.   4. Muslim families—United States.   5. United States—Ethnic
relations.   I. Title.
BP67.U6 B37 2006
297.0973'090511—dc22

                                                                              2006011404

First published in the United States by Farrar, Straus and Giroux

First Picador Edition: January 2008

10 9 8 7 6 5 4 3 2 1

Contents

AMERICAN

islam

Muslims in America

A visitor to the home of Mustafa and Sadaf Saied is promptly recruited by daughters Zaineb, seven, Sameeha, six, and Mariam, four, to read and discuss a colorful Disney book about the Little Mermaid. Enthusiasm and volume levels are high. The children, who attend public school in their hometown of Hialeah, Florida, wear jazzy American clothes. Asked for a favorite television program, they extol *Blue's Clues*, an educational show starring a puzzle-solving puppy.

Sadaf, the girls' mother, is in the kitchen preparing an aromatic feast of broiled salmon and chicken curry. She wears the Islamic *hijab*, or female head covering, and a concealing ankle-length turquoise wrap. Her husband, Mustafa, relaxes in the living room in denim jeans and a University of Tennessee football jersey. He explains cheerfully how his knowledge of college and professional sports helps break the ice with potential customers of the family company, All State Engineering & Testing. Mustafa's parents, visiting from India, keep an eye on Layla, the youngest Saied, born only a few months earlier.

Mustafa and Sadaf, who are in their early thirties, seem at ease as Americans, without having cut themselves off from their Muslim faith.

He came to the United States from India in 1990 to attend college and then decided to stay. She is the American-born child of prosperous Pakistani immigrants who settled in South Florida decades ago. The couple has decorated their living room wall with a large, framed rendition of Quranic verse in ornate Arabic calligraphy. Sadaf prays five times a day; her husband, less often. He takes the children trick-or-treating on Halloween, and they join school friends in celebrating Christmas. On Sundays the girls attend Islamic religious classes, but Mustafa has declared that the minute he hears anything about "infidels," he will keep them home. "I will stop it, cold turkey," he says. "I just want them to have a normal American life."

What, for Muslims, is a normal American life? That's a question many Muslims in this country are seeking to answer. Given the times, it's something that all thoughtful Americans ought to ponder. I had the question in mind when I set out after the attacks of September 11, 2001, to learn about Muslim life in the United States. My interviews took me from university campuses to maximum-security prisons, from elite corporate offices in midtown Manhattan to the fruit groves of Northern California. I spoke with hundreds of Muslims from a wide range of backgrounds about their startlingly varied American journeys. Much of the time I sat and listened as Muslims talked and debated with one another. I tagged along when they went to the neighbors' for dinner and to the mosque for Friday prayers. Just being there is often the best way to get your arms around someone's story. Some of the stories I gathered make up the chapters that follow.

Even after 9/11, assimilation remains a major theme in the lives of most American Muslims. Surveys show that most are middle class and that they graduate from college at roughly the same rate as other Americans. Increasingly they are involved in local and national politics. Given a chance to explain why they have come here, immigrant Muslims usually stress economic and educational opportunity, but also the constitutional protection of free speech and religion, ideals not upheld in most predominantly Muslim lands. In many ways, Muslims are an American immigration success story.

But there are subthemes to this story that are less reassuring. As a student at the University of Tennessee in the 1990s Mustafa Saied was drawn into a radical Islamic group that endorses suicide bombing and preaches hatred of non-Muslims, especially Jews. For a time he reveled in this extremism. By his own account, Saied's recruitment by the Muslim Brotherhood—in Knoxville, Tennessee, of all places—offers an illustration of the tension and flux within American Islam. Muslims in the United States represent an intricate mixture of creeds and cultures: immigrant and native-born, devout and secular, moderate and radical, integrated and isolated. Even as many American Muslims thrive in material terms, pockets of fanaticism fester.

Saied's excursion to the ideological fringe and then back again, to which I'll return, offers one illustration of the unease and conflict that mingle with the sunnier aspects of American Islam. The life and career of Osama Siblani, a Lebanese-immigrant publisher of a bilingual English-Arabic newspaper in Dearborn, Michigan, provide a different but equally instructive perspective. Siblani belongs to the heavily assimilated elite in Dearborn, the unofficial capital of Arab America. He lives in a comfortable home and drives a large black Mercedes. A courtly, registered Republican, he helped organize Arab-American support for George W. Bush in 2000. But the president's "war on terrorism" left Siblani feeling that his adopted country has turned against Muslims. He passionately opposed the invasion of Iraq and has even expressed sympathy for some home-grown Iraqi elements of the anti-American insurgency.

Large majorities of American Muslims, both Republicans and Democrats, disagree strongly with American policies in the Middle East, especially U.S. support for Israel. The conflicts in Afghanistan and Iraq have exacerbated this estrangement. But the domestic fallout from 9/11, beginning with the arrest and detention of twelve hundred Muslim and Arab men in late 2001 and the subsequent interrogation of eight thousand more, have played an even larger role in making many Muslims feel insecure and unwelcome. Certainly some Americans regard the Muslims in their midst with hostility. A Gallup poll in 2006 found that four in ten Americans admitted feeling prejudice against Muslims. Nearly one quarter said they would not like to have a Muslim as a neighbor. Four in ten would require Muslims to carry special identification cards and undergo more intensive security checks at airports. Among American Muslims, 40 percent told the Zogby International polling firm in 2004 that they had suffered discrimination since 9/11. Many Muslims in the United States have doubts about whether they are accepted as "real" Americans.

The complexity of Islam in the United States only deepens when African-Americans and their painful history are added to the picture. A cleric named Siraj Wahhaj leads a predominantly black mosque in the Bedford-Stuyvesant section of Brooklyn, where he is hailed as an antidrug activist and preacher of personal responsibility. Wahhaj's spiritual migration has taken him from the Baptist Church of his youth, where he was known as Jeffrey Kearse, through the racially separatist Nation of Islam, where he was known as Jeffrey 12X, to an understanding of the religion influenced by Sunni authorities in the Middle East. Today he represents two intertwined components of African-American Islam: a constructive do-for-self philosophy and a conspiratorial antagonism toward government and the white establishment. He has dined as an honored guest at the U.S. State Department and has given talks at some of the country's most prestigious universities. But he refuses to condemn Osama bin Laden for the attacks on Washington and New York. Does Wahhaj embody black Islam's arrival and acceptance in mainstream America or its lingering attachment to radicalism—or, somehow, both?

A few preliminaries: Two-thirds of American Muslims are immigrants; one-third, native born. Most American Muslims are not Arab, and most Americans of Arab descent are Christian, not Muslim. People of South Asian descent—those with roots in Pakistan, India, Bangladesh, and Afghanistan—make up 34 percent of American Muslims, according to the polling organization Zogby International. Arab-Americans constitute only 26 percent, while another 20 percent are native-born American blacks, most of whom are converts. The remaining 20 percent come from Africa, Iran, Turkey, and elsewhere.

Muslims have no equivalent to the Catholic pope and his cardinals. The faith is decentralized in the extreme, and some beliefs and practices vary depending on region and sect. In America, Muslims do not think and act alike any more than Christians do. That said, all observant Muslims acknowledge Islam's "five pillars": faith in one God, prayer, charity, fasting during Ramadan, and pilgrimage to Mecca. Muslims are also united in the way they pray. The basic choreography of crossing arms, bowing, kneeling, and prostrating oneself is more or less the same in mosques everywhere.

The two major subgroups of Muslims, Sunni and Shiite, are found in the United States in roughly their global proportions: 85 percent Sunni, 15 percent Shiite. Ancient history still animates the rivalry, which began in the struggle for Muslim leadership after the Prophet Muhammad's death in 632. Shiites believe that Muhammad intended for only his blood descendants to succeed him. Muhammad's beloved cousin and son-in-law Ali was the only male relative who qualified. Ali's followers became known as Shiites, a derivation of the Arabic phrase for "partisans of Ali." Things did not go smoothly for them.

The larger body of early Muslims, known as Sunnis, a word related to Sunnah, or way of the Prophet, had a more flexible notion of who should succeed Muhammad. In 661, an extremist assassinated Ali near Najaf in what is now Iraq. Nineteen years later Sunnis killed his son, Hussein, not far away in Karbala. These deaths permanently divided the aggrieved Shiite minority from the Sunni majority.

Sunnis historically have afflicted the weaker Shiites, accusing them of shaping a blasphemous cult around Ali and Hussein. At the Karbalaa Islamic Education Center in Dearborn, Michigan, a large mural depicts mourning women who have encountered the riderless horse of Hussein after his final battle. "You see our history and our situation in this," says Imam Husham al-Husainy, a Shiite Iraqi émigré who leads the center. In Dearborn, Shiite Iraqis initially backed the American invasion to depose Saddam Hussein, who persecuted Iraq's Shiite majority. Most Sunnis in Dearborn condemned the war as an exercise in American imperialism.

Sufism, another important strain of Islam, is also present in the United States. Sufis follow a spiritual, inward-looking path. Only a tiny percentage of American Muslims would identify themselves primarily as Sufis, in part because some more rigid Muslims condemn Sufism as heretical. But Sufi ideas crop up among the beliefs of many Muslims without being labeled as such. Sufism's emphasis on self-purification appeals to New Age seekers and has made it the most common avenue into Islam for white American converts such as Abdul Kabir Krambo of Yuba City, California. Krambo, an electrician who grew up in a conservative German Catholic family, helped build a mosque amidst the fruit arbors of the Sacramento Valley, only to see it burn down in a mysterious arson. Once rebuilt, the Islamic Center of Yuba City was engulfed again, this time by controversy over whether Krambo and his Sufi friends were trying to impose a "cult" on other worshipers.

Although there is a broad consensus that Islam is the fastest-growing religion in the country and the world, no one has provable numbers on just how many American Muslims there are. The Census Bureau doesn't count by religion, and private surveys of the Muslim population offer widely disparate conclusions. A study of four hundred mosques nationwide estimated that there are two million people in the United States "associated with" Islamic houses of worship. The authors of the survey, published in 2001 under the auspices of the Council on American-Islamic Relations (CAIR), a Muslim advocacy group, employed a common assumption that only one in three American Muslims associates with a mosque. In CAIR's view, that suggests there are at least six million Muslims in the country. (Perhaps not coincidentally the American Jewish population is estimated to be slightly below six million.) Other Muslim groups put the number higher, seeking to maximize the size and influence of their constituency.

Surveys conducted by non-Muslims have produced much lower estimates. The most recent major study, conducted in 2007 by the Pew Research Center, offered an estimate of 2.35 million. Such findings elicit anger from Muslim activists, who claim that many immigrant and poor black Muslims are overlooked. The Pew Center conceded that for this very reason its total may be low. On the basis of all the evidence, a very crude range of three million to six million seems reasonable. Rapid growth of the Muslim population is expected to continue, fueled mainly by immigration and high birthrates and, to a lesser extent, by conversion, overwhelmingly by African-Americans. In the next decade or two there probably will be more Muslims in the United States than Jews. Worldwide, the Muslim head count is estimated at 1.3 billion, second among religions only to the combined membership of Christian denominations.

American Muslims, like Americans generally, live mostly in cities and suburbs. Large concentrations are found in New York, Detroit, Chicago, and Los Angeles. But they also turn up in the Appalachian foothills and rural Idaho—the sites of two of the stories that follow—among other surprising places. Often the presence of several hundred Muslims in an out-of-the-way town can be explained by proximity to a large state university. Many of these schools have recruited foreign graduate students, including Muslims, since the 1960s. In the 1980s Washington doled out scholarships to Arab students as part of a campaign to counter the influence of the 1979 Iranian Revolution. Some of the Muslim beneficiaries have stayed and raised families.

In New York, Muslims are typecast as cab drivers; in Detroit, as owners of grocery stores and gas stations. The overall economic reality is very different. Surveys show that the majority of American Muslims are employed in technical, white-collar, and professional fields. These include information technology, corporate management, medicine, and education. About a quarter of Muslim adults in the United States have college degrees, roughly the same proportion as in the general public, according to the Pew survey in 2007. Pew found that Muslim families have incomes similar to that of the population as a whole. Among all adults nationwide, 44 percent report household income of fifty thousand dollars or more annually, as do 41 percent of Muslim American adults. Most Muslims own stock or mutual funds, either directly or through retirement plans. Sixty-three percent are registered to vote, compared to 76 percent of the general public.

Middle-class income, a college graduation rate on a par with that of the larger population, an inclination to vote that is impressive for a mostly immigrant group—all of these are indications of a minority population successfully integrating into the larger society. By comparison, immigrant Muslims in countries such as Britain, France, Holland, and Spain have remained poorer, less well educated, and socially marginalized. Western European Muslim populations are much larger in percentage terms. Nearly 10 percent of French residents are Muslim; in the United Kingdom the figure is 3 percent. In the more populous United States the Muslim share may be less than 1 percent or at most 2 percent, depending on which Muslim population estimate one assumes. It's unlikely that American cities will see the sort of densely packed, volatile Muslim slums that have cropped up on the outskirts of Paris, for example.

America's social safety net is stingy compared with those of Western Europe, but there is greater opportunity for new arrivals to get ahead in material terms. This may attract to the United States more ambitious immigrants willing to adjust to the customs of their new home and eager to acquire education that leads to better jobs. More generous welfare benefits in Europe allow Muslims and other immigrants to live indefinitely on the periphery of society, without steady jobs or social interaction with the majority. Europeans, who for decades encouraged Muslim immigration as a source of menial labor, have shown overt hostility toward the outsiders and little inclination to embrace them as full-fledged citizens. Partly as a result, violent Islamic extremism has found fertile ground in Western Europe.

The July 7, 2005, bus and underground train bombings in London, which roughly coincided with the end of my reporting for this book, were in some ways as unsettling as the 9/11 attacks that sparked my research. The London bombers weren't strange non-Westerners raised in insular Islamic lands. They were Muslims born and bred in Britain yet willing to murder their countrymen. This undeniable confirmation of a threat from *within* Islam in the West demands reflection on both sides of the Atlantic.

There are an estimated thirteen hundred mosques in America and several hundred Islamic religious schools. These institutions vary in religious approach and political ideology. But on the whole, Muslim houses of worship tend to be highly conservative compared with the larger culture. Like Orthodox Jews, almost all Muslim congregations separate the sexes during prayer and generally consign women to subordinate roles in communal rituals and social activity. Most observant Muslims view the Quran as the literal word of God, not a work of divine inspiration composed by humans, as most observant Jews and Christians describe their scriptures. Many Muslim preachers dwell on ideals that would be familiar to members of other faiths, such as treating the neighbors as you would have them treat you.

Some Muslim preachers, sad to say, give sermons condemning nonbelievers, but these messages are not that different in their essential theme from those delivered in some fundamentalist Christian churches. Similarly, surveys show that most American Muslims hold disapproving opinions about aspects of American society that parallel the views of conservative Christians. Two-thirds of American Muslims consider the United States "immoral" because of permissive attitudes toward sex outside marriage and toward alcohol, both of which Islam bans. Most Muslims also frown on accommodating homosexuality and permitting abortion. They favor outlawing pornography and allowing public funding for religious schools.

Islamic fundamentalism surged in the Middle East and South Asia in the 1970s, at roughly the same time that Christian fundamentalism became more prevalent in the United States. In Israel the Likud Party rose to power in the 1970s, asserting a biblical mandate to include the West Bank in the Jewish state. A mix of social, political, and economic stimuli caused each of these religious awakenings, but it is worth noting that Islam has not been alone in witnessing a powerful welling up of fundamentalism.

If there is one source of influence that bears special responsibility for exporting the Muslim world's worst ideas to the West, it is our equivocal ally Saudi Arabia. The kingdom that occupies the birthplace of Islam promotes a puritanical version of the religion called Wahhabism, named for Muhammad ibn Abd al-Wahhab, an eighteenth-century evangelist in

Arabia. Wahhab sought to cleanse Islam of corruptions he believed had caused Muslim fortunes to decline. Today an updated version of Wahhabism sometimes goes by other names (the Saudis take offense at the label). But Wahhabi ideas, including hostility to non-Muslims and more moderate Muslims, have persisted and fused with other strains of fundamentalism. One such strain, Salafism, the name of which refers to Muhammad's original righteous companions, seeks to reestablish a dominant Islamic empire based on the pure religion of the Prophet's era. In a misguided attempt to promote their Islamic legitimacy, the Saudi petroleum princes and their charities have financed the propagation of Wahhabi and Salafi radicalism around the world. In the United States, a Saudi-underwritten construction boom has produced scores of mosques and Islamic centers. They can be found in New York, Los Angeles, Washington, Chicago, Houston, Denver, San Francisco, Toledo, Tucson—the list goes on and on. One Saudi charity official based in the United States estimated in October 2001 that fully half the mosques and Islamic schools in the country had received Saudi money. Saudi religious organizations have funded the training of hundreds and maybe thousands of Muslim clerics and teachers sent to America. And Saudi publishers inundate American mosques with books and pamphlets. Inevitably, Wahhabi- and Salafi-influenced fundamentalism* has colored the thinking of some American Muslims. The breadth and degree of this influence are hotly disputed.

What to do about American Muslims who advocate extreme versions of Islam has become an urgent question of law and social policy in the

---

*As the adjective is often applied to Christians, most observant Muslims could be called fundamentalists: they believe the Quran is God's actual word and therefore literally true. When I refer to Islamic fundamentalism, I intend a much narrower meaning. I use the term to mean a strain of belief that includes several core ideas: that the fundamentalists' understanding of Islamic scripture is the only valid reading and that competing interpretations constitute apostasy; that the world is divided into a sanctified realm of Islam and a debauched realm of infidels; that Jews and Christians systematically seek to harm or eradicate Islam; and that Muslims will thrive only in a society modeled in a literal sense on Muhammad's community in Medina. Most observant Muslims in the United States (and elsewhere) *reject* some or all of these rigid views. Movements that I group beneath the banner of fundamentalism—though they have important differences—include Saudi Wahhabism, the much broader Salafism, and the extreme branches of the politicized Muslim Brotherhood. There are other variations, such as the militant Shiite creed of the Iranian mullahs. Islamic fundamentalism, as I define it, does *not* necessarily entail hostile action or violence against non-Muslims or Muslims viewed as apostate. But its ideas are susceptible to being used to justify such hostility and violence.

wake of 9/11. Sami Omar al-Hussayen was a popular graduate student of computer science at the University of Idaho, admired for leading fellow Muslims in mourning the victims of 9/11. But in February 2003 the FBI arrested the Saudi immigrant and charged him with supporting terrorism in connection with his role as webmaster for a Michigan-based group that disseminated extremist views, including murderous anti-Semitism and support for suicide bombing. An Idaho jury had to decide whether al-Hussayen had provided "material support" for terrorism or had been wrongly prosecuted for practicing free speech.

The alarming opinions that al-Hussayen helped spread—especially theological justifications for violence—have divided many American Muslim communities. The CAIR survey reported that 58 percent of American mosques acknowledged some internal conflict over religious issues, with 18 percent admitting that the turmoil was "moderate or very serious." Khaled Abou El Fadl, a reform-minded scholar of the Quran, has sparked as much of this discord as any other American Muslim. The Egyptian-American law professor at UCLA has become a hero to progressive members of his faith—and a reviled traitor in the eyes of many others—by reinterpreting Islamic scripture to justify equality of the sexes, tolerance of other religions, and opposition to religiously inspired bloodshed. Across the country in Morgantown, West Virginia, Asra Nomani has put Abou El Fadl's principles into action. Nomani, who arrived from India as a small child, has riled the mosque her father helped found by demanding the right to pray in the same space as men. The clash in Morgantown ignited similar debates across the country, and as they spread, far more scandalous questions have arisen: Can women ever lead a mixed congregation in prayer? Can an unmarried mother like Nomani, a worldly feminist, find a comfortable place in the religion of her parents and ancestors?

What one sees today in American mosques and Muslim homes, in Islamic centers and on university campuses is nothing less than a struggle for the soul of a religion.

ONE

The Publisher

hen Arabs arrived in Dearborn, Michigan, in the 1920s and 1930s, they encountered a complex cloud of bigotry mingling with the smoke and soot of the Ford auto factory. Henry Ford hated Jews and fretted about their influence. He had unflattering ideas about blacks as well but was willing to hire them as assembly line workers. By doing so, he helped accelerate the migration of southern sharecroppers to the North. This alarmed Dearborn's city fathers, who made it their business to bar blacks from settling within city limits. "They were so busy watching the front door for blacks," says Osama Siblani, a present-day newspaper publisher in Dearborn, "they didn't see the Arabs coming in through the side door."

The Arab migration from poor provinces of the crumbling Ottoman Empire, areas now within the borders of Lebanon and Syria, began in the late nineteenth century. Most of the transplants to the American Midwest were Christian; Muslims didn't become a majority of the continuing Arab influx until the 1980s. Mostly uneducated, the early immigrants worked in factories and sold housewares door to door. By the early 1900s some were marrying American women and bringing over relatives. "Peddlers were becoming store owners, and the Arabs found they could do business here and settle down," says Don Unis, a retired firefighter in Dearborn. His grandfather, a Lebanese tailor, operated a clothing factory in Mexico at the turn of the century before the family headed north toward the American industrial belt.

Some of the earliest accounts of Muslim immigrants gathering for communal prayer in the United States come from unlikely places to which intrepid Arab salesmen hauled suitcases filled with fabric and buttons to sell to farm families. By the 1920s tiny Ross, North Dakota, had about thirty Muslim families originally from Damascus by way of Minnesota. They built one of the country's first mosques, although it later fell into disuse, a victim of assimilation. Mosques also appeared in Cedar Rapids, Iowa, and Michigan City, Indiana.

Henry Ford's legendary five-dollar-a-day wage for autoworkers drew Arab émigrés along with Italians, Germans, and Poles. In the 1920s Ford had moved his main manufacturing operations from Highland Park, Michigan, to a complex on the Rouge River in his native Dearborn, west of Detroit. In contrast with his anti-Semitism, Ford displayed a paternalistic interest in non-Jewish immigrants. His company instructed them in English and personal hygiene. Syrian and Lebanese workers moved into Dearborn's heavily immigrant South End near the Ford plant. In 1938 the founders of the city's first mosque broke ground along gritty Dix Avenue. Today that mosque, expanded over the years, serves a religiously conservative Yemeni congregation, some of whose members assemble pickup trucks at the still-functioning Ford Rouge plant.

For Arabs, more distinctly than other immigrant groups, Dearborn has served as an Ellis Island, their point of entry into American society. More than a third of its hundred thousand residents today are Arab, the heaviest concentration of any place in the country. Most Dearborn Arabs are Muslim, and some neighborhoods there feel closer to Beirut than to Detroit.

Warren Avenue, a wide commercial boulevard, is lined with Lebanese restaurants and butcher shops selling halal meat (the Islamic version of kosher), as well as hardware stores, mobile phone outlets, and pharmacies, all with signs in Arabic. A dozen mosques welcome worshipers on Friday afternoon, the amplified call to prayer sounding from all directions. The public school cafeterias stopped serving pork in 1993, and varsity football heroes have Arab names. Across Michigan Avenue from City Hall, near where the overnight stagecoach from Detroit to Chicago once stopped, is the nation's only Arab-American museum, a modernistic stone and glass structure opened in 2005 and a source of tremendous local pride.

THE OTHER OSAMA

Another leading Dearborn institution is *The Arab American News*, founded in 1984 by Osama Siblani, who had arrived eight years earlier from Lebanon. The bilingual weekly newspaper chronicles life in Baghdad and the West Bank and watches events on Warren Avenue. Buying advertising in its pages are local mosques and Islamic schools, Arab-American car dealers and accountants, government agencies looking for Arabic speakers (including the CIA), and a nightclub featuring belly dancers. Siblani, now in his early fifties, is more than a publisher and editor. He is a driving force behind the local Arab-American political action committee. Because of the growing size and cohesiveness of the Arab-American vote, his backing is sought by county sheriffs, congressional representatives, and even candidates for the White House. He lobbies the school board (successfully) to name buildings after Arabs and leads protest marches against Israel. A Shiite Muslim, he rarely attends mosque but serves as a tenacious watchdog against anti-Muslim bias. His caustic wit surfaces even when the topic is deadly serious, as when he alluded on national television to his suddenly problematic first name. "Not everybody sitting there on their couch in the living room," he told ABC News on September 12, 2001, can "distinguish between Osama bin Laden and Osama Siblani, and that is scaring the hell out of us here."

As a business venture his newspaper has seen some lean times. But Siblani, a bulky man who dresses in grays and black, seems to be doing well enough. Like a number of Dearborn's influential Arab-Americans, he actually lives in a wealthier town farther out from Detroit. His spacious home has white neoclassical pillars in front and a large, well-tended yard in the back. His wife, Raja, serves sweet tea in a living room crowded with heavy, ornate furniture. Next to Osama's formidable Mercedes in the garage is Raja's gold Lexus SUV. She has a teenage son from a prior marriage, but Osama has no biological children, an absence he ascribes to his hectic schedule and one he now regrets.

Siblani speaks English in a rich baritone colored by his still-strong Arabic accent. He owes a lot to America, he says. "Here is where I established myself. Here is where I have been given opportunity." When he gives luncheon talks to local Lions and Rotary clubs, he tells them, "Arab-Americans understand more than anybody else how valuable is this freedom," because so many come from countries ruled by repressive governments.

But values and loyalties line up differently in Dearborn from most other American locales. Siblani, a man wooed by American governors and senators, openly endorses Hezbollah, the militant Shiite faction whose name means "Party of God." In Lebanon, Hezbollah fields political candidates and runs schools and orphanages for its supporters. But it also has provoked bloody conflict with Israel—most recently, in the summer of 2006—and has sponsored suicide bombers who have killed hundreds of Americans, including 241 peacekeeping marines in Beirut in 1983. The U.S. government brands the Iranian-backed group a terrorist organization. Siblani disagrees. Without applauding the deaths of U.S. soldiers, he nevertheless sees Hezbollah as having served as a legitimate liberating force and foe of foreign occupation. A naturalized American citizen, he says he loves his adopted country—and he is persuasive on the point—but his is a complicated kind of patriotism, to say the least.

Some of Dearborn's Arab-Americans are more determined to detach from the ingrained antagonisms of the Middle East, an inclination that can bring them into conflict with Siblani. But his outlook isn't unusual in Dearborn or in Arab and Muslim communities elsewhere. He and others say they are frustrated to see American perceptions slipping back to those of the 1970s and 1980s, when the word "Arab" automatically conjured up hostage takers or car bombers. Yet Siblani and others like him, who seem in some ways very comfortable in America, retain their respect for certain extremists in the Middle East.

The contradiction surfaces in the routines of Arab comedians who play on the theme of being an outsider in an era of fear. Entertaining guests at the twentieth-anniversary banquet of *The Arab American News* in December 2004, a comic from Chicago named Ray Hanania joked that his hobby is hanging around airports: "I'm not traveling; I just go there to scare the crap out of people. You guys should try it. It's a lot of fun." This brought guffaws. The comedian noted that his wife is Jewish. "She's turned me in to the FBI three times in the past week," he said, provoking more laughter.

Siblani's newspaper, especially in its local articles, tries to replace violent stereotypes with images of integration and ordinariness: successful Arab schoolteachers, store owners, and county prosecutors. Some of the paper's analysis of foreign events offers the valuable skepticism of writers who do not take American support for Israel as a given. But at other times Siblani and the writers he publishes project a grim conspiratorial worldview. In June 2005 the guest columnist Gary Leupp summed up American involvement in the Middle East in this way: "Yes, ladies and gentlemen, this is indeed a Crusade, an anti-Muslim project conducted from a Judeo-Christian command center of a particularly unholy type."

Siblani was born in 1955 in a poor village near Beirut. Birth records weren't kept, so he doesn't know the date. He was the youngest of the eleven children of a seamstress and a policeman. His father later became the village's mayor and, to Osama's disapproval, took a second wife. Osama's mother was the family's mainstay. "She was not really a designer, a Versace," he told me. "She was working for the very, very poor and making a living to support us." For a time Osama attended a two-room school in Beirut owned by an older brother. At night he slept on a thin mattress on the school's cold floor.

Even as a child he followed Lebanese politics and world events, especially the Arab fight against Israel. In high school he became a leader in student government and idolized Gamal Abdel Nasser, the Egyptian military ruler who promised to build a strong, modern Arab bloc. But not long after Siblani graduated, Lebanon's civil war erupted, the division among Arabs providing one more reminder of Nasser's failure. Enlisted in the national army, Siblani "was sitting there in the middle of all the fighting," a confusing clash of Christian, Muslim, and secular forces. "I was in the crossfire," he recalled. "All of the army was in the crossfire."

In 1976, when he was twenty or twenty-one, his family sent him to the United States, where another brother was living. He arrived in Detroit with $180 in his pocket and little else. Within days he had three jobs: parking cars, pumping gas, and delivering pizza. At the same time, he earned a degree at the University of Detroit in electrical engineering, one of the practical fields preferred by male Arab immigrants whose families expect them to send money home. Upon graduation, he took an entry-level engineering job at General Motors. He "wanted to be the president of GM the next day," and when, after six months, he hadn't moved up quickly enough, he quit. He eventually joined an import-export company that served as a broker between American manufacturers and Middle Eastern contractors. Siblani jetted to Riyadh, Cairo, and Beirut, selling ventilation and air-conditioning equipment. He earned more than enough money to fix up his childhood home in Lebanon, where his aged mother still lived. He bought her new furniture, a washer-dryer set, and a television.

"This is the American dream," Siblani said years later. "It doesn't matter who you are or whether you have anything to start. You can make something of yourself." He bought a comfortable suburban home near Detroit and a vacation condo near Lake St. Clair. He dated American women, including, for a while, one who was Jewish. Probusiness and antiabortion, he looked forward to gaining American citizenship and supporting Ronald Reagan's reelection campaign.

In early June 1982 Siblani wrapped up some business in Saudi Arabia and went to Lebanon to visit his mother. The civil war continued: Christian factions fought Muslim. Palestinian guerrillas in the south attacked Israel, drawing Israeli retaliation. Ordinary Lebanese lived in chaos. On June 6, Siblani said goodbye to his mother and boarded a flight to Paris, beginning the trip back to the United States. That day Israeli forces invaded Lebanon, seeking to crush the Palestine Liberation Organization and install a friendly Christian government in Beirut. An Israeli aerial bomb destroyed Siblani's mother's house. She and other family members survived unhurt, but the dwelling and its contents were left in cinders. "The furniture was burned," he told me. "My letters from lovers I had when I was in school, my pictures. I don't have any pictures from when I was little." How many thousands of times had he told this story? "Who burned it?" he asked. "*Israeli* jets."

He has never forgiven the country that attacked his family, even though Israeli pilots surely had other targets in mind. He sees Israel as the illegitimate offspring of European colonialism and Zionism, a combination that, in his view, has devalued and destroyed Arab lives for sixty years. This opinion pervades Dearborn's Arab Muslim circles. Compounding the hatred for Israel is the sense of humiliation over feckless Arab leadership. And making the frustration even worse is that the United States has chosen to protect Israel and prop up repressive Arab dictators. Siblani sees American Middle East policy as a form of bipartisan moral corruption, attributable, above all, to the influence of Israel's American Jewish backers. A 2003 headline in his *Arab American News*: "U.S., U.K. and Israel: The Real Axis of Evil."

After the Israeli invasion of Lebanon in 1982, Siblani recalled searching American newspapers and television for accounts of what was happening there. Lebanon "is a country that is independent and another state is invading its capital," he said. "Nobody is defending the Arab point of view, saying you can't do that." In fact there was some debate, but overall Israel received its usual respectful coverage from the American press. In Siblani's eyes, American journalists were too lazy or co-opted, or both, to present a balanced picture of Middle East events.

Then he had an idea. "I said, instead of waiting for someone to step in, why don't I do it?" He decided to start a newspaper. "I would never pretend that I am a journalist out to tell the story without feelings, without bias," he said. "I am a biased journalist. I am a journalist on a mission. I want to tell my story. I don't want somebody else to come and tell it." He also had a political goal: "to bring the Arab-American community together, to form a bloc, and to start generating organizations and lobby.

"I believe in the philosophy [that] the United States is a corporation," he said. "You need to buy shares in order to have influence." The newspaper would be his investment.

Fellow Arab immigrants predicted he would fail and make a fool of himself. The lack of confidence had some foundation. Siblani had no publishing experience. His main deputy was his girlfriend, an American and a Christian who knew little about the Middle East or journalism. Early Arab-immigrant hires brought credentials of varying sorts to the task but shared a churlish resistance to working with a woman, let alone a non-Arab. Siblani had to go to England and Saudi Arabia to find Arabic typesetting equipment. In Dearborn few Arab store owners wanted to pay for newspaper ads. Siblani poured almost all his own savings as well as bank loans—hundreds of thousands of dollars, all told—into the long-shot venture.

The first regular issue of Siblani's newspaper appeared on February 11, 1985. It was then called *Sada Alwatan*, or "The Nation's Echo," which is now the name of only the Arabic-language section. The paper opens like a book. The English version begins on the front; the Arabic section, with writing from right to left, starts from the back. In its inaugural edition the paper covered topics that became staples: Lebanese strife, Palestinian strife, and Iraqi strife. Looking back, Siblani told me, "It seems like it's today. The same things are happening."

Less than a year after the newspaper's start, a standoff that transfixed the Middle East and much of the rest of the world provided the story that put *The Arab American News* and Osama Siblani on the map. On June 14, 1985, armed men seized control of TWA Flight 847, which was taking 153 passengers and crew from Athens to Rome. The hijackers forced the plane to Beirut instead. They released most of the passengers but kept 40 Americans, whom they proposed to swap for hundreds of Lebanese being held prisoner by Israel. Demonstrating their seriousness, the militants murdered a U.S. Navy petty officer on the flight.

It turned out the hijackers were Shiite Muslims with ties to an organization called Hezbollah, about which most Americans knew very little. Lebanese fundamentalists backed by the Shiite government of Iran had formed Hezbollah in the early 1980s to drive the Israeli military out of Lebanon. With Iranian arms and financing, the group rapidly gained strength in a lawless country. Hezbollah challenged Israeli forces in southern Lebanon and lashed out repeatedly at American civilians and soldiers, including, in 1983, killing the 241 marines sent to Beirut as peacekeepers. Viewed as terrorists by Washington, Hezbollah fighters were hailed as heroes by many Lebanese Muslims.

For three weeks in 1985 the taking of TWA Flight 847 was the lead news story around the world. Nabih Berri, the leader of Amal, another Shiite militia, ended up with control of the plane in Beirut. His relationship with the hijackers was murky. At times he seemed to be mediating between them and the United States; at other times he appeared to be negotiating on the hijackers' behalf. As tension built, Berri had passengers removed from the plane and scattered to secret locations. American journalists desperate to sort out the Lebanese connections discovered that Berri had family ties to Dearborn. The media eye turned toward the American Rust Belt.

A commercial lawyer by training, Berri had lived in Dearborn in the 1970s. His ex-wife and their children still lived there, along with a much larger circle of Berri relatives, some of whom had Americanized their name to Berry. Sought out by reporters and television crews, Dearborn's Berrys and their neighbors admitted ambivalence over what was going on in Beirut. "Maybe the hijackings were wrong. We didn't choose that way, but the cause was just," one local leader told the *Chicago Tribune*. A member of the Berry clan posed for a picture holding an AK-47, which the *New York Post* used to illustrate a dispatch about a supposed fifteen-hundred-member Shiite militia in Dearborn. Embarrassed Berry family members said the man had been joking. But the *Post* article, headlined "Beirut,

USA," helped fuel hysteria about what turned out to be a nonexistent Muslim paramilitary force in the Midwest.

In this hectic atmosphere, reporters found their way to the still-new *Arab American News*. They discovered that its publisher and editor in chief, Osama Siblani, could provide pithy, informed explanations of his homeland's convoluted politics. In interviews, he condemned the taking of hostages while defending the hijackers' demand that Israel free its prisoners. "I think we should be more evenhanded in the Middle East," he told one local television station. "I think we should look at the Palestinian question and resolve it and put some pressure on Israel to withdraw from Lebanon, to have good allies in the Middle East. It will increase our friends and decrease our enemies."

U.S. State Department officials decided they too could learn something from Siblani. The government brought him to Washington, where he was taken to see Undersecretary of State Michael Armacost and then, briefly, Secretary of State George Shultz. American warships were massing in the Mediterranean, but Siblani urged the officials to let Nabih Berri sort things out. What the American officials didn't know was that Siblani's older brother Ghassan was one of Berri's top aides. Osama told me that no one at the State Department asked him about the family connection, so he didn't bring it up. He and his brother weren't talking at the time, he said, because they disagreed over the hostage taking.

After seventeen days and the release of thirty-one Lebanese prisoners by Israel, the last of the American hostages were finally freed. During a subsequent visit to Beirut, Siblani said, he lectured his brother that the hostage affair had alienated Americans and confirmed the image of Arabs as fanatics.

For the publisher, the TWA 847 hijacking marked a turning point. His expertise and availability won him a place in journalist Rolodexes nationwide. *The Arab American News* became an "address," as he put it, where mainstream reporters could go for authoritative analysis on how international events played among Arab-Americans. Locally, his small paper gained stature as its circulation grew from five thousand to ten thousand and then higher.

But prominence had a dark side. Siblani gained national notice only because of Dearborn's connections to the taking of American hostages. The highest levels of American government had sought his advice, but radio hosts used the hostage situation to stir suspicions of a phantom fundamentalist militia. Letters to the editors of some papers had called for Arab-Americans to be taken hostage until the U.S. citizens were released in Beirut. Dearborn police reported bomb threats aimed at Lebanese residents and mosques, though none was carried out.

"Our community is very pro-U.S.," a frustrated Siblani told *The Globe and Mail* of Toronto shortly after the TWA 847 episode. "But once again we're being portrayed as enemies of the U.S. The message is: 'Arabs are terrorists. Get them out of the country.'"

As Lebanese families in Dearborn saved and prospered, some began moving out of the South End to the greener neighborhoods of East Dearborn. They bought sturdy brick houses from Catholic German- and Italian-Americans moving farther from Detroit and its many poor blacks. Statues of Jesus and Mary disappeared from East Dearborn's orderly lawns. Muslims revere Jesus and his mother, who, the Quran says, conceived him immaculately. But Muslims avoid religious statuary as a form of idol worship. In place of the Virgin and Child, many homeowners built front porches surrounded by white wrought-iron fences, a dignified place to drink sweet tea with neighbors.

Dearborn's old guard, descended from European immigrants, maintains a residential enclave on the west side of town. But some of its members weren't happy to see Arabs moving up the socioeconomic ladder. In the summer of 1985, just as the TWA 847 drama drew to a close, Michael Guido, a thirty-one-year-old city councilman running for mayor, gave voice to the discontent. He sent residents a brochure that suggested they focus on "the Arab problem." Guido, whose parents had emigrated from Italy and still lived in town, claimed in the pamphlet that he wasn't "anti-Arab," but he went on to accuse Arabs of promoting "a system and an attitude which threaten our neighborhoods, the value of our property, and a darned good way of life."

Arab-Americans denounced Guido's swipe. Siblani personally delivered a copy of an angry editorial to the candidate's headquarters. But Arab-Americans weren't yet organized enough to have much effect. Guido won the 1985 election handily, never apologizing for the brochure. For Siblani, this was a lesson that he needed to focus more on local events, not just the Middle East.

He already published features like the historically oriented "Know Your New Country." Now he got more serious about promoting Muslim and Arab-American political candidates. One was Dearborn restaurateur Suzanne Sareini, a fellow Lebanese and Republican, who stirred excitement with her 1985 race for city council. Guido's brochure didn't help Sareini. At coffee hours and barbecues, the secular American-born Muslim had to reassure voters that she wouldn't represent "just Arabs." She reminded people of her four children in the public schools and her years of PTA service. She thought of herself as "a typical Dearbornite. Then I found out I was 'foreign.'" Sareini lost that first race, but four years later, she came back and, with Siblani's endorsement, won a city council seat. That made her a pioneer among Muslim politicians in the United States, and she has been returned to city hall four times since.

With Arab-Americans still only about 20 percent of registered voters, Mayor Guido hasn't had any trouble getting reelected five times. A barrel-chested man who wears pin-striped suits and suspenders, he still defends his notorious brochure. "People in the neighborhoods, nonimmigrants, were frustrated" in 1985 that Arab immigrants were not upholding "Dearborn community morals," he told me when we spoke in his office at City Hall. But as the Arab influx has continued, Guido has adjusted his rhetoric and proved himself to be an agile politician. He visits mosques and spices speeches with Arabic phrases. He has cultivated Lebanese businessmen—Muslim and Christian—who have deemed it pragmatic to contribute to his campaigns. In 2001, two months after 9/11, he soundly defeated a capable Lebanese-American challenger backed by Osama Siblani. In 2003 the mayor took a five-day trip to Lebanon, with some of his wealthy

Lebanese-American supporters paying his way and accompanying him. (Siblani declined to participate.) Two years later Guido was returned to office without opposition.

Others may have forgotten or forgiven the "Arab problem" brochure, two decades after its appearance, but not Siblani. "Eventually it's going to come back to haunt him," Siblani predicted, pointing to the proliferation of Arab families and the votes they represent. Certainly things in Dearborn have changed. Candidates can no longer get away with open attacks on Arabs. In 1997 a city council candidate suggested in campaign literature that her Arab opponent was guilty of "political terrorism." Siblani and some of his allies "decided it was time for her to be defeated," he said, and he used *The Arab American News* to make sure that happened. The next year, when the same woman ran for state senate, the paper came back and helped beat her again. But Arab voters didn't get another chance to oust Mayor Guido. He died in office in December 2006 and was replaced by the long-time city council president, John Jack O'Reilly.

SECRET EVIDENCE

In the late 1980s Siblani met a garrulous social worker named Imad Hamad, who would become a symbol to many local Muslims of the excesses of government terrorist hunters. For Hamad, as for Siblani, the 1982 Israeli invasion of Lebanon had been a crucial event. Hamad's participation in protests of the invasion led years later to murky U.S. government accusations that he was tied to a militant Palestinian group. This trouble brought him to Siblani's doorstep, and the two became friends. In Dearborn such stories aren't that unusual. Quite a few residents with good jobs and reputations suddenly have found themselves under suspicion—sometimes for good reason, other times not.

Hamad's extended family fled a small village in the Upper Galilee in 1948 during the Israeli-Arab war over the establishment of Israel. The Hamads landed in a refugee settlement in Lebanon, and that is where Imad was born in 1961. His father, a teacher, eventually moved the family to a proper home and sent Imad to the United States to study engineering.

In the early 1980s Imad bounced among several American universities, never earning his degree, but he eventually landed an electrical engineering job in Northern California. He married an American Jewish woman— her family took it better than his, he said—but they divorced after a few years. He decided to start fresh in Dearborn. He knew no one in the small city but heard it was the center of Arab life in America, so in 1987 he picked up and moved. "I wanted to see myself there," he told me. Having never really enjoyed engineering, he became a social worker for Arab immigrants. In 1991 he married a woman of Yemeni descent and applied for American citizenship. Life seemed to be falling into place.

Then, in 1996, after years of delay, the Immigration and Naturalization Service informed Hamad that no, he couldn't become a U.S. citizen. In fact the agency said it intended to deport him. Hamad's past, or a small piece of it, had caught up with him. The government said he was a threat to national security because of his ties to the Popular Front for the Liberation of Palestine (PFLP), a Marxist-Leninist faction involved in hijackings and killings that over the years have cost at least twenty American lives. In 2001 the group assassinated the Israeli minister of tourism.

The allegation against Hamad traced back to 1982, when as a student in San Francisco he had participated in protests of the Israeli invasion of Lebanon. Now, fourteen years later, the INS said that the protests had been linked to the PFLP and that Hamad had helped raise money for the group. He denied knowingly doing any such thing, insisting that he merely attended events that others planned and led. The INS said it had "secret evidence" to back up its charges and invoked a 1996 antiterrorism law that allowed it to rely on such evidence without disclosing it to deportation targets or their lawyers. The case was one of the first in which the government employed the new secret evidence authority, which is still in use today.

Hamad was desperate. His wife was expecting their third child, and her primary family attachments were in America. He had a lawyer, but he knew he needed more than courtroom arguments. He appealed to members of Congress and to influential Arab-Americans. Then he went to the office of *The Arab American News*. Siblani was eager to help. "I knew what kind of a person was Imad," the publisher said. "They made a big deal out of nothing." Siblani's paper had been following the case, portraying Hamad very much as he comes across in person, a good-humored man with no affection for the state of Israel but no fantasy about seeing it disappear. Siblani went beyond covering the case. He helped enlist political support, cochaired a legal defense committee, held press conferences, and attended court sessions. He feared that if Hamad were deported, "it would have been a precedent that would have taken maybe half of this community, because he was a typical example of an activist in that community accused of being a supporter of the Palestinian cause."

Many Muslims in Dearborn and the rest of the Detroit area sympathize with and, at one time or another, have given money to factions in the Middle East that the U.S. government considers terrorist. Religious Muslims often give the money as part of their *zakat*, or annual charitable contribution, which is usually set at 2.5 percent of net worth. The stated intention is typically to support the social service affiliates of such organizations as the Palestinian Hamas and the Lebanese Hezbollah. Often such contributions have gone through intermediary charities with humanitarian-sounding names. Much of this financial support ceased after 9/11, as the federal government shut down several U.S.-based Muslim charities because of their alleged connections to foreign terrorists.

Siblani grew up in an area outside Beirut that later became a Hezbollah stronghold. During visits back to Lebanon he has dropped in on schools and orphanages sponsored by the organization. These institutions "do wonders for the Lebanese in the absence of government services," he said. On the paramilitary side Hezbollah fighters command admiration, he explained, because they have put their lives on the line against the Israeli military.

This pride in Hezbollah, common among Arab-Americans, is hard to square with the group's long and bloody record of fanaticism. In the 1990s Hezbollah became more geographically adventurous. It was blamed for the 1994 bombing of a Jewish Community Center in Buenos Aires that killed ninety-six people and the 1996 attack on Khobar Towers in Saudi Arabia that killed nineteen U.S. servicemen. In early 2005 Israeli and moderate Palestinian officials complained that Hezbollah was trying to undermine the shaky Palestinian-Israeli truce by sponsoring suicide bombing attacks by Palestinian militants. Siblani emphasized that he disapproves of any violence against civilians and of any Hezbollah operations not directly aimed at defending Lebanon. He told me that he has never given any money to Hezbollah.

The campaign to generate political support for Imad Hamad yielded impressive results. Members of Michigan's congressional delegation, including Representatives David Bonior, John Conyers, and John Dingell and Senators Spencer Abraham and Carl Levin, lined up behind Hamad. All these politicians have relied on Arab-American voters. In 1997 the Washington-based American-Arab Anti Discrimination Committee opened a Midwest office in Dearborn and signaled its support by hiring Hamad as regional director. In October of that year an immigration judge looked at the government's secret evidence and ruled that Hamad should not be deported. But the INS appealed. In May 1998, while the INS was still trying to deport him, the Secret Service gave Hamad a security clearance to attend a meeting at the White House to discuss Arab-American concerns with senior Clinton administration officials.

As court papers flew back and forth, fragments of the secret files gradually came into public view. Hamad and his lawyer learned that the Detroit office of the FBI had closed its investigation of him all the way back in 1990, concluding he wasn't a threat. The classified evidence turned out to include blurry undercover photos of him arranging furniture for a Palestinian fund-raiser. The Board of Immigration Appeals was not impressed. In February 1999 it exonerated Hamad, ruling that his alleged association with the Popular Front for the Liberation of Palestine hadn't been proven. It took years to clear remaining red tape, but in September 2002 Hamad finally became a U.S. citizen at a special swearing in conducted by U.S. District Judge George Steeh, who is of Lebanese descent.

Local TV news cameras recorded the festive event at the Lebanese American Heritage Manor in Dearborn. "Only in America could this happen," Hamad told the *Detroit Free Press*. In honor of his work with the government as the regional director of the Anti Discrimination Committee, the Detroit FBI office gave him a framed American flag. That memento sits on a shelf in Hamad's office near a photo of him shaking hands with a smiling President Bill Clinton.

Osama Siblani duly published articles on all these events in his newspaper, but looking back, he was less than celebratory. "If they had succeeded in portraying under the secret evidence law Imad Hamad as a dangerous man, to remove him," he said, "imagine what they could have done against me or some people who really are activist and strong people in this community." Or imagine if all this had transpired after 9/11, he added, when hundreds of Detroit-area Muslims were detained and some whisked out of the country on the basis of secret evidence. Hamad would have been long gone.

After accusation and vindication, the Hamad story ended with a curious twist. Despite his harrowing experience with the federal government, Hamad distinguished himself after 9/11 by encouraging communication between a frightened Arab-American community and the FBI. He helped set up monthly meetings in Detroit at which law enforcement and community representatives discussed concerns about terrorist investigations and hate crimes. This quiet cooperation improved Arab-American compliance with voluntary questioning by the government and provided a forum for rectifying investigative excesses. In 2003 a grateful FBI called Hamad to say that he would receive an Exceptional Public Service Award for his constructive role. Hamad's co-honoree was to be the late Madeline Sweeney, a flight attendant on one of the hijacked planes that struck the World Trade Center. Sweeney had had the presence of mind to call the FBI on a mobile phone and describe the hijackers, a first step in the investigation of the atrocity. The symbolism would be potent: juxtaposing the memory of the heroic Sweeney with a short Palestinian immigrant who wears a scruffy beard, speaks with an Arab accent, and carries Muslim prayer beads.

Osama Siblani told Hamad to turn it down. "Arab civil rights groups should not be in bed with the FBI or with the local authorities," the publisher later said to me, recounting his advice. "They should be a watchdog and should always maintain a distance between them and the security officials." He worried that Hamad would be seen by his constituency as a "loyal FBI boy."

Hamad was willing to take that risk. He arranged to fly to Washington at government expense to pick up the award. But then a fringe Jewish group, the Zionist Organization of America, along with the conservative columnist Debbie Schlussel, writing in the *New York Post*, raised the old PFLP allegations. The publicity-conscious FBI awkwardly rescinded the award offer while reiterating that it "commended" Hamad for "bridging the gap" between Muslim Americans and law enforcement. The brave Madeline Sweeney would be the sole honoree.

Hamad took the whole thing in stride. He laughed that perhaps he needed a TV reality show "extreme makeover" to lose the terrorist image. More seriously, he said, "The fact that I am a nominee, I'm still proud of it. I use it like Emmy Awards—a nominee for this. I was there. I was on the list." Sure, some acquaintances told him that he deserved the humiliation for foolishly trusting the government. But he didn't feel humiliated. "Ms. Sweeney sacrificed her life," he said. "She deserves an award more than I do."

Speaking publicly on behalf of a coalition of Arab-American organizations, Osama Siblani denounced the prize withdrawal as "a slap in the face to the entire Arab-American community." But he said privately that having the award pulled back was for the best: "Many people in our community are suspicious of Imad's activities" because of his friendly relations with the government. "I dismiss it all the time. I don't believe that he is this kind of person. He is trying out of his good heart . . . to have a good relationship with everybody." But better to be seen at a distance from the FBI.

MARRIED TO OSAMA

In April 1997 *The Arab American News* broached the sensitive topic of Arab-American manners. The article was a tough-love scolding from M. Kay Siblani, the non-Arab woman who had helped start the newspaper and was by then the ex-wife of Osama Siblani. "Things Must Change in Dearborn," her headline stated. Kay Siblani, who had tried earnestly to embrace Arab-immigrant culture, recalled Mayor Michael Guido's "Arab problem" brochure and how hurtful it had been. But then she said that Dearborn's Arabs needed to ask themselves some questions:

"What about how to stand in line at the bank?" she wrote. "What about speaking English if possible when around non-Arabic speaking people? What about not being on welfare if you're living in a $200,000 home? What about not taking advantage of young non-Muslim women simply because they haven't had the blessing of the teachings of Islam?" (She appeared *not* to be referring to her ex-husband.) "What about having some consideration for neighbors who have to get up at 5 a.m. to go to work and aren't invited to your yard party anyway?"

Readers reacted strongly, some applauding Kay's courage, others denouncing her as "ridiculous" and "insulting." In response, she wrote another piece, saying the examples she had cited were the least of the problem. "On top of behavior that alienates people socially, we have had an Arab crime wave, Arab gangs, and Arab drug dealing in Dearborn at crisis levels for years. How can we blame American culture for this while simultaneously excluding ourselves from the country's moral, social, and legal standards?"

Readers continued to split over Kay's critique, but some Muslim parents regretfully agreed with her. Osama Siblani, the editor in chief, encouraged the debate by publishing the articles and letters. The paper wouldn't come out without his ex-wife—in fact it might never have taken off without her—so he was inclined to let her blow off steam. He also agreed with some of what she had to say. While her description of a crime "crisis" may have been hyperbole, *The Arab American News* was indeed reporting break-ins and robberies in Dearborn's Arab neighborhoods. Every group has its lowlifes as well as its solid citizens, Osama Siblani said, and Arabs are no different.

↩

Kay Kendall grew up in Detroit, a tall, fair-skinned girl of German and Italian ancestry who had a fascination with minarets and Bedouins. She became a nurse and met Osama in the late 1970s through mutual acquaintances. They began dating. By 1984 she had tired of nursing, so she plunged into her boyfriend's newspaper project with a neophyte's zeal, becoming the paper's English-language editor. There were high points, including the couple's excursions to the Middle East to interview Arab heads of state. In 1986 they jetted to Kuwait and then Baghdad to catch up with then-exiled PLO leader Yasser Arafat, one of the perennial heroes in the pages of *The Arab American News*. Kay became a strong supporter of Arab causes, although her unsparing assessment of Arab manners eleven years later showed that she was not a slavish one.

Running a small newspaper is grueling work. Osama depended heavily on Kay to cull articles from Arab-friendly news services and a far-flung network of freelance writers. In 1989, when she was recovering from cancer surgery, Osama came to her hospital bed with page proofs for her to read. After twelve years as a couple, they finally decided to marry in 1992.

The paper had grown to a circulation of twenty thousand and a staff of sixteen. But Osama's strength wasn't as a manager, and revenues weren't covering growing costs. Part of the problem was Dearborn's odd economy. Businesses on the city's middle- and working-class east and west sides are mostly small and won't pay high advertising rates. In the center of the city are the sprawling world headquarters of Ford and its many satellite offices. These draw thousands of white-collar workers who commute from more affluent towns. Henry Ford left behind other local legacies, including mammoth collections of Americana at the Henry Ford Museum and an adjacent historical theme park called Greenfield Village. Busloads of tourists pull up every day and help support hotels and shopping malls in central

Dearborn. But none of the Ford-related establishments advertise very much in *The Arab American News*.

In 1994, when the Siblanis' credit cards hit their limits and the banks wouldn't make any more loans, Osama was forced to declare personal bankruptcy. He and Kay lost their home and vacation condo, as well as their cars. The next year their marriage ended in divorce. The paper barely survived with its payroll cut in half and its distribution area reduced. But advertising revenue gradually grew, and Osama got back on his feet financially with the help of an outside consulting job for a local Arab social service agency.

The Arab American News operates today from its own one-story building on a commercial side street. Most staff members sell ads and conduct phone interviews from a small, messy newsroom. Osama works in a comfortable office decorated with photos of his father and his hero, Nasser. A decorative Arab-style water pipe sits on a side table next to several promotional coffee mugs that say "Army of One," a gift from a military recruiter who paid a goodwill visit.

Kay persevered in her post at the paper. After the divorce she took the surprising step of converting to Islam and donning the hijab, a transformation that still causes her secular ex-husband to shake his head with bewilderment. For a while she prayed five times a day and attended Friday services at Shiite mosques. She liked the Islamic idea of religion structuring all aspects of life, from diet to hygiene. But after 9/11 she received a scary anti-Muslim threat and abruptly shed her veil and head covering. Although their relationship is complicated and sometimes tense, she still works closely with Osama. Her name appears in the masthead just below his, and she still uses the byline M. Kay Siblani.

Raja Siblani, Osama's current wife, is a Lebanese-born former United Nations staff member who wishes she lived in Rome, Paris, or Beirut— rather than Michigan. Americans, she told me between puffs on a cigarette, are "arrogant, impolite, and racist." The French, Raja added, are preferable company. She spoke in a light tone, intending, it seemed, to tease more than insult. Many sophisticated Lebanese who blame American "imperialism" for the Middle East's woes nevertheless harbor affection for their former colonial patrons, the French.

Osama smiled indulgently. "Americans are good people," he insisted, praising the country's economic opportunity, free speech, and real, if imperfect, democracy. America is where he and Raja and her teenage son, Adrian, live in a spacious house with white pillars in front. The problem, Osama said, is that the American media fail to challenge the country's actions overseas, where the United States, in his view, often supports the bad guys. Americans, he added, are ignorant about foreign affairs and allow their government to manipulate them.

The conversation took place over dinner at La Shish, an Arabic restaurant in an upscale strip mall near the Siblanis' home in prosperous West Bloomfield. Raja, who doesn't cover her long copper red hair, wore a stylish denim jumpsuit. Her husband, who had recently quit smoking, eyed her cigarettes longingly. Osama had on a silky black golf shirt and nicely tailored charcoal slacks.

He said that until 9/11 Raja had been warming to America, but since the attacks on New York and Washington she had grown anxious that "some nut" would try to kill him. Listening quietly was Adrian, Raja's sixteen-year-old son. A big fan of Michael Moore's conspiratorial anti-Bush movie *Fahrenheit 911*, the teenager wore the hip-hop uniform: tentlike white T-shirt, drooping baggy pants, sideways ball cap, and oversize silver link necklace. Ours was the only table employing English, for my benefit; everyone else spoke Arabic.

Raja and Osama had met in school in Lebanon in 1973. She was wealthy and Sunni. His poor Shiite family grumbled that her people were trying to "buy" Osama—"tribal bullshit," in his words. When civil war broke out in 1975, her family took Raja to France. Osama later left for the United States. After years of secret conversations and missed connections, they drifted apart, and each married someone else.

In 1995 one of Osama's older brothers ran into Raja at a reception in Beirut. She had divorced; Osama had divorced. They married in 1996, and Raja reluctantly moved to Michigan. In theory they could live in Beirut.

Osama could work as a fixer for an American car maker or defense contractor, dealing with local politicians and power brokers. He had received offers for such jobs, he told me. But he felt a responsibility to Dearborn and his readers. By now he has lived longer in the American Midwest than in the Middle East. "I can't live there," he said of Beirut. When he visits, the traffic noise keeps him awake at night. "I am a stranger in my town. Within my family I am a stranger."

UP AND DOWN WITH BUSH

For Osama Siblani, as for many relatively assimilated Arab men in the United States, American politics has become like politics back in the Middle East, an obsession. But in the 1980s and 1990s, Arab-Americans thought that each advance they made in national politics was canceled out by a major insult—until 2000.

In 1984 Jesse Jackson embraced Yasser Arafat, drawing fervent support from Arab-Americans and Muslims for his quixotic third-party presidential campaign, while the Democratic nominee, Walter Mondale, returned contributions from Arab-Americans out of fear he would alienate Jews. In 1988 George H. W. Bush repaid Lebanese-American John Sununu for helping his campaign by making the New Hampshire governor his White House chief of staff; Democratic candidate Michael Dukakis turned down the proffered endorsement of an Arab-American organization. In 1996 GOP candidate Bob Dole alienated potential Arab-American backers by canceling a big meeting in Washington without even offering an excuse. And in 2000 Hillary Clinton, on her way to the Senate, showily returned fifty thousand dollars raised for her by the American Muslim Alliance. Then, in the 2000 presidential race, George W. Bush appealed to Arabs, especially Muslims, with an ardor not seen before from a major-party presidential candidate.

Historically Arabs and Muslims have split roughly 40 percent to 40 percent in their professed party affiliations, with 20 percent saying they were independent. After Bob Dole offended Muslim leaders in 1996, Muslims increasingly charmed by Bill Clinton tilted toward the incumbent, 57 to 22 percent. But Clinton did not secure long-term allegiance to the Democratic Party.

The 2000 election map showed that some of the closest races would be in Michigan, Ohio, and Florida, states with Muslim populations numbering in the hundreds of thousands each. The Bush campaign's pitch was that Muslims and Republicans shared conservative values: opposition to gay marriage and abortion and support for publicly funded religious schools and free market economic policies (although the last is sticky for strictly observant Muslims who observe the Islamic ban on paying or collecting interest). George W. Bush visited Islamic centers and referred in speeches to the faithful who attend "church, synagogue, *or mosque.*" Grover Norquist, a well-known conservative operative in Washington and an ally of top Bush political strategist Karl Rove, launched a nonprofit group called the Islamic Free Market Institute to help court the Muslim vote.

No place felt the newly kindled Republican warmth for Islam more than Dearborn. Michigan's Arabs and Muslims traditionally support politicians who pay attention to them, regardless of party affiliation. They have strongly backed veteran Michigan Democrats, such as U.S. Representatives John Conyers and John Dingell, but also prominent Republicans, such as former Governor John Engler and former U.S. Senator Spencer Abraham. All these politicians have catered to immigrant concerns and expressed empathy for the Arab cause in the Middle East.

Osama Siblani, a longtime registered Republican, had flip-flopped like fellow Arab voters in Michigan. In the 1980s he applauded Ronald Reagan as "the right person to move the United States from a position of weakness to a position of strength" in its standoff with the Soviet Union. He cast his first presidential vote in 1988 for George H. W. Bush. But the elder Bush's decision to wage the first Gulf War prompted Siblani to choose Bill Clinton in 1992, and he stuck with Clinton in 1996.

In 1997 Siblani and some friends formed the Arab American Political Action Committee (AAPAC). Through its prolific endorsements, campaign contributions, and voter guides, the committee quickly became a local powerhouse and a barometer of Arab-American predilections in

Michigan and nationally. The group has more Democrats than Republicans, but the Democratic candidate in 2000, Al Gore, didn't seem to notice the AAPAC. This irritated Siblani and his colleagues. It didn't help Gore with this crowd that his running mate, Senator Joseph Lieberman of Connecticut, was Jewish. The AAPAC claimed that it didn't oppose the idea of a Jew in the White House; Siblani and others said they worried that *some* Jews, including Lieberman, placed the interests of Israel ahead of those of America. Green Party candidate Ralph Nader, the son of Lebanese immigrants, has many friends in Dearborn, including Siblani. But Nader attracted surprisingly modest backing, probably because of the sense that 2000 was the year that Arabs and Muslims could influence the outcome, rather than cast mere protest votes.

George W. Bush campaigned in and around Dearborn a half dozen times in 2000, while his staff patrolled the area like cops on a beat. According to Siblani, the candidate made a startling promise when he met the publisher for the first time at a GOP fund-raiser in nearby Troy, Michigan. After small talk about the newspaper business, the conversation turned to the future of Iraq. Siblani urged caution. But Bush, he said, bluntly vowed he would "take out" Saddam Hussein. This was in April 2000.

"With all due respect, Governor, I don't think you should be the one who takes Saddam Hussein out," Siblani said. "Maybe what you should do is help the Iraqis to make their choice."

Bush, he recalled, "looked at me with surprise" and then said they would discuss the matter later.

Siblani deduced that Bush thought he was speaking with a Shiite Iraqi immigrant, many of whom live in Dearborn and favored American military action to depose Saddam Hussein. Still, it was more important to Siblani that Bush was trying hard to appeal to Arabs and Muslims. The publisher assumed that when Bush got into the Oval Office, he would become more cautious about invading other countries.

In October 2000, Siblani said he and Bush spoke again at a closed-door meeting with a small group of Arab-Americans at the Hyatt Regency in Dearborn. This time the publisher tried to focus the candidate's attention on the Palestinians. "Cats and dogs get more respect for their lives in this country than Palestinians," Siblani told Bush. "Did you see the twelve-year-old child who was killed in cold blood?" Horrific news footage broadcast on major American networks had shown a Palestinian boy caught in crossfire between Israeli soldiers and Palestinian militants.

"I saw the video of the 12-year-old child being killed," Bush said, according to an account in *The Arab American News*. "It is sad. It is sad."

They also talked about the way Arabs and Muslims were treated in the United States. "Airport profiling and secret evidence are insults to the Constitution," Siblani told Bush.

Bush nodded, seeming to listen, Siblani said. (Asked for comment on these accounts, a White House spokesman said they were "kind of one-sided," declining to elaborate.)

Six days after Siblani complained to candidate Bush about profiling and secret evidence, Bush and Gore held the second of their three face-to-face debates. At one point in the exchange, Bush suddenly changed the subject to say: "Arab-Americans are racially profiled in what's called secret evidence. People are stopped, and we've got to do something about that. My friend, Senator Spencer Abraham of Michigan, is pushing a law to make sure that Arab-Americans are treated with respect."

Most viewers probably didn't focus on what sounded like a throwaway line, but Muslim and Arab-Americans did. Siblani said he received two dozen congratulatory phone calls that night. It hardly mattered to the celebrants that Bush had confused racial profiling at airports, when police single out Arabs for scrutiny, with secret evidence cases, such as the one against Imad Hamad.

"He didn't know what he was talking about, but he raised it," Siblani said. As far as he was concerned, Bush had listened and made a public gesture. It wasn't Bush's opposition to abortion or gay marriage that won over Arab Dearborn. His position on Israel was basically the same as Gore's. What made the difference was that Arabs and Muslims felt Bush had invited them into the club.

"Having a place at the table, at the White House, at the highest level, was for me a dream," Siblani recalled. The AAPAC, the political action committee, and *The Arab American News* gushingly endorsed Bush. The paper editorialized that Bush had "moved our domestic issues to the national scene and captured the hearts and minds of Arabs around the country."

Al Gore took Michigan in 2000, but exit polling showed that voters in predominantly Arab-American precincts in Dearborn went for Bush by ratios of more than three to one. Nationally, Arab-Americans preferred Bush to Gore by 45.5 to 38 percent, according to the Zogby International polling firm. Looking at the Muslim vote, Zogby found an even stronger leaning for Bush: 58 to 22.5 percent. That reversed the results from 1996, when Muslims had chosen Clinton over Dole by a similar margin.

After weeks of legal wrangling over the vote count in Florida and Bush's victory before the U.S. Supreme Court, he was deemed the winner by a mere 537 votes. One could argue that any group of 537 Florida voters who chose Bush could take credit for his win. But Grover Norquist, the Republican strategist and emissary to Muslims, estimated afterward that Muslims in Florida preferred Bush by a margin of thousands, perhaps tens of thousands. In other words, Muslims might have made the difference.

Days before the election, *The Weekly Standard*, a conservative Washington magazine reliably plugged in to Republican thinking, lauded Siblani for helping steer Bush toward his debate remarks on profiling and secret evidence. If Bush won, the magazine said, he would have many people to thank. "One of them is Osama Siblani."

Across town from Siblani's newspaper office, the Iraqi immigrants who congregate at the Karbalaa Islamic Education Center also backed Bush in 2000, but not for the same reason as Siblani, a difference that led to conflict with the publisher. The Iraqis *did* want the United States to "take out" Saddam Hussein. "We knew all along it would have to be a Republican president to do something with this guy," said Ihsan Mirza, an environmental engineer who lives in Dearborn Heights. "When Bush took office, that hope almost started blooming again: This guy has the guts to do something."

Mirza, a Shiite Muslim in his early forties, grew up in a middle-class family in the holy Shiite city of Najaf, south of Baghdad. His wealthier relatives were the first to import American cars and tires to the city. Older generations of the extended family didn't make waves under Saddam Hussein, but Ihsan and his peers began to clash with local Baath authorities. There were death threats, and he decided to pursue his college education in the United States. He arrived in 1982.

In Dearborn, he met his future wife, Ifaa, another expat Iraqi; both are now naturalized American citizens. Ihsan became part of the small anti-Saddam student movement in America. The Iraqi dictator had thousands of loyalists in the country in the 1980s. Mirza and his friends confronted them at Middle East symposia on university campuses and on the street in front of the Iraqi Embassy in Washington. There were fistfights and arrests. Mirza said he was shot at once while passing out leaflets near a pro-Saddam social organization that used to have an office on Seven Mile Road in Detroit. The United States supported Saddam in his war against Iran in the 1980s, so the FBI, according to Mirza, tailed the anti-Saddam activists and subjected them to periodic questioning. But American loyalties flipped when Iraq invaded Kuwait in 1990 and the first Bush administration went to war against the former U.S. client. Suddenly federal authorities stopped chasing Mirza's group and instead invited them to wave their picket signs directly in front of the Iraqi Embassy. Mirza, a tall man who wears carefully ironed shirts and khaki pants, shook his head and chuckled at American fickleness.

Between demonstrations, he squeezed in college classes and started a family—he and Ifaa have five children now—but life in Dearborn was difficult for a new Iraqi immigrant in the 1980s. Shiites fleeing Iraq came to Dearborn because of the large number of Lebanese Shiites already living there. But in Dearborn, Mirza recalled, some of the earliest Iraqi arrivals earned a reputation for cheating insurance companies and other types of fraud. "I hated that," he said. "You go to the bank, and they don't trust your signature." He and his family moved to Philadelphia for two years.

By the time they returned to Dearborn in 1992, he had built a financial profile that won quick respect from loan officers. Today they live in an ethnically mixed middle-class neighborhood and send their kids to the local public schools.

Iraqi émigré activists were distraught in 1991 when the first President Bush encouraged Shiites to rise up against Saddam after the Gulf War but then failed to support the revolt. Saddam brutally defeated the rebels. Then, "when Clinton took office, hope just vanished," Mirza said. The Iraqis in Dearborn correctly calculated that the moderate Democrat wouldn't invade.

Iraqi Shiites felt betrayed by the United States but not entirely surprised, according to Mirza's brother-in-law Husham al-Husainy. Betrayal and oppression are woven into Shiite tradition, he told me. Husainy, a former aeronautical engineer with a biography roughly similar to Mirza's, became a Shiite *imam*, or prayer leader, after arriving in the United States. He wears a white turban and an embroidered cream-colored clerical robe. Like some other Shiite clerics, he sometimes writes flowery poems about divine love in the Persian tradition. In 1993, Husainy turned a former nightclub on Warren Avenue into the Karbalaa center.

The mosque's name is an idiosyncratic transliteration of Karbala, the Shiite holy city in southern Iraq where Hussein, the son of Ali, was killed by Sunnis, inaugurating centuries of conflict still frighteningly raw in contemporary Iraq. "The Shiites are always waiting, you see, very patient, all these years and centuries," Husainy said, "for the time when we will be in Karbala and in Najaf and our other holy places and free of the oppression of the ones like Saddam." The United States raised Shiite hopes in 1991, only to dash them. "The Shiites know a long history of betrayal and martyrdom," Husainy said. "We have seen this kind of thing before." Today Iran and Iraq have Shiite majorities. Lebanon, Saudi Arabia, Afghanistan, Pakistan, and India also have sizable Shiite populations.

"We voted for President Bush in 2000 because we sense he is a man who will topple Saddam; this is the reason," Husainy said. The Iraqis in Dearborn weren't much concerned about how an American invasion would be justified. When the 9/11 attacks occurred, they felt horror at the carnage, but they also quickly realized their moment had arrived. They perceived that anti-American terrorism provided an excuse for President Bush to invade Iraq. "Saddam was the fall guy. What more can you ask for?" Ihsan Mirza said.

～

On the morning of September 11, 2001, Osama Siblani rose early to put up primary day signs for his friend, Abed Hammoud, an assistant county prosecutor running for mayor of Dearborn. The city's Arab-Americans felt great pride that one of their own stood a chance of getting into a runoff with the incumbent, Michael Guido. After decorating dozens of lawns with HAMMOUD FOR MAYOR signs, Siblani drove to his newspaper office and made get-out-the-vote calls, hoping to catch people before they left for work. Then word came that something had happened at the World Trade Center.

The threats began only minutes later. "Pray to God that Arabs did not do this," one caller said, "because if they did, your ass will be next." Shaken by the hatred pouring in by phone and e-mail, a woman on the paper's staff broke down and wept. Siblani sent her home. He draped the front of his one-story newspaper building with a giant American flag. Some drivers stopped their cars to thank him. But others demanded to know how Siblani dared wrap himself in the flag when Arabs had attacked the country. "Take the fucking flag! I'm not going to be intimidated by this shit," the publisher responded. Within a week he took it down himself.

In the next issue of his paper, dated September 15, 2001, Siblani published two full pages of patriotic statements under the headline "Arab & Muslim Americans Stand with America." His political action committee, AAPAC, declared, "We fully support the president and all law enforcement agencies in their efforts to protect our country from tragic and vicious terrorist acts and to punish those who do perpetrate them." But on his editorial page Siblani carried a column with a very different emphasis. "This is not the war of democracy vs. terror that the world will be asked to believe in the coming days," Robert Fisk, a British journalist, wrote. "It is also about American missiles slamming into Palestinian homes and U.S. helicopters firing missiles into a Lebanese ambulance in 1996, and American shells crashing into a village called Qana, and about a Lebanese militia—paid and uniformed by America's Israeli ally—hacking and raping and murdering their way through refugee camps."

In the September 11 mayoral primary Siblani's friend Hammoud squeaked past a retired Dearborn police chief to qualify for the runoff. But in the November general election Hammoud lost to Mayor Guido, 79 to 21 percent, a defeat exacerbated, in Siblani's opinion, by backlash from 9/11. Around the country there were reports of hundreds of incidents of mosque vandalism and physical and verbal assaults on Muslims. Three men were killed in mindless acts of revenge in the days following the attacks: a Pakistani Muslim grocer in Dallas; an Egyptian store owner in San Gabriel, California, who was Christian; and an Indian Sikh who ran a gas station in Mesa, Arizona. The latter two apparently were mistaken for Muslims. Pinning down the precise number of "backlash" incidents is difficult. In early 2005 the U.S. Department of Justice said that after investigating hundreds of allegations since 9/11, it had brought federal charges against 27 defendants, resulting in the conviction of 22. State and local authorities had brought another 150 criminal prosecutions. The Council on American-Islamic Relations, which keeps its own annual hate crime statistics, said that in 2002 it counted 42 physical attacks on Muslims based on their religion.

In Dearborn, there were accounts of angry words on the street, Muslim children harassed at playgrounds, and Arab workers hassled on the job. But the local police were out in force, and there wasn't any serious violence. Still, the emotional toll was heavy. Dearborn's Arab Community Center for Economic and Social Services reported an unprecedented number of people seeking help for depression and anxiety.

Siblani's mood grew grimmer as the FBI swiftly rounded up twelve hundred Arab and Muslim men, including several hundred from the Detroit area. Ultimately, more than eighty thousand Arabs and Muslim foreign nationals were required to register after 9/11; eight thousand were summoned for "voluntary" questioning. The government hasn't pointed to a single significant terrorism prosecution that resulted directly from this process, but deportation proceedings were initiated against nearly thirteen thousand people deemed to be illegal. The registration and interrogation program showed that in the name of fighting terrorism, President Bush had abandoned his campaign promise to stop ethnic profiling and end the use of secret evidence. "By using the tragedy of the 9/11 attacks, the Bush administration abrogated the civil rights of Arab-Americans and Muslim Americans," Siblani editorialized in his newspaper. "George Bush has shaken the very foundations of this country with his assault on civil rights."

Arab-Americans and Muslims all over the country shared this anger. In Dearborn, they had a chance to register their frustration at the highest levels of the Bush administration. Siblani, Imad Hamad, and several other Detroit-area Arab-American leaders sat down in December 2001 with Attorney General John Ashcroft at the U.S. attorney's office in Detroit. At one point during the conversation, Siblani told me, Ashcroft had looked at him and said Arab-Americans should be "thankful" that they hadn't been sent to internment camps as Japanese immigrants were during World War II.

"I resent the comparison!" Siblani said he responded. "You're telling me Arab-Americans are responsible? No, they did not attack. Arab countries? No, they did not attack. Nineteen thugs attacked."

Ashcroft quickly backed down and apologized, Siblani said. But this didn't mollify the publisher, who was convinced that the attorney general had revealed the administration's true thinking before trying to eat his words. (Later asked about the incident, Ashcroft, through a spokesman, declined to comment.)

The FBI announced its intention to intensify investigations of anyone in the United States supporting terrorist groups—whether the groups had anything to do with 9/11 or not. One might have assumed that in this atmosphere Siblani and others in Dearborn would back away from controversial associations in the Middle East. Many did stop making contributions to Muslim charitable groups that came under scrutiny. But even as FBI agents fanned out, Siblani reminded *The Detroit News* of the street celebrations in Dearborn just the previous year, when the Israeli military ended its long occupation of southern Lebanon. "There were people waving the flags of Hezbollah," he said. "How could you not support a group that has driven an occupier from your country?" (Former U.S. national security officials have said Hezbollah provided training and explosives to al Qaeda members in the 1990s, but the Lebanese group hasn't been linked to the attacks of September 11, 2001.)

In the wake of 9/11, several Dearborn residents were convicted of crimes related to Hezbollah. One man went to prison for hosting Hezbollah fund-raising meetings at his home in 2002. Another was put behind bars for sending proceeds from a cigarette-smuggling ring to the Lebanese group. Siblani dismissed such infractions as insignificant, as he had in an earlier case. In a pre-9/11 prosecution he had offered an affidavit on behalf of a pair of brothers named Boumelhem who were accused of trying to ship firearms to Lebanon for use by Hezbollah. The defendants allegedly tried to send two shotguns, components of automatic rifles, and ammunition, all hidden among auto parts. "I tell the judge [in the written affidavit], why would Hezbollah need two shotguns?" Siblani recounted to me. The militant faction receives ample arms and logistical support from Iran and Syria.

One brother, Mike Boumelhem, was acquitted. The other, Ali, had been arrested at the airport in possession of a one-way ticket to Lebanon, a black ski mask, and identification cards with three different names, according to federal agents. He was convicted on September 10, 2001, and sentenced to nearly four years in prison. "These people have nothing to do with Hezbollah," Siblani assured me. "They are just trying to make a buck."

∽

September 11 brought into sharper focus a Muslim concern that Siblani and his newspaper have dwelled on for years: the raw bigotry that flows from the mouths of some fundamentalist Christians. President Bush tells the nation that Islam is not the enemy, but he has done little, if anything, in public to discourage his fundamentalist allies from demeaning Islam.

Televangelist Pat Robertson has called the Prophet Muhammad "an absolute wild-eyed fanatic," with no apparent damage to Robertson's reputation in Republican or Christian circles. Likewise, the Reverend Jerry Vines, the past president of the Southern Baptist Convention, has portrayed the Prophet as "a demon-possessed pedophile." And preacher Franklin Graham, who gave the invocation at Bush's first inauguration and is Billy Graham's son, has called Islam "a very evil and wicked religion."

Many Muslims assume that the fundamentalists speak for Christians generally and that evangelical animus drives the war on terrorism. As *The Arab American News* has reported, the scary truth is that there are Christian fundamentalists who talk about a war against Islam as an essential step toward Armageddon and the return of Jesus. Siblani doesn't think this kind of doomsday thinking has actually motivated America's efforts to protect itself against terrorism. Nor was the invasion of Iraq, whatever its merits, part of a scheme to bring on Judgment Day. But Muslims can see like anyone else the deference fundamentalist Christians receive in the Republican Party.

Siblani's paper covered the case of Lieutenant General William Boykin, a top Pentagon intelligence official. While in uniform, Boykin told Christian audiences after 9/11 that fighting Islamic militants was a religious cause. America would triumph, the general said, only "if we come at them in the name of Jesus." Boykin was forced to apologize when the media aired his comments, but he didn't lose his job. Beyond the sheer insult and alienation it causes, the Christian hostility provides ammunition to those Muslims who are eager to assail America as evil from top to bottom.

By late 2002 the Bush administration had begun in earnest trying to drum up public enthusiasm for invading Iraq. Officials described the prospective invasion as a preemptive strike to neutralize weapons of mass destruction, or as a part of the antiterrorism fight, or as a way to liberate oppressed Iraqis—or all three, depending on what the White House thought would fly at any given moment. Dearborn became a central part of this campaign, as top administration aides huddled with Iraqi expats who favored militarily deposing Saddam. Husham al-Husainy, the imam at the Karbalaa Islamic Education Center, attended meetings in Washington and Dearborn with Defense Secretary Donald Rumsfeld, his top deputy, Paul Wolfowitz, and National Security Adviser Condoleezza Rice, who was later promoted to secretary of state. Wolfowitz, a leading advocate for war, repeatedly invoked the Dearborn Iraqis in his speeches and television appearances. "I wish you could hear some of their stories," he told a Veterans of Foreign Wars convention, "so you could appreciate what those people and their families have gone through and how much they and their relatives back in Iraq want to be freed of Saddam Hussein and freed of the offensive weapons that threaten to terrorize the Middle East and the world."

The attention thrilled members of Dearborn's Karbalaa Islamic Education Center. It disgusted Osama Siblani. He saw the move toward war as one more betrayal by Bush—even though as a candidate Bush had unequivocally told Siblani of his intention to "take out" Saddam. The publisher became an eloquent television opponent of the impending invasion. In a January 2003 exchange, Fox News star Bill O'Reilly demanded to know whether Siblani considered Saddam a "villain."

"Well, I think that he is a bad guy," Siblani said. "He's a dictator." For good measure, he added, "I would be ashamed of most of the leaders of the Arab world." That momentarily thwarted the verbal theatrics O'Reilly seemed eager to start. When the TV host suggested that Saddam might obtain nuclear weapons, Siblani noted, "We really don't know he has weapons of mass destruction."

"That's a canard," O'Reilly snapped. Saddam couldn't account for "a big inventory of weaponry."

"Not according to the United Nations inspectors," Siblani said. "They said they have destroyed ninety-five percent of this stockpile."

O'Reilly tried, implausibly, to cast Hans Blix, then the chief UN inspector, as someone spoiling for war, but Siblani said the host was distorting Blix's comments. Siblani turned out to be correct, of course. The U.S. military never found Saddam's supposed stash of weapons of mass destruction.

At home in Dearborn, the publisher's tone toward the Bush White House grew harsher. "We are against the brutal regime in Iraq, but we are also against the regime in the United States!" he told a cheering crowd of five hundred Arab- and Muslim American antiwar protesters who gathered near Dearborn City Hall in March 2003, as the U.S. invasion was getting under way.

Across Michigan Avenue, two hundred Iraqis held a counterdemonstration, shouting, "One, two, three—set Iraqis free!" Imam Husainy of the Karbalaa center, leading the prowar contingent, said, "Whatever it takes to remove Saddam, let it be. We've got to fight this criminal."

On April 9, when U.S. troops pulled down the statue of Saddam in Firdos Square, Dearborn Iraqis danced on Warren Avenue. But Siblani didn't share the joy. The Iraqi émigrés "do not deserve" to see their dictator deposed by the United States, he told a French journalist. "You want to overthrow Saddam? Then do it yourselves!"

As for the president whose election victory had brought Siblani national recognition, the publisher now saw him as no better than a terrorist. Speaking as if he were addressing the man in the Oval Office, Siblani told me: "What's the difference between you and Osama bin Laden? His God tells him to bomb the World Trade Center. Your God tells you, bomb Baghdad. No difference. You're the same." Siblani, as many Muslims do, expressed indignation over the president's occasional claims that his agenda is divinely inspired. Still, most Americans would not view the intentional killing of thousands of civilians as similar to launching a war—however wisely or unwisely—against a murderous dictator hated by a large majority of his subjects.

Siblani published columns in his paper such as "Slipping Toward Armageddon: Israel in Iraq," which argued that the United States had cleared the way for an imminent Israeli *nuclear* offensive of inconceivable proportions:

Bush's Iraq policy has imploded. In fact, there never was a coherent policy, apart from grabbing the oil. It was always just a bunch of lies packaged as patriotic slogans for popular consumption here at home. And the Israelis, who wanted the war (just about any war is OK with them) are now where they've wanted to be for years, that is, on Iran's border, i.e., positioning themselves for the next round when the shinola really hits the fan: the shooting match that will make everything we've seen up until now look like a warm-up.

The publisher's friends in Dearborn, people who relied on his political acumen, wanted to know why he had failed them by endorsing Bush. He had no good answer. "I have apologized," he told me. Anger poisoned his embarrassment. "Since 9/11," Siblani said, "I have felt choked. I can't breathe, like the Atlantic Ocean is right under my nose and rising. The world has really closed in on me."

SEEDS OF PEACE

In late 2003, in the midst of the controversy over the American adventure in Iraq, Dearborn took time out to feud over Israel. An organization called Seeds of Peace announced that it would hold a gala fund-raising dinner at Dearborn's Ritz-Carlton Hotel. Founded in the early 1990s, the American group brought together Israeli and Palestinian teenagers in hopes of nurturing a generation that could live and work without bloodshed. Seeds of Peace announced that at the dinner it would give an award to former Israeli prime minister Shimon Peres, a Labor Party stalwart who shared the 1994 Nobel Peace Prize. With its penchant for political symmetry, the group said it would give the same award to Sari Nusseibeh, a Palestinian peace activist and president of Al-Quds University.

The very thought of this ceremony infuriated Siblani. He claimed that he had nothing against the basic concept of Palestinian and Israeli teenagers becoming acquainted. But with Ariel Sharon, an architect of the Israeli occupation of Lebanon, in the prime minister's office and Israeli commandos hunting Palestinian militants in Gaza, "Seeds of Peace was no longer a proper vehicle," he asserted. "You can't seed on the rock. You have to have fertile ground."

Peres in particular sparked anger. "Peres's record is full of criminal actions against Palestinians and Arabs," Siblani said in an article in *The Arab American News* headlined "Honoring Peres in Dearborn Causes Outrage." Many Jews would say something similar about a cowinner of the Nobel Peace Prize in 1994, Yasser Arafat, but he wasn't invited to the dinner.

One act specifically made Peres a villain in the eyes of many Arabs in Dearborn. In 1996, when he served as prime minister, Israeli forces fighting Hezbollah guerrillas in southern Lebanon shelled a United Nations compound in the town of Qana, inadvertently killing more than a hundred civilians who had taken shelter there. Among the dead were two boys from a Dearborn family visiting their grandmother for the summer. The deaths became a symbol in Dearborn of Israeli cruelty. Dearborn and Qana established a sister city relationship. With the Peres invitation, *The Arab American News* editorialized, "Seeds of Peace officials have demonstrated an incomprehensible lack of understanding and respect for this community."

Tim Attalla, an organizer of the Seeds of Peace dinner and its twin awards for Peres and Nusseibeh, was surprised by the ferocity of the opposition. "We thought those two would be a good attraction for the Arabs and Jews here in Detroit," he recalled.

Seeds of Peace, which is based in New York, first approached Attalla in 1997 because of his reputation as a moderate Palestinian Muslim. The organization invited him to visit its camp in Maine. "We met these unbelievable kids," Palestinians and Israelis who were bright and open-minded, Attalla said. "It really sent shivers down my spine . . . I was looking at what I envisioned as the future."

Attalla's father, Ahmad, had come to the United States from the Palestinian town of El Bireh in 1950. The old man sold linen from a suitcase until he landed an assembly line job at Ford that eventually put Tim through law school and his brother through medical school. Ahmad built a house on family property in El Bireh to maintain an anchor there. "The Palestinian conflict, to me, is not about land," Tim told me (a view that may seem more obvious to Palestinians still in possession of ancestral property). "It's about rights," he continued. "It's about treating me the same way as anyone else is treated." He looks at the Palestinian plight in very American terms: "I want the same things you want. I want to be able to go to work in the morning and provide for my family. I want to be able to become a consumer and buy that DVD player, and that TV, and a car, and send my kids to school. It's the same thing. There's no difference between Palestinians and Israelis. I feel that once they can get past this wall of hatred and start focusing on what they can be together, they would be an economic force that would transform the entire Middle East."

Even after 9/11 and its fallout, Attalla, an attorney in Dearborn, worked hard to defend his optimistic perspective. He naturally feared for his family's safety. His wife wears the hijab, and his three young sons attend public school in the nearby town of Northville. The boys use their Arabic first names, unlike their father, whose Arabic name is Hatim. But unlike Siblani's bleak account of the local reaction to 9/11, the Attallas report only a single bad encounter: Two older kids told Yusuf Attalla, then ten, "Islam sucks." But the school promptly consoled Yusuf, punished the perpetrators, and informed their parents. "They nipped it in the bud, and that was the only incident," Tim Attalla said. "I guess that's what's great about America. For the most part, there wasn't guilt by association."

He helped start a Detroit-area branch of Seeds of Peace, which launched its own series of lucrative annual fund-raising events. "I'm not going to throw rocks. I'm not going to shoot anybody," he said. "I'm going to find what we have in common and build on that." He paid a personal price for his volunteerism. Many Arab-Americans are wary of any conciliation with Israel, and business at his small law firm fell off every year around the time the Seeds of Peace event appeared in local newspapers. "He gets it from everyone; I feel sorry for him," said Imad Hamad, the civil rights activist, who has himself criticized Attalla. On occasion, after an Israeli military or political action that has met with disapproval in

Dearborn, Attalla has been sitting in a local restaurant and someone has walked by and said, "So, where's your Seeds of Peace now?"

⚊⚊

In the weeks before the Peres/Nusseibeh appearance in December 2003, Osama Siblani organized a town hall–style meeting at which a number of Arab-American leaders announced opposition to the event. In an act of public shaming, *The Arab American News* published the names and business affiliations of members of the Seeds of Peace host committee, including that of Attalla and his law firm. "They slowly began, one by one, pulling out," the attorney remembered. Siblani, he said, "succeeded in intimidating them." The publisher countered that he was only reporting the facts. But this wasn't just about Shimon Peres, Attalla believed. "I don't recall [Siblani's] supporting Seeds of Peace" in earlier years either, the attorney said. Attalla called his imam, Mohamed Mardini, who is from Lebanon and had agreed to offer a prayer at the dinner. Mardini had come under intense pressure to stay away. "I take my orders from a higher authority," the cleric told Attalla. "I will be there tomorrow."

Despite some cancellations by Arab-Americans, the dinner still attracted about six hundred people who contributed at least $250 each. Ford and General Motors led a host of business sponsors that kicked in thousands more apiece. "The greatest enemy of peace is skepticism," Peres told the gathering. "If we are children of Abraham and have the same father, I can't understand why we cannot behave like a family."

Outside the Ritz-Carlton, Osama Siblani led a protest. A hundred picketers stood in the December cold, some holding placards with pictures of Abdul-Muhsen Bitar, nine, and his brother, Hadi, eight, the boys killed in the Israeli bombardment. "Shimon Peres is a war criminal, not a peacemaker," Haidar Bitar, their father, told reporters. "This is an insult," added Siblani. "Honoring a man such as Peres in the middle of our city is a slap in the face of the Arab community."

Two days later, in the early morning before business hours, someone tossed a Molotov cocktail at the back of the *Arab American News* building. The small firebomb did some damage to a bulletproof door, but the building didn't ignite, and there was no one around to be injured. Local police and the FBI investigated but never identified a suspect. Siblani attributed the attack to payback for his protest of Peres. Scores of people contacted the publisher to offer support. Siblani published a letter from Sharona Shapiro, Michigan director of the American Jewish Committee, in which she condemned the firebombing as "an attack upon what we hold most dear," the freedoms of speech and press.

Attalla continued to hear carping about Peres for months. But his law firm business bounced back, as it had in the past. What pained him is that because of the Peres conflict, some people may have concluded that he doesn't understand Palestinian suffering. But this isn't so, he said. He has taken Jewish colleagues to see the Israeli checkpoints where Palestinians wait all day for a chance to visit a sick relative. He has shown his guests the Palestinian towns where the Israelis have redirected the water supply so Arabs go thirsty and dirty. People who lose hope turn to violence, he tells the Americans. The way out, he believes, is to build connections that will lead to trust.

ELECTION DAYS

There never was much doubt about who Osama Siblani and his AAPAC friends would back in the 2004 presidential election: whomever the Democrats nominated to run against Bush. But the publisher relished making the Democrats beg—or at least work—for it. In a telephone conversation in January before the Iowa caucuses, he teased candidate John Kerry: "Looks like you don't have enough fuel to make it to Michigan." Months later, when Kerry did make it to Michigan, Siblani reminded the candidate that Arab-Americans had favored Bush in 2000, only to be disappointed: "I hope you don't disappoint us." Kerry, he said, responded that he would find a way to bring peace to the Middle East.

This didn't impress Siblani. He had little faith that the Democratic candidate would significantly shift U.S. foreign policy. "Kerry Offers Nothing New on Iraq," said one election season report in *The Arab American News*. "John Kerry's Misperception of Palestine," said another. Siblani laughed at

Kerry's stump speech vow that John Ashcroft wouldn't be the attorney general under his command. "You know, of *course* not," Siblani said, rolling his eyes. The question was, would profiling of Arab-Americans and use of secret evidence stop? Unlikely, Siblani thought. "Arabs & Muslims Drift, Not Run, Towards Kerry," his newspaper said in September.

In the end, the AAPAC and *The Arab American News* offered Kerry tepid endorsements that stressed the need to remove Bush. The Republican "administration has proven to be the most arrogant administration in recent history," the paper editorialized. "The only thing Bush has united is the rest of the world against us." In a put-down that to Siblani's great pleasure got wide circulation on the Internet, he said of the administration's Madison Avenue–style campaign to improve America's image in the Middle East: "They could have the Prophet Muhammad doing public relations, and it wouldn't help."

His paper's news coverage of the campaign was often thoughtful, offering Bush loyalists a chance to make their case and sorting through Kerry's record with some care. There were reasonable articles arguing for a quick American retreat from Iraq. But Siblani also published articles that seemed to savor American failure—"Iraq Is Ready to Explode"—and some that indulged variations of opaque conspiracy. Regular contributor Mahmoud M. Awad's anti-Bush screed—"What Happened to My America?"—rolled along predictably until this jumped out: "I still do not know who is responsible for 9/11." In September 2004 this was a bizarre statement. How often did Osama bin Laden have to take credit?

Talking with Siblani in his office, I heard the same kind of jarring dissonance: astute observations about Kerry's incurable diffidence mixed with Siblani's sinister musings about the Middle East. "I support the resistance to an occupation, not only in Lebanon, but anywhere in the world," he said. "In fact I support right now the Iraqi resistance against American forces there."

Favoring attacks on U.S. soldiers? Most Americans would find that repulsive, regardless of their opinion of the U.S. invasion. Did Siblani really mean it?

He dodged the question. "I don't care what the Americans think," he said. "I think what's important here is the principle. The principle is not that when we are the occupier it's okay, when we are not the occupier it's not okay."

Months later, when I asked once more about the Iraqi insurgency, Siblani took a half step back. "I did not support the insurgents," he said. "I supported their right to fight occupation, not necessarily agreeing with their method—like, for example, killing innocent civilians," he continued. "Those people who are genuinely fighting occupation by disobedience, by fighting the army that is occupying directly—those people, they get my support. Not those who are killing innocent civilians and bombing Shiite mosques." He denounced Abu Musab al-Zarqawi, the insurgent leader associated with al Qaeda. In his newspaper Siblani suggested that the United States had allowed the occupation to slide into chaos and violence as part of a secret plan to prevent Iraq from becoming "an Arab superpower."

That some Arab- or Muslim Americans would hold such opinions isn't shocking. But it seems remarkable that someone who does would have been a key Bush supporter in 2000 and then, four years later, host a banquet for more than five hundred people to celebrate his political action committee's endorsement of John Kerry. Yet in October 2004 there was master of ceremonies Osama Siblani, holding forth from the dais of a large Dearborn social hall. Waiters delivered platters of grilled chicken, roasted lamb, and hummus, along with pitchers of Coca-Cola (no alcohol). An Arab-American high school student sang the national anthem.

Members of Congress, Michigan Governor Jennifer Granholm, and Kerry's brother Cameron all accorded Siblani the elaborate deference due a political boss on endorsement day. "It's much better to have him on your side," Representative John Dingell joked to the appreciative audience. "This great publisher," Representative John Conyers called him. The Democratic presidential candidate "is honored, and he is grateful for this endorsement," Cameron Kerry said, applauding the gathering's "deeply felt patriotism."

"George Bush betrayed us!" Siblani bellowed when it was his turn. "Take our country back from those Taliban in Washington!"

Most of the crowd cheered. But at his table Cameron Kerry looked un-

easy, silently tolerating this rant as part of the compromise that both major parties have decided to make in the competition for Arab and Muslim
votes. Siblani's Taliban metaphor might have been a touch stronger than
what others in the room would have chosen for a public event, but his
views evidently enjoyed wide appeal within Dearborn's political class.

⌇⌇

After Bush's victory it didn't seem to bother Siblani very much that Arab-
Americans had bet on the loser this time. He ticked off accomplishments:
Once again there was a cohesive Arab/Muslim vote. Other Arab and Muslim groups around the country, in his opinion, had followed the AAPAC's
lead. Arab-Americans had shown the national parties that they could deliver on a promise. "We cannot be discounted," he said.

On the basis of a poll of voters in four battleground states—Michigan,
Ohio, Pennsylvania, and Florida—Zogby International found that Kerry
won among Arab-Americans by a margin of 63 to 28.5 percent. Muslims
preferred Kerry to Bush by an even more lopsided 83 to 6 percent. Kerry
took Michigan by 166,000 votes and easily won Dearborn.

In the days that followed, Siblani seemed particularly pleased that
GOP operatives were contacting him to try to mend fences. "The Republicans got the message," he told me. Grover Norquist, the Karl Rove ally
and cofounder of the Islamic Free Market Institute in Washington, had
just called. He was flying out to Dearborn to meet with Siblani and some
of his buddies. They would talk about the 2006 midterm elections and
beyond.

⌇⌇

Some of the Shiite Iraqis at the Karbalaa Islamic Education Center who
had been so enthusiastic about President Bush and the Iraq invasion also
shifted their view in 2004. In June, fifteen months after they held their
prowar demonstration to compete with Siblani's antiwar protest, the
Iraqis returned to Dearborn City Hall to denounce the American invasion. "I was pro-war a year ago because we wanted Saddam out, but we
never thought it would get this bad," protester Mohammad Chachour

told *The Arab American News.* "Now the U.S. is out of control, and they must leave." Siblani did not disguise his pleasure at this turn of events. The article carried the headline "Local About-Face on Support of Iraq War."

The bedlam in Iraq had to be intentional, Iraqis at the Karbalaa center said. "We're sure there was a hidden plan," Husham al-Husainy, the aeronautical engineer turned imam, explained. The goal, as it has been for centuries, was to prevent Shiites from gaining power, he said. The Karbalaa center is aligned with the powerful Iraqi Shiite party, the Supreme Council for Islamic Revolution in Iraq. Portraits of its late leader, Ayatollah Muhammad Bakr al-Hakim, hang throughout the mosque. Hakim returned to Iraq from exile in Iran after Saddam was imprisoned, but in August 2003 he was killed in Najaf by a huge car bomb that also took the lives of ninety of his followers.

"They"—the forces of chaos—"want a secular regime to come in, so they change Saddam's face to another Saddam with a different face," Husainy said. "America itself is a victim of a special interest group that doesn't want it to have a good relationship with the Muslim world. Bush himself is a victim, I believe." At the heart of the conspiracy is something he called "the Zionist special group," which opposes "the improvement of relationship between Christians and Muslims."

Trying to take the sting out of this anti-Semitic indictment, the imam's brother-in-law Ihsan Mirza affirmed how much he and his family and friends enjoy living in the United States: "There's honesty in people. There's honesty in the judicial system, civilized country, civilized people with values." He wished more Muslims knew what life in this country is really like. "America is something inside," Mirza said, alluding to his admiration for the order and values of day-to-day existence in his adopted country. But "it's completely contradictory outside," he said, registering his disapproval of the aggressive stance the United States often takes in its foreign relations.

～

On January 28, 2005, I accompanied Mirza and his wife to a cavernous former home improvement store near Dearborn, where they voted in an

Iraqi election for the first time in their lives. (Iraq now recognizes the votes of people overseas who are eighteen and older and whose fathers were born in Iraq.) That morning, the Mirzas said, they were enjoying America's better side, even as they worried about the safety of relatives who would try to cast ballots in Baghdad and Najaf. They confided that two months earlier they had split from Imam Husainy to vote again for George W. Bush. They were suspicious of why the United States had allowed Iraq to descend into disorder after deposing Saddam. Mere incompetence and arrogance weren't possibilities they took seriously. But the important thing was that Saddam was gone. "If it wasn't for the U.S., Hussein's grandson would be ruling fifteen or twenty years from now," Ihsan said. If things calm down, the Mirzas said, they would go back to Iraq, at least for a few years, so they could show it to their children.

Osama Siblani dismissed the Iraqi voting as a sham, part of a cynical public relations campaign by "those Taliban in Washington" to conceal a collapsing occupation. The Mirzas disagreed. They saw the vote as an important step toward democracy in Iraq and a cause for joy.

The drafty polling place for Iraqi-Americans was divided by cloth partitions into voting stations. Magic Marker signs in Arabic offered directions. There were metal detectors, bomb-sniffing dogs, and uniformed police and plainclothes security guards—all reminders of the fierce Sunni insurgency challenging Iraq's tentative move toward democracy. But in Dearborn the Iraqi vote still felt like a celebration. Extended families, many dressed formally, greeted and gossiped. At midday some men laid down cardboard on a corner of the gray concrete floor and prayed in Arabic.

There were III slates of candidates seeking seats in an interim assembly that would draft a constitution. The Mirzas knew which one they wanted: number 169, the main Shiite slate that included the late Ayatollah Hakim's party. When they pushed their folded paper ballots into the large plastic collection boxes, the all-Iraqi staff in their partitioned voting station stood and applauded. Every few seconds, all day, a burst of applause went up for each ballot deposited, about nine thousand of them in Michigan. Nationwide, twenty-four thousand Iraqi-Americans went to the polls, less than 10 percent of those thought to be eligible. But Ihsan saw it as a start. He smiled and held up his index finger, stained with purple ink, an antifraud precaution that became a mark of pride.

"Tell me how it felt to vote," an eager TV news reporter said to Ihsan.

"We're speechless," Ihsan responded. "It's a dream come true."

Ifaa, his wife, was on her mobile phone. "Guess where I am!" she said to her mother in Dearborn. "I'm voting!"

TWO

The Scholar

race Song couldn't stop listening to the tapes. She listened at home and in the car. To have more time, she took the long way to work in suburban New Jersey. The tapes were lectures about some of the most obscure figures imaginable: Muslim women jurists of the medieval era. Song, a marketing executive with an Ivy League M.B.A., sat in her car in the Johnson & Johnson company parking lot, transfixed.

The daughter of Taiwanese immigrants, she was born in 1967 and grew up in Northern California. Her mother had gone to Catholic school and had Grace baptized, but they never went to church. Religion played no role in her "very Americanized" upbringing. Grace excelled at Palo Alto High School, Berkeley, and Cornell Business School. She was smart, athletic, and attractive, with long, sleek black hair.

Still, something was missing. She found herself thinking about God and the meaning of life. Familiar faiths didn't add up for her. She couldn't grasp the Catholic concept of a divine trinity, mystically combined. The Jewish idea of a chosen people didn't work either. What happened to all the people who weren't chosen?

Through encounters with two Muslim foreign students at Cornell—
one, a Pakistani man who prayed five times a day—she learned that Islam
offered what she saw as a simpler, more coherent vision of God. She liked
the idea that Islam honored the prophets of both Jews and Christians. In
snowy Ithaca, New York, she began reading the Quran. There Song discovered a central principle that she found appealing: accountability. She
had always questioned "this Christian notion of everything is okay: God is
love, God is this, God is that. As long as you accept God, everything is fine.
It made more inherent sense to me that if nothing else, God is fair." There
were consequences, good and bad, for people's actions. Eventually she
tried praying on her own. The bowing and kneeling felt awkward, but for
the first time in her life she experienced a sense of spirituality that seemed
authentic, "a sweet exhilaration" she had never felt before. She tried giving up alcohol in the Muslim fashion, and that too felt right. Years later she
self-deprecatingly described this solitary process as a "book conversion" to
Islam.

She graduated from business school with honors in 1993 and went to
work in marketing for Johnson & Johnson. For the first time she began occasionally attending Muslim prayer services at the Islamic Center of New
Jersey, on Route 1 in South Brunswick. In 1994 she asked a friendly and
knowledgeable Muslim man she met there what she needed to do to convert officially. The man, whose name was Mazen, posed a series of questions about faith, ending with "Do you believe that God is the one God
and Muhammad is His final Prophet?" She had always assumed that there
was only one supreme power, and through her reading and introspection
she had come to accept that Muhammad was the final Prophet. So she
said yes. "Congratulations," Mazen said, "you're a Muslim!" That basic
declaration, known as the *shahadah*, is all that Islam formally requires.

Only after proclaiming her faith did Song start worshiping regularly at
the Islamic Center. Pleased as she was to find religion, she quietly questioned some of the rules. Women were sent to a basement room to pray.
They were told to cover their hair at all times. Her conservative white
business blouses, which left her neck exposed, were said to reveal her

"chest"—not allowed. "Women have this aura, this sexuality," her friend Mazen told her. "You've got to cover it." Avert your eyes, she was told. Keep your distance from men.

She felt alienated from the faith she had just joined. She prayed with the other women downstairs but refused to cover her hair outside the mosque or trade her corporate wardrobe for one that Mazen might approve. "You live one life while you're at work. You're a serious businessperson in what you do," Song said years later. "Then you go to the mosque, and it's like, check your brain at the door." She wondered if she could in good faith continue attending communal prayer.

Then she got the audiotapes. At a high school reunion in Palo Alto in fall 1994, Song mentioned her conversion to a female classmate born into an observant Muslim family. The classmate recommended that Song listen to a taped lecture series entitled *Muslim Women Jurists in Islamic History*, by Khaled Abou El Fadl. This is something you're not going to hear at the mosque, her high school classmate told Song. On the recordings, Abou El Fadl recounts the lives of long-ago women scholars. He explains how influential these women were, how they contributed to centuries of vigorous debate within the religion. "Women and law were married to each other," Abou El Fadl says. He tells of the jurists' marriages, divorces, and remarriages; the schools and orphanages they ran. Abou El Fadl says he isn't trying to boost Muslim spirits. "I am not proving to you that women were not oppressed in Islamic history, and I am not proving to you that they were liberated in Islamic history," he lectures. "What I am proving to you is the precedent in Islamic history of different forms of femininity than the ones we are accustomed to today."

"When I started listening to these tapes, my mind exploded," Song recalled. Women could be strong, independent figures within Islam. "It was like, oh, my God, my brain is working again—someone who finally said something. This is the Islam that I came to, what I believe in. This is challenging. This is like, wow!" Behind the wheel one day, she found herself answering the voice on the tape. "I started yelling, 'I love you! I haven't met you, and I *love* you!'"

A LIGHT IN A "DARK AGE"

Khaled Abou El Fadl has that effect on some Muslims. It's not his appearance. In his mid-forties, he is short, balding, and soft. He chugs Diet Coke and smokes heavily, despite a slew of chronic illnesses. Preoccupied by his work, he doesn't drive and can't keep track of keys or a checkbook. Grace Song didn't know any of that at first, but it wouldn't have deterred her. She tracked him down at Princeton University, where he was a Ph.D. candidate in Islamic studies. They met at a bookstore and spent the day together. Within months they were engaged.

Song remained an observant Muslim, one of a number whom, by their accounts, Abou El Fadl has kept from losing their faith. In 2003, Eahab Ibrahim of San Diego wrote to Abou El Fadl, by then a tenured professor of Islamic jurisprudence at the University of California at Los Angeles. "It was an excerpt from one of your books that a friend of mine read to me that I felt took a shield off of my head and allowed one of God's greatest gifts to function, my brain," Ibrahim said. Assim Mohammed had a similar experience. In the midst of what he calls his enlightening phase a few years back, Mohammed read some of Abou El Fadl's essays and was so bowled over that he traveled from his home in Chicago to Los Angeles to meet the scholar. "I was very impressed by his honesty," Mohammed said.

An American-born Christian man considering conversion to Islam e-mailed the professor in 2004: "When I read your work, I feel there may be some room for hope—perhaps even some room in Islam for people like me, who feel the truth of the Prophet's message, but cannot accept that embracing a religion would mean surrendering our intellects at the door of the mosque."

Muslims today, Abou El Fadl says, "are living through the Dark Ages." Amid the gloom, some discontented believers see hope in his effort to smash the shell of narrow-mindedness that he contends Muslims have built around their religion. He has published a half dozen books and more than fifty articles in English that display a mastery of classical Islamic scholarship and a humanistic sensibility he is not ashamed to call Western as well as Islamic. With these, he argues, one can bring to light the beauty at the core of Islam. At its height, a millennium ago, the religion honored intellectual debate. He wants to recover that quality.

Abou El Fadl rejects the game of Good Quran vs. Bad Quran that is played out daily on the newsstand, Internet, and cable television. On one side are Muslim apologists who describe a holy text suffused with only sweetness and light. Muslims who commit terrorism can claim no support from Islam, according to this simplistic view. Meanwhile, such antagonists as right-wing radio hosts and Christian televangelist Pat Robertson dissect the Quran solely to find evidence of cruelty and repression. As the Islamophobes read it, the holy book sounds like an instruction manual for terrorists.

A devout Muslim, Abou El Fadl concedes that Islamic scripture contains passages that can be interpreted in an ugly way. "Oh, you who believe," the Quran instructs at one point, "do not take Jews and Christians as allies. They are allies of each other, and he amongst you who becomes their ally is one of them. God does not guide such evildoers" (5:51). Over the centuries some religious authorities have read this and similar passages in ways that would strike many people today, including many Muslims, as barbaric. Abou El Fadl acknowledges that extremists can find support within the traditions of Islam but defines his job as undermining that support and showing that stronger Islamic arguments exist for tolerance and moderation. These arguments are drawn from the Quran itself—verses such as "God has created you from male and female and made you into diverse nations and tribes so that you may come to know each other" (49:13)—and from an interpretive method that marginalizes more vituperative scriptural passages and seventh-century social practices.

He holds common Muslim views on many contemporary political issues, backing the Palestinian cause and condemning Bush administration foreign policy. But he is a rare, nondogmatic guide in the realm of Islamic history and belief, someone who points the way toward common ground among religions and a means for Muslims to live modern lives without abandoning their faith. And yet within Islam, he encounters disapproval from those who resent his challenging views, especially his contention that Muslims must take moral responsibility for terrorism committed in the name of the Quran.

OF DOGS AND BOOKS

Khaled Abou El Fadl and his family live in what appears from the outside to be an ordinary three-bedroom suburban house in a middle-class neighborhood in the San Fernando Valley. Sprinklers water parched lawns. Nearby commercial avenues are lined by fast-food restaurants. But inside the Abou El Fadl residence an unexpected world exists.

Volumes in Arabic line every wall in every room except the bathrooms. In addition to sections on Islamic jurisprudence and history, there are collections in English on Judaism, Christianity, Western philosophy, and classical music. One of the first things Abou El Fadl did upon my arrival was provide a tour of the stacks. In public he dresses in conventional Western clothing: khaki slacks, turtleneck, and corduroy jacket. At home he wore a black clerical robe over an embroidered white ankle-length gown. He leaned heavily on a carved wooden cane; chronic neurological and bone ailments have hindered his movement. Accompanying us on the tour were Baby, a black Labrador-shepherd mix, and Lulu, a nearly blind terrier who navigates by trial and error. These two dogs remained respectfully silent, but from elsewhere in the house came the yapping of what turned out to be a small pack of additional canines, all rescued, like Baby and Lulu, from the local pound. Mostly mutts, they spend most of their time in a clean, glassed-in area off the kitchen and in an adjacent yard.

A thousand years ago, Abou El Fadl said, gesturing toward his ancient texts, the Islamic world vibrated with scholarly disputation. In more recent centuries this tolerance for disagreement has been largely extinguished. "Muslims have lost the ethos of knowledge, as well as their moral and intellectual grounding," he has argued. He puts much of the blame on Saudi-funded proselytizers who have spread Wahhabism, the kingdom's intolerant strain of Islam. As Abou El Fadl has witnessed personally, Wahhabis encourage the belief that there is only one true approach to Islam, based on a rigid set of dos and don'ts. But if you look back far enough, he said, Islamic intellectual heritage offers far more flexibility than most present-day Muslims realize or care to admit.

Consider the dog. Growing up in the Middle East, Abou El Fadl observed hostility to dogs based on a common Muslim belief that the animals are unclean—specifically, that their saliva voids the ritual purity needed for prayer. This conviction has carried over to Muslims in America, many of whom refuse on religious grounds to keep dogs as pets. Abou El Fadl always found this contrary to common sense. How could Islam abhor animals so loyal and so responsive to human affection? Years ago he investigated the religion's surprisingly prolific literature on the topic. The Quran, first of all, does not condemn dogs as impure or evil. Several well-known historical reports of the Prophet Muhammad's statements and actions (a body of hallowed writing collectively known as *hadith*) do suggest that dogs are impure. But Abou El Fadl found seemingly contradictory hadith indicating the Prophet's gentleness toward the species. Some medieval Islamic scholars portrayed the animals as symbols of faithfulness and self-sacrifice, as suggested by the title of Ibn al-Marzuban's book *The Superiority of Dogs over Many of Those Who Wear Clothes*, published in the tenth century. In his own scholarly article on the topic, "Dogs in the Islamic Tradition and Nature," published in 2004, Abou El Fadl emphasizes the diversity of opinion on the topic down through the ages. "It is clear from the evolution of these discourses," he writes, "that as nature became more susceptible to rational understanding, complex and potentially dangerous creatures, such as dogs, became less threatening to Muslim jurists." Most modern Muslims are unaware of this evolution because "puritanical movements in contemporary Islam," such as Wahhabism, have choked off debate and imposed simplistic notions about what Islam dictates.

What goes for dogs, in his view, goes for non-Muslims, music, women, and warfare: The widely held "Islamic position" is frequently open to question. And just as Abou El Fadl cannot resist acquiring any obscure Islamic tome that makes this point, so he and Grace have difficulty passing the local pound without adopting yet another of humankind's (and Muhammad's) four-legged friends.

∽⊃

Growing up in Kuwait, Abou El Fadl woke to the Quran being recited on the radio. His mother, Afaf El Nimr, listened in the kitchen as she sliced bread for breakfast. She introduced her son to the holy book while her husband tended to his law practice. Abraham, Moses, and Jesus all revered the one God, she taught, and Allah had sent Muhammad as His last messenger. She fed Khaled and his brother and sister pita stuffed with honey, which they called superjihad sandwiches. "Jihad" can mean physical battle in defense of Islam, but it is also commonly used to mean a personal exertion or inner struggle. Khaled's mother prayed aloud for her children: "Oh, God, allow them to enjoy the fruits of their jihad on this earth and in the hereafter."

A social worker by training, she had been sent from Egypt in the mid-1950s by the Egyptian government to pre–oil boom Kuwait, then an underdeveloped patch of desert. Her mission, to help start a mental health hospital, was part of a larger effort by Egypt's President Nasser to assert influence over the postcolonial Arab world. Her family boasts that Afaf received the first Kuwaiti driver's license ever issued to a woman. In Kuwait she met Medhat Abou El Fadl, an idealistic Egyptian lawyer. His prodemocracy agitation had elicited the dark side of Nasserism: Medhat had been tortured by the government and banished to Kuwait. The couple raised their three children in semi-exile, "constantly in waiting, waiting to go back to Egypt," as Khaled later recalled.

The boy hungered for books. He appropriated his father's biographies of Churchill, Roosevelt, and Nehru. He also excelled in religious studies, attending Islamic classes at night after a full day of secular school. During Kuwaiti school vacations his parents sent him to Egypt for additional religious training. He says he had memorized the entire Quran by age fourteen.

At the mosque he attended in Kuwait, students gathered in circles around sheikhs hired to train them. There were often several circles going at once, and gradually Khaled's attention was drawn to one of the other groups. "They were constantly getting these sermons in which they were yelling and screaming, and they looked like they were having much more fun than us," he remembered. The discussion in this raucous circle focused on politics more than on books. Muslims, the students shouted, were oppressed everywhere and by everyone. "But at the same time, they made you feel really good about yourself individually," Abou El Fadl recalled. "They always talked about how God promised victory to His true soldiers, and you are the true soldiers, and it's through you that the liberators of Islam will come."

This combination of defeatism and insistence that "Islam is the answer" exerted a strong pull on Abou El Fadl, as it did on many young Arabs in the 1970s. By then Nasser's pan-Arab program had collapsed. Every day, it seemed, the radio announced new Israeli military advances, while Arab dictators brutalized their own people. Islamic revivalists preached that only a society relying on the Quran as its constitution would be able to defeat the Zionists, overcome the Arab tyrants, and escape the secularizing influences of the Americans and Soviets. Abou El Fadl moved over to join the true soldiers.

He grew the beginnings of a scraggly beard. In the pocket of his short white robe he kept a twig known as a *miswak*, similar to what Muhammad and his companions had used to brush their teeth. Imitation of even the mundane habits of the Prophet was thought to heighten piety. If Muslims would return to the "straight path of Islam," all problems afflicting them would abate. Islam, it was preached, offered a self-sufficient alternative to capitalism and Marxism. This Islamic Dream, as he later called it, enveloped Khaled at age fourteen. He announced to his parents one day that there would be no more mixing of male and female guests at their home. He destroyed his sister's Rod Stewart tapes and mocked his father's conviction that elections and free speech would strengthen Arab societies.

His father responded with a challenge: If Khaled would attend a certain sheikh's classes on Islamic law and answer all questions correctly, the family would bow to the teenager's commands. On the appointed day Khaled sat with the sheikh and his students. Rather than spew political slogans, the scholar posed questions in the Socratic style. Always there was another query, a contradiction, or a paradox. Khaled, unaccustomed to the absence of simple answers, became flummoxed. Others were better informed and more eloquent. He ran home afterward and crawled under his bed. His father came in and told him his only problem was arrogance.

Khaled continued to study but stopped looking for easy answers. He woke from the Islamic Dream. Eventually he accumulated two dozen *ijazas*, or licenses, to teach such technical topics as Quranic grammar and the authentication of hadith. He also wrote poetry, some critical of the Egyptian government. The country's security forces, ever attuned to dissent, noticed when he published some of his work in newspapers and magazines. Twice while he was visiting Egypt as a teenager, the secret police arrested and beat him, warning that he should stick to explicating the Quran. "I was going to get an ulcer," Abou El Fadl recalled. "I just sat around and worried all day, every time I heard footsteps, especially after midnight, because they always showed up after midnight."

A family friend who had served as a government minister recommended that he abandon his plans to study law in Egypt. The ex-official had connections at Yale University, to which a hastily assembled application was sent. Soon a telegram arrived from New Haven, Connecticut, saying Khaled was accepted as a freshman for the class of 1986.

Tempted by religious extremism and bullied by the guardians of despotism, Abou El Fadl might well have chosen a militant path. Many other Arabs of his generation did. Instead, in 1982, at the age of eighteen, he headed for America to continue his studies and take advantage of the chance to speak and write as he chose.

He arrived with broken English and little preparation for American college life. Group shower rooms, drunken parties, smug preppies: they all shocked the shy Egyptian. He felt at home in the Beinecke Library, though, and became fascinated by political science. His English improved. In the spring of his junior year he was named a Scholar of the House, one of Yale's top undergraduate academic honors.

While his classmates spent summers backpacking in France or interning on Capitol Hill, Abou El Fadl took the risk of returning to Egypt. He was determined to earn enough ijazas to merit the title of sheikh. The best place to do that was al-Azhar in Cairo, an ancient mosque and university known as the premier educational institution in the Middle East. He kept his head down and hoped the police had more important people to harass.

He studied primarily with sheikhs from the disappearing Usuli school of jurisprudence. Islamic legal scholars have historically played a leading role in interpreting the Quran and hadith to determine how God wishes believers to live. During the religion's early centuries, various schools of thought offered competing methods for discerning divine intentions. Most withered over time, and in the past half century variations of fundamentalism have gained dominant influence. Abou El Fadl's Usuli teachers held out against the fundamentalist view that the Quran has one clear meaning and that any differing view is false. The Usulis believe that mere mortals must take tremendous care not to misconstrue the Quran. They worry that human scholars can't possibly appreciate God's full meaning, and therefore any interpretation must remain tentative. "As long as God is in the picture, the ethic is humility," Abou El Fadl explained.

One verse that illustrates this difference concerns the nature of the Quran itself. It states that some passages of the holy book are clear and form its foundation but that others are more ambiguous. "Those in whose hearts is perversity follow the part that is not of established and clear meaning, seeking discord and searching for its concealed meanings," the verse states. "In truth, only God knows its true meaning" (3:7).

The passage acknowledges ambiguity in the Quran but seems to condemn those who focus excessively on vagueness. Fundamentalists rely on the passage to attack any effort to reinterpret the Quran in a modern context, insisting that the one and only true Islam is their literalist understanding of how the religion was practiced by the Prophet and his companions.

Abou El Fadl takes a much more open-ended view, offering several alternative interpretations of the verse. First, it's possible that God meant it to apply only to the specific context of seventh-century Medina, where "hypocrites" misused divine revelations to attack the fledgling Muslim community. Another possibility is that the verse asserts that there is a core of clear meaning in the Quran, surrounded by an unspecified amount of ambiguous material, the purpose of which only God understands. Readers must apply their rational faculties to distinguish between the two.

In much the same vein, Abou El Fadl recounts a lunch years ago at the home of an Usuli sheikh and his wife in Cairo. Abou El Fadl portrays himself as an overly eager student, shifting the discussion to the many contradictions in historical accounts of what the Prophet said and did. "I read reports that the Prophet never struck, cursed, or insulted anyone," the young Abou El Fadl said, "and then I find these reports that claim he permitted men to beat their wives or something equally immoral."

The sheikh's wife interrupted him. "There are a million reports that the Prophet never struck or insulted anyone, and any self-respecting Muslim woman would not stay a single day with her husband if he dared strike her!"

"Khaled," the Usuli scholar added, "the Prophet is reported to have said that after his death, there will be many reports about him, and many of these reports will be pure inventions. The Prophet instructed that we must examine these reports in light of the Quran." In the Quran, the sheikh continued, God describes the Prophet as a man of mercy and compassion. Any historical report to the contrary "should give us a serious pause," the sheikh said.

The lesson: When confronted with ambiguity, the Usuli scholar states only what he knows for sure, which may be little. As for the rest, he suspends judgment and considers contrary opinions.

WAHHAB'S LEGACY

But the cautious Usuli way has largely disappeared from the Muslim world. In ascendance have been Wahhabism and its fundamentalist cousins.

Wahhab, the harsh eighteenth-century evangelist, formed an alliance with an ambitious desert clan named Saud. Together they launched a rebellion against the Ottoman Empire. Operating in what today is Saudi Arabia, the Wahhabi-Saud forces slaughtered thousands of Muslims they deemed apostates, as well as many non-Muslims. The rebellion was ultimately put down, but in the twentieth century the Wahhabi-Saud alliance revived. With encouragement from an oil-thirsty West—initially Britain and later the United States—it became the foundation of the modern Saudi state. In the 1960s and 1970s the House of Saud promoted Wahhabism to counter the secular pan-Arabism popularized by Egypt's charismatic President Nasser. Saudi proselytizing became even more vigorous after the 1979 Islamic Revolution in neighboring Iran. The Saudis, who are Sunni, viewed the radical Shiite Iranian mullahs as rivals in a contest to dominate Islam internationally. In the decades since, Saudi oil profits have fueled the spread of fundamentalism throughout the Muslim world and the West. One example: the Saudi-funded Islamic Assembly of North America. Started in 1993 and based in Ypsilanti, Michigan, the *dawa*, or proselytizing, group gained a national following among immigrant Muslim college and graduate students. Persian Gulf preachers featured on IANA-supported Arabic-language Web sites have endorsed violent jihad, the slaughter of Jews, and the idea that the United States is the enemy of Islam.

Abou El Fadl observed the Wahhabi ideological takeover firsthand. One of his favorite teachers at al-Azhar, he said, took more than a million dollars in Saudi money and dutifully produced a pro-Wahhabi book. The Saudis paid for imams and jurists from around the world to take sabbaticals in Mecca. To maintain his independence, Abou El Fadl told me, he had turned down Saudi offers of hundreds of thousands of dollars in grants and prize money over the years. The unlikely aspect of his religious education is that he emerged untainted by rigid fundamentalism, thanks largely to his parents and a handful of elderly scholars loyal to a nearly extinct school of thought.

The summer after Yale named him a Scholar of the House, Abou El Fadl returned to Cairo, where his luck ran out with the Egyptian police.

One evening, as he left his study circle in Cairo, several men in plain clothes grabbed him, the way government thugs had taken his father decades earlier. The authorities held him for three weeks in a Cairo jail, never naming his supposed offense. For long periods they suspended him from the ceiling by one arm. They gave him electric shocks and pulled out his fingernails. But there was nothing for him to confess. His achievements at Yale did nothing to protect him in a secret Egyptian jail cell. If anything, his captors' taunts indicated that his success in America had made him seem like more of a threat in the eyes of the Egyptian government. One day the security forces let him go, still with no explanation.

He went back to New Haven and kept silent in public about what had happened. He worried he would endanger relatives still living in Egypt if he made an issue of having been tortured. The experience confirmed his pessimism about the prospects for freedom in the Middle East. Upon graduating from Yale in 1986, he resolved that he owed it to his parents and the Usuli sheikhs to try to spark an Islamic intellectual rebirth and that the place to do it was in the predominantly Christian United States.

"Western education," Abou El Fadl said in one of our long conversations, "gave me keys to be able to approach the classical [Islamic] tradition and understand and see it in a way that I could not see it when I was approaching that tradition from the perspective of a defeated and insecure people, from the perspective of a present-day Muslim." He learned methods of literary criticism that question the roles of author and reader. He became adept at the analysis used by American constitutional scholars when they debate whether texts can "evolve" with changing societal standards. And he gained confidence in the use of human reason in the search for divine meaning. Along the way he earned a law degree from the University of Pennsylvania in addition to his Ph.D. in Islamic studies from Princeton.

He led a complicated personal life. A first marriage to a Muslim woman ended in divorce (which is permitted in Islam), leaving him with custody of a young son. Abou El Fadl supported himself and the boy by working as a lawyer on immigration cases while completing his doctorate. His mother came from Egypt to help look after the child.

While still in his twenties, he began to receive pleas from other Muslims in America for guidance on Islamic law. The people who came to his door often were women unhappy with how they had been treated by Muslim men. One, a convert, about thirty years old, visited him in his office at the University of Texas in Austin, where he landed a job teaching Islamic law. On her first visit to the mosque, the visitor said, men told her she could greet them, but only if they greeted her first. Otherwise she should remain silent. "Yet another woman attracted to the religion and repulsed by the followers—validated by the Quran and voided by the Muslims," Abou El Fadl recalled. It was an echo of his wife Grace's frustrating experience.

He informed his visitor that a number of Islamic sages over the centuries have manipulated reports about the Prophet's words and deeds to come up with rules that oppress women. In Abou El Fadl's view, the dignity God granted His female servants was taken away by later generations of Muslim men. "The evidence conflicts, and the jurists disagree," he told his visitor. But return to the Quran, he advised, where God told Muhammad, "When you enter houses, greet each other with a greeting from Allah, pure and blessed" (24:61).

But what of the men at the mosque? the young woman asked.

"I think you say, 'Peace be unto you, we do not seek after the ignorant,'" Abou El Fadl replied. That too is from the Quran (28:55).

AN HOUR'S REFLECTION

When portraying the Prophet, Abou El Fadl describes a man dedicated not just to faith but to knowledge. Muhammad is said to have declared that "an hour's reflection is better than a year's worship." Puzzled, followers asked the Prophet whether reflection was better than reading the Quran. "Can the Quran be useful without knowledge?" Muhammad answered. Abou El Fadl interprets the anecdote as teaching that even the devout must learn about the world and think independently.

He enlists the Prophet as an ally in the great intelle
divides Islam, that pitting rationalists (including the l
mentalists (including the Wahhabis). Scholars will quib
which are admittedly crude. But broadly speaking, ration
thinkers have argued that the Quran can be understood as both the
word of God and a historical document whose larger meaning migh.
progress with the times. That evolution requires the reader's participation, the "hour's reflection" to which Muhammad referred. Fundamentalists have insisted that the Quran has a single fixed meaning, not open to
reconsideration. In this rigid view, the ideal society grows not so much
out of intangible principles derived from God's word as from the repro-
duction of a particular place and time, the early Muslim community led
by the Prophet and then, after his death in 632, by his companions.

The rationalists of the Muslim world are losing this contest, but Abou
El Fadl refuses to surrender. He wants to renew the debate in the West.
He reminds Muslims, and anyone else who is interested, that what today
seem like dissenting voices once spoke loudly and, in the case of the
Prophet, with more authority than any fundamentalist preacher or mili-
tant.

Muhammad's full name was Abu al-Qasim Muhammad ibn 'Abd Allah
ibn 'abd al-Muttalib ibn Hashim. He led caravans for a living. His home,
the desert city of Mecca, served as both a commercial crossroads known
for loose morals and a religious center to which pilgrims trekked to worship scores of gods and goddesses. While some Meccans grew wealthy
from trading and hosting pagan rites, others chose a different path. Con-
templative men known as *hanifs* went off on their own to worship a powerful deity known as Allah, or "the God." Muhammad, though engaged in
commerce, apparently had reservations about Mecca's religion business.
He would have learned about the alternative of monotheism not only
from local hanifs but also from Jews and Christians he met during his
travels.

Between journeys Muhammad began spending extended periods

ditating in a cave near Mecca, and at the age of forty, he reported receiving revelations from Allah, as delivered by the angel Gabriel. These
messages—laying out a reformulated religion of one deity, along with
stringent guidelines for human conduct—continued over twenty-two
years, until Muhammad's death. The Prophet repeated the revelations to
his companions and wives. Years later these utterances were compiled
as the Quran, which means "recitation." According to Islamic tradition,
Muhammad was illiterate and played no role in composing the Quran. He
merely recited God's word.

A bit shorter than the New Testament, the Quran contains 114 chapters that are arranged neither chronologically nor by theme (posing a
challenge to a first-time reader expecting linear narrative). Divine guidance conferred in Mecca, where Muhammad and his early converts were
persecuted, tends to have a tolerant and ameliorative tone. Some scholars
have observed that the conciliatory approach may reflect the situation of
a new and struggling sect. In 622 the Muslims fled to Medina, where they
thrived and grew in numbers. Many of the revelations Muhammad is
thought to have announced in Medina seem more like immediate guidance for an ambitious community jostling with its rivals. Allah sometimes
spoke in a belligerent manner during this period.

As with any holy book, knotty questions of interpretation arise. Muslims clash, for example, over whether later, more bellicose verses cancel
out earlier revelations that limited jihad to a strictly defensive war. Was
God editing Himself? One passage that has been used to legitimate un-
conditional warfare against non-Muslims is: "When the sacred months
have passed, slay the idolaters wherever you find them, and take them cap-
tive, and besiege them, and lie in wait for them at every conceivable
place" (9:5). Often overlooked by those who quote that instruction, whether
to justify aggression or paint the Quran as inciting violence, is the very
next sentence, which states that if the idolaters "repent and take to
prayer" and pay a religious tax to the Muslims, they should be allowed to
go on their way, "for God is forgiving and kind" (9:5). By the standards of
the seventh century, the latter injunction was fairly humane. To what

degree should the Quran's teachings on just warfare, or relations between the sexes, be read in historical context?

Abou El Fadl reads the Quran's basic themes of justice, compassion, and mercy as timeless but considers their *application* a subject worthy of perpetual reexamination. He argues that the specific instructions on how the first Muslims should act that God revealed to Muhammad should be interpreted in light of practices of that time. The Quran, like the Bible, offers no prohibition of slavery, a common practice among ancient Arab tribes. That doesn't mean that Muslims today ought to practice slavery. Abou El Fadl suggests focusing instead on the encouragement the Quran and a number of hadith offer to those who treat slaves well or free them. Promoting freedom, he argues, is the enduring lesson.

Islam means "peace" or "submission," and Muslims are those who submit to God. At the end of time, He will sit in judgment of all people. The essential moral teaching of the Quran echoes that of Jewish and Christian scripture: Treat others as you would have them treat you. Muhammad taught that the God of the Quran is the same God worshiped by Jews and Christians. The Quran recognizes those earlier faiths and offers itself as a corrective document, clarifying the crucial teachings of the Jews and Christians. It sets the record straight on questions such as the divinity of Jesus (a prophet but not the son of God) and reminds Muslims to seek justice: "You are the best community evolved for mankind, enjoining what is right and forbidding what is wrong" (3:110).

Portions of the Quran, like portions of Jewish and Christian scriptures, appear to be very much in tension. Chapter 5 of the Quran generously instructs that Jews, Christians, and "any who believe in God and the Final Day, and do good" will achieve salvation (5:69). Yet the same chapter offers the verse I cited earlier about not taking Jews and Christians as allies. Can these passages be reconciled? Perhaps the more generous revelation indicates that at first God (and Muhammad) expected the Jews and Christians to embrace Islam. But after the earlier monotheists resisted conversion, the later revelation conveyed a growing divine (and prophetic) impatience.

Abou El Fadl rejects this interpretation as reflecting Western condescension toward Islam and its scripture. He argues that the seemingly conflicting messages of chapter 5 in fact contain a unified, if complicated, message. These revelations are thought to have come as Muhammad was establishing his community in Medina, sometimes competing with and battling Jewish and Christian tribes. Abou El Fadl reads the chapter as a whole as presenting a "layered discourse about reciprocity." In part, the chapter calls on Muslims to rally behind their leader. "But its point is not to issue a blanket condemnation against Jews and Christians," in his view. "Instead it accepts the distinctiveness of the Jewish and Christian communities and their laws, while also insisting that Muslims are entitled to the same treatment as those other communities. Thus it sets out an expectation of reciprocity for Muslims: While calling upon Muslims to support the Prophet of Islam against his Jewish and Christian detractors, it also recognizes the moral worth and rights of the non-Muslim."

Plucked out of context, as it often is, the verse warning against alliances with Jews and Christians sounds like a prescription for religious bigotry. In the wrong hands it becomes an instrument to persuade the malleable that attacking Jews and Christians doesn't violate Islam's sacred word. "Clearly these possibilities are exploited by the contemporary puritans and supremacists," Abou El Fadl acknowledges. "But the text does not command such intolerant readings." His Usuli teachers had cautioned that any time a Quranic interpretation pointed away from mercy and compassion it deserved reconsideration.

When addressing the Quran's apparent inconsistency on the question of non-Muslims, Abou El Fadl's talk of reciprocity seems far preferable to an edict forbidding any dealings with the infidels, or worse. All the same, in this example, and others, one suspects that Abou El Fadl has his thumb on the scale, tilting any "layered discourse" in the direction of the laudable results he seeks. Whether those results flow naturally from the text is another question.

While still a graduate student at Princeton, Abou El Fadl began lecturing at mosques and Islamic centers around the country. His audiences, mostly younger, responded enthusiastically to his call for reexamination of what many Muslims in America take to be settled questions about marriage, relations with non-Muslims, and living in the West. He argued that his humanist views have roots in traditional Islamic values. He told his listeners that while the leaders of their local mosques may reduce Islam to a simplistic list of rules, scholars of much earlier eras had debated the religion in a freewheeling manner. Abou El Fadl traces the squelching of this healthy discussion to the rise of Wahhabism in the eighteenth century and its latter-day revival. Other scholars have argued that the closing off of reinterpretation and debate began much earlier in Muslim history. The resolution of that debate doesn't affect Abou El Fadl's liberating message for American Muslims: Their intellectual heritage contains ample precedent for creative thought.

In his talks, he scoffed at how much time and energy Muslims in the United States spend debating whether women should always cover their hair in public or whether during communal prayer they should be separated from men by a physical barrier. Neither practice is an absolute religious requirement, according to the Quran and hadith, he said. He blamed the obsession with what he considers trivial questions on the fact that immigrant Muslim communities in America are typically led by engineers, doctors, and computer experts who conceal their lack of deep theological understanding with superficial displays of religiosity.

A seventeen-year-old son of Egyptian immigrants, Eahab Ibrahim first heard Abou El Fadl lecture in 1997 at the Islamic Center of Southern California. Ibrahim later recalled viewing Abou El Fadl as "part of the Zionist conspiracy to prevent Muslims from sticking to their religion." The teenager felt uncomfortable at the lecture because men and women sat together in the audience. In college Ibrahim stayed away from the humanities because he thought that a Muslim had nothing to learn from the philosophy and literature of unbelievers. The attacks of 9/11, however, prompted him to look anew at his faith—and at Abou El Fadl. A friend read him an excerpt from one of Abou El Fadl's books. "It had a profound effect on me," Ibrahim told me. "I learned that Muslims didn't always agree on everything." Today, a software engineer in San Diego, he attends Friday prayers but also reads about Western philosophy and history. He sees reflections of divinity in religions other than Islam. "This is quite a shift from someone who loathed reading all his life and whose mosque religious training had taught him to be scared of any books except the Quran," Ibrahim wrote in a letter to Abou El Fadl in 2003, thanking the professor for changing his life. "I ask Allah to give you and others like you patience to continue your work in helping to resurrect Islamic intellect and civilization."

In 1997 the leaders of the Islamic Center of Greater Austin decided they had heard enough from Abou El Fadl. He was teaching at the University of Texas and winning a following among some Muslim students. One Friday he was invited to the conference room of the center, which served as the mosque for the Austin area. He recalled that when he arrived, he found fifteen engineers and computer science experts, Muslim men he knew, arrayed around the table. They didn't hold back. His ideas were impermissible innovations, one man told him. Another called Abou El Fadl the Great Satan. They told him to leave the premises and never return. Men followed him out the door and onto the street, repeating their condemnations with increasing vehemence. One took off his shoe and began swinging it at Abou El Fadl. "I made a point to turn and stare at him—to show him that I was not afraid—and then calmly walked away," the scholar told me. (The mosque's current board of trustees said no one there recalled the encounter, and there was no record of it.)

It particularly galled Abou El Fadl that he faced resistance from American Muslims he considered arrogant but ignorant about their religion. "I know from experience that Muslims hardly read—not even the Quran for that matter," he wrote in a 1997 essay that referred obliquely to the episode in Austin. Too many immigrant Muslims isolated themselves from secular society, in his view: "They build Islamic centers, organize camps and conferences, and pretend that the mainstream does not exist.

Although Islamic centers are necessary for generating a basic sense of community and identity, they are rarely a serious avenue for knowledge or discourse on Islam. As to the camps, conventions, and conferences, all too often they are no more than pep rallies or cheerleading events." The essay, entitled "On Knowledge," was later included in *Conference of the Books: The Search for Beauty in Islam*, a collection of short writings that Abou El Fadl published in 2001. The book, by turns acerbic, melancholy, and funny, became popular among college-educated Muslims who are religiously observant but skeptical of Islamic organizations.

A couple of years after the Austin incident Abou El Fadl encountered a group of Muslims protesting a talk he was giving at UCLA's Hillel House, the Jewish student center. The picketers condemned any friendly contact with the Jewish organization, he recalled. "We do not want to lose respect for you!" some of the demonstrators told him. "Since when has the desire for respect motivated me?" he replied.

He often found Muslim rejection of Western customs and culture inane. Many American Muslims believe their religion bans music because it is an enticement to carnality. In fact the Quran includes no such prohibition. Sayings attributed to the Prophet Muhammad caution against women singers, flutes, and stringed instruments. But there is debate over these attributions, and as Islam spread over the centuries and mingled with a range of societies, music became a venerated art form among many Muslims. Only over the last three or four decades have the exceptionally austere traditions of the Saudi Wahhabis and other fundamentalists, who proscribe music and public jollity, exerted an impressive and little-understood influence on Muslim attitudes worldwide. American Muslims who forbid music act out of ignorance of Islam's cultural history or a misguided desire to demonstrate their piousness, according to Abou El Fadl. He, by contrast, hears evidence of the divine in Brahms and Chopin.

Some American Muslims who reject music also disdain such innocuous Western customs as audiences clapping in appreciation. The Prophet is said to have prohibited clapping when believers ritualistically circled the Kaaba, the ancient cube-shaped shrine in Mecca. But how, Abou El Fadl asks, "did this become a prohibition against ovations or acclaim or merriment or festivity?" His answer: "I move from mosque to mosque, and I encounter Muslims who seem to think that the harsher and the more perverse the law, the more its Islamic authenticity." There is an expression of mass appreciation that passes muster with Muslims concerned about such matters. Rather than applaud, an audience member will shout, "Takbir!" and other spectators will respond, "Allahu akbar!" (God is great!). The call-and-response is repeated three times. "God is always great," argues Abou El Fadl, who has heard the salute after numerous talks. "But I recoil at the unfortunate impression that my lecture is somehow sanctified by God's greatness."

He grew scornful. Educated Muslims in the United States and around the world, he wrote in a December 1999 essay, "adore activism, abhor intellectualism, and happily learn our religion from pamphleteers." Gradually his audiences picked up on his contempt, and Abou El Fadl's speaking invitations came less frequently. Even as he disparaged Muslim gatherings, though, he mourned his exclusion and worried about being consumed by bitterness. "I chide myself," he wrote, "for the pessimism that threatens to descend into misanthropy."

"Khaled is not a person to mince words," according to Assim Mohammed, a young insurance company executive who became friendly with him in the late 1990s. "He is not a very patient personality," Mohammed said, and "that is not very appealing to average Muslims who are looking for scholars who are more respectful." Islamic conferences that combine religion and socializing are a staple of immigrant Muslim life. But these events typically don't challenge audiences so much as try to reassure them. Abou El Fadl didn't fit in, and that's why Assim Mohammed and some other open-minded young Muslims found him so fascinating. Born in the Chicago suburbs to a Pakistani-immigrant family, Mohammed had led the Muslim Students Association at the University of Illinois. Then, in his mid-twenties, he grew disillusioned by what he saw as the narrowness of many American Islamic groups. "I was looking for intellectual honesty, looking for thinking not locked into a specifically Muslim political mind-set," Mohammed told me. Abou El Fadl argued

persuasively that Islamic tradition permits, even/
restlessness.

knowled
with
pass

FIGHTING "UGLINI

On February 23, 1998, Osama bin Laden issued a ju..
entitled "Declaration of Jihad Against Jews and Crusaders." Di..
by fax and on the Internet by radical Muslim groups, it states, in part.
"The ruling to kill the Americans and their allies—civilians and military—
is an individual duty for every Muslim who can do it in any country in
which it is possible to do it. This is in accordance with the words of
Almighty Allah, 'and fight the pagans all together as they fight you all together' and 'fight them until there is no more tumult or oppression, and
there prevail justice and faith in Allah.'" Few Americans paid attention to
bin Laden until after his minions struck on 9/11. At that point many
people wanted to know whether the words of the Quran really meant
anything close to what the wealthy Saudi jihadist claimed.

The inescapable fact, according to Abou El Fadl, is that the Quran
does contain a healthy supply of bellicose exhortation. Bin Laden's quota-
tions are more or less accurate in a literal sense, giving him and al Qaeda
legitimacy in the eyes of many millions of Muslims. Abou El Fadl, who
condemns all terrorism, argues that bin Laden relies on the Quran selec-
tively and without attention to historical context. But squaring Abou El
Fadl's position with the ancient Islamic text requires work.

In chapters revealed during the Medinan period of expanding Muslim
power, the Prophet's followers were instructed, as bin Laden claimed, to
fight unbelievers until all "oppression" had ended (8:39, 9:36). The Quran
forbids "aggression" and requires that any hostilities be proportional to
the provocation, but it urges Muslims to slay "those who wage war against
you . . . wherever you may come upon them, and drive them away from
wherever they drove you away—for oppression is worse than killing"
(2:190–191). Likewise: "Fight those among the People of the Book [Jews
and Christians] who do not believe in God or the hereafter, who do not
forbid what God and His Prophet have forbidden, and who do not ac-

ge the religion of truth—fight them until they pay the poll tax
illing submission and feel themselves subdued" (9:29). Yet another
age popular with fundamentalist Muslims states, "Whomsoever fol-
ows a religion other than Islam, this will not be accepted from him, and
in the hereafter he will be among the losers" (3:85).

Abou El Fadl points to the troubling fact that bin Laden and his ilk
aren't the first to invoke these passages as a rationale for violence. "Many
classical [Islamic] jurists adopted an imperialist orientation, which divided
the world into the abode of Islam and the abode of war, and supported ex-
pansionist wars against the unbelievers," Abou El Fadl writes in *The Place
of Tolerance in Islam*, a collection of essays published in 2002. Wahhab revived some of these ideas in the eighteenth century, and later, in a very different setting, so did the Muslim Brotherhood of Egypt. In 1928 the
Egyptian schoolteacher Hassan al-Banna established the Muslim Brotherhood with two goals: providing social services to the poor and steering a
modernizing Egypt back toward a society dominated by Islam in every respect. This conviction that Islam contains the solution to all social and political problems produced the bumper sticker ideology—"Islam is the
answer"—that Abou El Fadl encountered as a teenager in Kuwait. As it
attracted popular support, the Brotherhood also ran into stiff official
resistance. Some in the movement turned to violence. After a group of
Muslim Brothers tried to kill President Nasser in 1954, the Egyptian dictator banned the organization and locked up thousands of its followers.
Muslim Brothers scattered across the Middle East, spreading a mixture of
religious fundamentalism and radical political ideology.

One of those Nasser imprisoned, a philosopher and writer named
Sayyid Qutb, crystallized a violent strategy for Islamic resurgence that has
motivated Muslim terrorist groups ever since. Qutb saw Islam in perpetual conflict with Judaism, Christianity, and secular modernity. The Cru-
sades had never really ended, in his view, and neither had the West's desire
to destroy Islam. His prescriptions were jihad, the obligatory military defense of Islam, and, for the individual Muslim, pursuit of martyrdom, a
form of death that pleased God and inspired others to give their lives too.

The Nasser government executed Qutb in 1966, turnin[g]
and burnishing the Brotherhood's revolutionary aur[a]
Saudis hosted and funded Brotherhood émigrés as par[t]
counter Nasser's spreading influence. Although Wahh[ab]
ideology have different historical and cultural roots, ele[ments]
combined to help create the surge of Islamic fundamentalism that began
in the 1970s. As mentioned earlier, this fundamentalism sometimes has
marched under the banners of Salafism and other movements.

Today the Brotherhood continues to agitate across the Middle East, its
status varying from country to country. In Egypt, where it is officially
banned but informally tolerated, it provides the only significant political
opposition to the repressive government of President Hosni Mubarak.
Brotherhood spokesmen now profess nonviolence, while declaring that
America is manipulated by "the sons of Zion" and that the Holocaust is a
myth. Offshoots of the group have followed Qutb's exhortations about jihad and martyrdom, leaving a bloody trail that includes the assassination
of Egyptian President Anwar Sadat in 1981. Muslim Brothers formed the
prolific Palestinian terrorist organizations Hamas and Islamic Jihad. Yet
another vicious outgrowth, Egyptian Islamic Jihad, was led by Osama bin
Laden's top lieutenant, Ayman al-Zawahiri, who merged his organization
into the al Qaeda network in 1998. Bin Laden's condemnation of the West
and celebration of martyrdom echo his ideological forefather, Sayyid Qutb.

Abou El Fadl admirably confronts these developments and the dangerous ways that fundamentalists of various pedigrees can use ancient texts.
"Do the bin Ladens of the Muslim world actually find justification for the
ugliness that they perpetuate in any interpretative tradition in Islam?" he
asks. "Does this level of intolerance and criminality find support, regardless of how flimsy or absurd, in some of the traditional interpretations? I
think that unfortunately, the answer must be yes; it would be dishonest to
say otherwise." The God of Israel of course can sound every bit as pitiless
in the Hebrew Bible as the divine voice of the Quran. In the Book of Exo-
dus, the Lord encourages the followers of Moses to slaughter opposing
nations and even destroy Israelite cities that had reverted to paganism.

Without ignoring the more ominous strains of Islamic thought, Abou El Fadl argues that there are competing, and more compelling, approaches to the Quran. "Classical Muslim jurists debated whether unbelief is a sufficient justification for warfare, with a sizable number of classical jurists arguing that non-Muslims may not be fought unless they pose a physical threat to Muslims," he writes. The Quran contains a number of broad-sounding admonitions favoring freedom from strife. "If your enemy inclines toward peace, then you should seek peace and trust in God," according to one revelation, which, like the more militant ones, came during the Medinan period (8:61). "These discussions of peace would not make sense," according to Abou El Fadl, "if Muslims were in a permanent state of war with nonbelievers, and if nonbelievers were a permanent enemy and always a legitimate target."

Extremists, in Abou El Fadl's opinion, mistakenly read the Quran as a list of isolated legal commands. Instead the problematic verses should be read in historical context and "in light of the overall moral thrust of the Quranic message." He defines that message as focusing on "general moral imperatives such as mercy, justice, kindness, or goodness." God instructs: "Oh, you who believe, stand firmly for justice, as witnesses for God, even if it means testifying against yourselves, or your parents, or your kin, and whether it is against the rich or poor, for God prevails upon all" (4:135).

On the topic of religious tolerance and diversity, Abou El Fadl recounts a historical anecdote from the time of the Prophet. A group of Jews, Christians, and Muslims met in the market in Medina. They argued over who would be entitled to enter heaven. Followers of each faith made the case for their exclusive eligibility. In response, Muhammad revealed divine guidance that salvation awaited not members of any particular religion but all those who do good deeds and believe in the one God (4:123–124). According to the lore, Jews and Christians would teasingly remind Muslims that this teaching made them all equals.

In fact Medina in the time of the Prophet had its share of religious strife. Muhammad employed the common tactic of raiding rival caravans as part of his protracted struggle against pagan foes. In times of conflict he exiled from Medina Jewish tribes that opposed him and in one instance executed hundreds of their men. But in theory the Quran envisions peaceful coexistence. Recall the verse noting that God apportioned mortals into "diverse nations and tribes so that you may come to know each other" (49:13). The legitimacy of differing beliefs receives this divine endorsement: "To each of you God has prescribed a Law and a Way. If God would have willed, He would have made you a single people. But God's purpose is to test you in what he has given each of you, so strive in the pursuit of virtue" (5:48).

Fundamentalist Muslims—and non-Muslim critics of Islam—have discounted the Quran's more ecumenical themes by pointing to history. First, there was the unpleasantness with the Jews in Medina. Then, within a century after Muhammad's death, Muslim armies conquered an empire that reached from the Atlantic Ocean to China. Compared with others of their time, Islamic generals and rulers were benevolent toward most of those they controlled. Peaceful trade helped spread the religion in some areas. But overall there was plenty of bloodshed, the Quran's teachings notwithstanding.

Regarding this history Abou El Fadl argues, "Muslims acted according to the order of their time and place. Conquest and invasion were the norm at that time." He goes on to say that today, believers "must have the moral courage to recognize situations in which the ethics and moral principles of the Quran were derailed or continue to be derailed by either the technical doctrines of law or the historical practice of Muslims."

One reason that some of the Quran's more humanistic passages have been insufficiently appreciated is that the Prophet's revelations didn't come with specific guidance on *how* diverse nations and tribes should "come to know each other." Influential Muslim scholars during the centuries of Islam's expansion and imperial power didn't fully develop these ideas, according to Abou El Fadl, because they lacked an immediate incentive to do so. The "political dominance and superiority of the Islamic civilization" during its first five hundred years "left Muslim scholars with a sense of self-sufficient confidence," he contends. They saw Islam's vast power as divinely conferred authority to rule others. Early Jews and Christians, scrambling to survive within other people's empires, lacked that kind of security and smugness as they elaborated on their foundational principles.

Abou El Fadl admits that his interpretation of Islamic scripture requires more than a literal reading of the Quran and hadith. "Ultimately the Quran, or any text, speaks through its readers," he argues, echoing a central tenet of late-twentieth-century Western literary criticism. He doesn't take postmodernism to extremes and assert that texts are infinitely malleable. But he does insist that "any text, including those that are Islamic, provides possibilities for meaning, not inevitabilities. And those possibilities are exploited, developed and ultimately determined by the reader's efforts—good faith efforts, we hope—at making sense of the text's complexities. Consequently, the meaning of the text is often only as moral as its reader. If the reader is intolerant, hateful, or oppressive, so will be the interpretation of the text."

On September 10, 2001, Abou El Fadl took a flight home to Los Angeles from New York. He and his father, who still practiced law, had been working together for several days on a legal dispute concerning Egyptian antiquities. They had stayed in a hotel across the street from the World Trade Center. Early on the morning of September 11, Grace Song woke her husband. He stared at the television. "Oh, God, not Muslims," he said to himself. "Please don't let it be Muslims."

That week he delivered his class lectures at UCLA's law school as if in a trance. He could tell that his students were desperate for some explanation. After all, it was a course on Islamic law. "I can't, I just can't," he told them, unable to comprehend, much less rationally explain the devastation wrought in the name of his beloved religion.

Only in the late-night silence of his study at home was he able to collect his thoughts. On September 14 the *Los Angeles Times* published his commentary on Muslims in America after 9/11. The thinking that could justify these horrific acts, he wrote, had connections to mainstream Islam that American Muslims could not simply shrug off. "I like many other Muslims grew up with an unhealthy dose of highly opportunistic and belligerent rhetoric, not only in the official [Arab] media but also at popular cultural venues such as local mosques," he wrote. "Even in the U.S., it is not unusual to hear irresponsible and unethical rhetoric repeated in local Islamic centers or Muslim student organizations at universities." The slaughter on 9/11 revealed the effects of a slow-growing illness at the heart of the faith. "Terrorism is not a virus that suddenly infects the brain of a person," he continued. "Rather, it is the result of long-standing and cumulative cultural and rhetorical dynamics." Resistance to colonialism and secular Arab despots had bred "a dogmatic, puritanical, and ethically oblivious form of Islam," he asserted. "The extreme form of this puritanical Islam does not represent most Muslims today." But for generations Muslim intellectuals, including those in America, had fed extremist tendencies by devoting themselves to "rampant apologetics" that "produced a culture that eschews self-critical and introspective insight and embraces projection of blame and a fantasy-like level of confidence and arrogance."

Abou El Fadl's commentary brought two very distinct reactions. The mainstream media swarmed him, eager to hear from a learned, self-critical Muslim, while some Muslims angrily accused him of seeking celebrity by consoling distraught Americans at the expense of Islam. The main Muslim newspaper in Los Angeles, *The Minaret*, ended his monthly column. Condemnations appeared on the Internet. The bill of particulars: befriending Jews and other non-Muslims, supporting Muslim apostates, endorsing music, assisting Muslim women claiming spousal abuse, and owning forbidden dogs.

He began to get anonymous phone calls and e-mail. "You know us. Don't push us," one caller said. "You're dead. You know what we're capable of," threatened an e-mail from an electronically masked sender. On several occasions a car or a panel truck loitered in front of his house. Abou El Fadl called the police, but the vehicles sped away before officers arrived. The police said whoever was watching probably had a radio scanner and heard the dispatcher sending the squad car. One evening that fall, after seeing a movie, Abou El Fadl and his family found the windshield of their

SUV smashed. No other cars in the parking lot had been vandalized. After the FBI launched an investigation and installed a phone tap, the harassment stopped. No one was ever caught, but the muffled voices on the phone had Arab accents.

During the worst of the intimidation, when Khaled and Grace feared it would have a horrible ending, the Orthodox rabbi Yitzchok Adlerstein offered to help. He and Khaled had lectured together, and they disagreed on almost everything about the Arab-Israeli conflict. But out of mutual intellectual respect, a friendship had grown. Rabbi Adlerstein suggested that Abou El Fadl, his wife, and son come stay with his family elsewhere in the Los Angeles area. "You can make this your home," the rabbi said.

Deeply touched, Abou El Fadl nevertheless declined, not wishing to impose. As time passed, he grew angry that he received no other offers like the rabbi's. "Not a single Muslim offered me refuge," he said. Once he had been an honored lecturer at the Islamic Center of Southern California, a major Los Angeles mosque. But his caustic assessments of American Muslims had made him unwelcome there. In Southern California's large and varied Muslim society, he was now more or less on his own.

His wife didn't understand. "This is a scholar producing thought," she said. "You take a scholar in any other tradition—the Jewish tradition, whatever—you would find a community of supporters stepping in and saying this is wrong."

Years earlier Grace Song had stepped out of the corporate world to devote most of her time to serving as her husband's editor, office assistant, and chauffeur. She carries a cassette recorder everywhere and tapes anything of substance he says, both to make a record for posterity and to protect him against being misquoted. Abou El Fadl doesn't keep track of appointments or when to take the many pills he consumes each day. Song does all of that, with the aid of a paid secretary. Song sits in the back of some of her husband's law classes, and she helps run a Web site, scholarofthehouse.org, that sells his books and audiotapes.

With allowances for his fragile health, Abou El Fadl works almost all his waking hours. One of the few people who can interrupt him is his son, Cherif, a shy teenager, who, like his father at his age, composes poetry. Father and son talk about Cherif's writing and schoolwork, and occasionally they indulge a mutual weakness for video game combat, an endearing wrinkle in Abou El Fadl's hyperserious persona.

At prayer time one evening when I was visiting, Grace unfolded several small Persian-style rugs, which she laid out in a corner of the living room, facing toward Mecca. She covered her shiny black hair with a pale yellow scarf. Khaled, in his black clerical robe, stood between his wife and son. They formed a single line, shoulder to shoulder, defying the tradition of women praying behind men. Grace and Cherif had to help Khaled lower himself to kneel. The only sound in the house was the soft chanting of Arabic. The dogs Baby and Lulu snoozed nearby.

After 9/11 the scholar's routine became a victim of his sudden celebrity. *The New York Times*, CBS News, National Public Radio, *The Wall Street Journal, Chicago Tribune, The Dallas Morning News, The New Republic,* and many others sought him out for interviews. His lonely confrontation with what appeared to have been Muslim stalkers fueled admiring profiles. "Battling Islamic Puritans," the *Los Angeles Times* headlined its page 1 portrait. The paper billed him as "a leading scholarly voice against intolerance among Muslims," adding, "Death threats don't deter him."

Abou El Fadl saw 9/11 as grim confirmation of what he had been saying about the poverty of contemporary Muslim thought and the growing influence of a twisted fundamentalism. As appalled as he was by the violence, he couldn't help feeling vindicated. "This gave me a lot of confidence," he told me, "a lot of sense of 'I saw it, I called it, I knew it'—even 'I told you so' . . . It was an 'I told you so' that gave no pleasure."

He used his newfound access to the national media to emphasize the restrictions the Quran and the Prophet's teachings placed on stealth attacks, rebellion, and harm to noncombatants. He told CBS News: "You cannot kill a woman, you cannot kill a child, you cannot kill a senior individual, you cannot kill a hermit, you cannot kill a member of the clergy, you cannot even kill peasants who are not fighters." That translated in modern terms into a ban on all terrorism.

Addressing the conservative Ethics and Public Policy Center in Washington, D.C., he argued that the Quran's concept of divine sovereignty doesn't preclude democracy, as some fundamentalists contend. At a conference, in Doha, Qatar, sponsored by the liberal Brookings Institution, he debated Sheikh Youssef al-Qaradawi, a religious leader of the Muslim Brotherhood well known on Arab television as a dispenser of sacred teachings. Al-Qaradawi argued against terrorism in general but made an exception for attacks on Israeli citizens. "The Quran says, 'Fight those who fight you, and do not transgress against others,' " he noted.

Abou El Fadl agreed that the Palestinians have a right to defend themselves against Israeli aggression. But referring to suicide bombings of Israeli civilians, he said, "When as an intellectual living in the United States I hear about a group that goes in during a bar mitzvah and slaughters a group of religious practitioners, I cannot fit it within my readings of Islamic ethics or Islamic law."

Some Muslim leaders viewed Abou El Fadl's sudden mainstream prominence as a betrayal. Maher Hathout, a retired cardiologist from Egypt, had been a close friend of Abou El Fadl's father. "Khaled was like a son to me," Hathout said. "I watched with excitement his progress and his success." Hathout came to the United States in 1971, settled in Los Angeles, and became a leader of the growing Muslim community there. He helped build the Islamic Center of Southern California into a prominent institution and, in earlier years, invited Abou El Fadl to give lectures there.

After 9/11 a fissure opened. Hathout felt that a young man he had encouraged returned the favor by turning on his own people. First there was the *Los Angeles Times* piece linking terrorism to intellectual and moral decay within Islam. Then there were the media appearances reiterating the devastating analysis. For the coup de grâce, ten months after 9/11, Abou El Fadl wrote another commentary for the *Los Angeles Times*, this one attacking Muslim leaders—implicitly including Hathout—for failing "to convince the American public of the outrage felt by most Muslims over the tragedy of September 11. Various individuals and particular organizations have issued isolated condemnations, but to date there has not been something unified and overwhelming. Muslim leadership has failed, and it has blamed everyone but itself for this failure." Abou El Fadl suggested, among other steps, a huge Muslim demonstration of mourning at the World Trade Center site, something truly dramatic and designed to attract television coverage, so the world would have to take notice.

The criticism went off like a bomb within Muslim circles. "When you find a statement like that from an insider, it creates anger," Hathout told me, still seething two years later. He said he reviled the 9/11 hijackers. "If those people claim to be Muslims, this is against every fiber in Islam," he said. But American Muslims had done enough after the attacks. "We spoke very loudly against that. We made a quilt with all of the names of victims. Some of them, I think, were Muslims. We sent the quilt to Ground Zero; then we put it in a church in New York. We went out of our way to express this sentiment, not only in search of safety but also to defend the religion."

Abou El Fadl broke ranks "at the very time that a lot of Muslims [felt] very injured and very much under siege," Hathout explained. "You have so many people, self-proclaimed experts, [who] are saying awful things about Islam." He referred to the televangelist Pat Robertson, who had publicly called the Prophet Muhammad "an absolute wild-eyed fanatic." For Abou El Fadl "to come within that time of great vulnerability and say that . . ." Hathout couldn't bring himself to finish the thought.

Hathout takes particular offense over Abou El Fadl's challenge because the older man sees himself as having devoted much of his life to promoting Muslim integration into American society. His adult children are successful professionals. The Islamic center he helps lead flies the American flag and discourages harangues against Christians and Jews. But notice that when Hathout lashes out at the hijackers, he suggests that they weren't Muslims at all. In his circular reasoning, real Muslims can have no connection to terrorism carried out in the name of Islam because Islam forbids terrorism. Notice as well that he frames the Muslim reaction to 9/11 in terms of securing the safety of Muslims and defending their religion. Consideration of the significance of Muslim complicity in the atrocity seems not to interest Hathout.

Abou El Fadl's perspective differs in an important way. The hijackers acted out of a religious zeal that perverts Islam, he contends, but that twisted view of Islam can't be neatly isolated from the religion. As much as they were repelled by the carnage, he asserts, American Muslims needed to take a certain degree of responsibility for the ideological corrosion eating away at Islam. That corrosion helped form the environment in which the 9/11 plot was hatched.

In Abou El Fadl's view, Hathout insists on being a perpetual victim in a way that American Muslims ought to abandon. Abou El Fadl asks whether Hathout and other American Muslim leaders have infused their public statements about mass death in America with the same fervor that animates their frequent denunciations of killings of Muslims in Palestine, Chechnya, and Kashmir. After 9/11, Abou El Fadl maintains, "Muslims were still playing the political game of on the one hand, saying, 'Don't blame us,' [but] on the other hand, not being passionate about their anger because the victims were not [predominantly] Muslim." This tendency diluted Muslim condemnations of 9/11. More broadly, the weakness of American Muslim leaders—their tendency to back into a defensive crouch—has left ordinary Muslims without credible representatives on issues ranging from American foreign policy to domestic law enforcement.

The insular voices of Muslim America overwhelmingly sided with Maher Hathout against his former protégé. The Council on American-Islamic Relations, a media-savvy defender of Muslim civil rights, said, "It seems to us that Dr. Abou El Fadl's busy schedule at UCLA might have caused him to miss numerous statements and actions that CAIR and many other American Muslim organizations have undertaken since the 9/11 terrorist attacks." Even Assim Mohammed, the young Muslim from Chicago, began to question Abou El Fadl's motives. After 9/11, Abou El Fadl "began to play a certain role. It seemed he wanted to develop a constituency," Mohammed said. Scholars praised his work as "challenging" and "inspiring." But among rank-and-file Muslims, Abou El Fadl lost fans, "including myself, I'm afraid," Mohammed told me. He attributed his disillusionment to what he perceived as Abou El Fadl's trying to become "the American Muslim mullah, the authority senators and congressmen and leaders would go to for years to come."

Jealousy, Abou El Fadl said, had poisoned his relations with some former admirers. "It's often like that story about the crabs in the barrel that are always pulling each other down, so no one gets out," he said. "It's very much a defeatist attitude."

Abou El Fadl challenged other Muslim American leaders after 9/11, but he didn't abandon Muslims or their causes. He continued to criticize Israeli actions toward the Palestinians and, for that matter, most of U.S. foreign policy in the Middle East. Ambivalent at first about the invasion of Iraq, he turned negative when American forces didn't quickly transfer authority to Iraqis. He accused the United States of hypocrisy for tolerating despotism in Saudi Arabia and Egypt while trying to intimidate Iran and Syria. "The policy of double standards that Bush seems intent on sustaining and promoting will backfire in the long term, and we will create something like the Iranian revolution all over the Middle East," he wrote in a commentary in *The Boston Phoenix* in April 2003. In *The New York Times*, he attacked the Bush administration for "systematically undermining" the civil liberties of Muslim Americans. He testified before the bipartisan 9/11 Commission that the United States had scorned American values by punishing Muslims on the basis of secret evidence and by shipping certain terrorism suspects to countries known to use torture in interrogation. What he didn't do in each of his many press interviews and commentaries—although he did it sometimes—was set off any comment he made about al Qaeda against a criticism of Israel or the Patriot Act. He answered questions directly and offered a critique of Muslim thinking rarely heard from inside the faith.

His bluntness didn't buy him immunity from non-Muslim suspicion, however. He wears Western clothes in public, but his tan skin and facial features suggest the Middle East. On airplanes he sensed the nervousness of fellow passengers: the whispers and sideways glances when he reached for his carry-on briefcase. Some conservatives suggested that he had tricked the mass media into believing he was ideologically moderate when in fact he was a closet militant. The right-leaning *Weekly Standard* magazine quoted the pundit Daniel Pipes's argument that calling Abou El Fadl a "moderate" is like making a distinction "between a moderate Nazi and a radical Nazi."

Likening Abou El Fadl to a militant, let alone a Nazi, is appalling. But the experience of being judged guilty until proved innocent became depressingly common. After he had delivered a conciliatory lecture on human rights in New York in 2002, an elderly lady rose from the audience. She said she had nightmares about Muslims. "After 9/11 and all that happened, as a Jew and a supporter of Israel I have become scared of people who look like you," she told Abou El Fadl. "So, what can you say to make people like me feel safer?"

Abou El Fadl told the woman it wasn't his duty to reassure her. *He* was the one with reason to be afraid, he thought but left unsaid.

DEMOLITION MAN

Abou El Fadl's story offers reason for hope—to Muslims and all Americans. His work suggests that Muslims are beginning a healthy internal debate about the future of their religion in American society. The positive reaction to his writings from some younger Muslims signals an eagerness to challenge beliefs that deserve reexamination. He has helped inspire what some ambitiously call a progressive Muslim movement, scholars, writers, and other young professionals who are questioning many aspects of Islam as it is practiced in this country. The 2003 essay collection *Progressive Muslims*, to which Abou El Fadl contributed the lead piece, features a number of provocative thinkers, some of whom go far beyond anything he has written. One chapter makes a case for the acceptance of gay and lesbian Muslims, an unheard-of notion in American mosques, where one finds the sort of homophobia common in conservative Christian churches and Orthodox synagogues. All of the book's contributors, as well as its readers, owe Abou El Fadl a debt of gratitude for his pioneering assault on the fortress of fundamentalist jurisprudence.

Abou El Fadl has distinguished himself as an intellectual demolition man. He knocks down archaic assumptions and the rigid defenses of pedantry. His work has shown a way to rethink Islam from the foundations up. With the meanings of Quran and hadith more open to reinterpretation, Muslims in America and elsewhere can build in new directions, finding moral solutions to contemporary problems. The nascent movement of progressive Muslims presumably will have something to say about those solutions. Perhaps Abou El Fadl will as well.

THREE

The Imam

There may be no better place to take the measure of African-American Islam than at Masjid At-Taqwa in Brooklyn, New York. Formerly a clothing store, then a junkies' shooting gallery, Taqwa sits at the busy intersection of Fulton Street and Bedford Avenue. In the mid-nineteenth century free blacks had helped settle the area, now known as Bedford-Stuyvesant. In the 1930s a new subway line from Manhattan encouraged African-Americans to move to the neighborhood from a crowded and deteriorating Harlem. As the number of blacks in Bedford-Stuyvesant tripled over the next three decades, most whites fled to the suburbs. Housing projects and crime went up; businesses disappeared. Today black professionals are starting to gentrify some blocks, but much of the area remains bleak.

At one o'clock one summer Friday afternoon the jostling to get into the mosque and find a space to sit was getting intense. The imam was in town and would be delivering the *khutbah*, or sermon. Some five hundred men eventually crowded into the windowless main hall. Among them were cabdrivers and security guards, ex-convicts in do-rag stocking caps and merchants wearing embroidered West African robes of crimson and gold. There were schoolteachers, municipal clerks, and mobile phone salesmen. Most were American-born blacks; the rest, immigrants from Africa, South Asia, and the Middle East. Their shoes were stored in green plastic bags set on long shelves near the door. They sat on dingy gray-striped carpeting laid to indicate the *qibla*, or direction of prayer toward Mecca. The walls, painted mustard yellow and green, were bare except for a torn poster of the holy city. Invisible from the main hall, a small group of women in headscarves and ankle-length dresses entered through a side door. They sat in a separate room connected via closed-circuit TV.

A wiry black man with a reddish orange beard—some Muslim men tint their whiskers with henna, imitating a practice of the Prophet Muhammad—picked up a microphone and repeated the plaintive invitation to prayer, beginning, "Allahu akbar, Allahu akbar/ Ashahadu an la ilaha ill Allah" (God is great, God is great/ I declare there is no god but God). This was the *jummah* service, the main communal prayer of the week.

From a rear door two burly men emerged to clear a path for Siraj Wahhaj, the imam. Over his white tunic and trouser ensemble, he wore a long chocolate-colored robe. He carried a stack of religious texts under one arm. Seated worshipers swiveled to follow his progress, several reaching to touch him as he passed. Wahhaj is a tall, handsome man in his mid-fifties with a full beard tending toward gray. He carries himself like someone who knows he is the pride of the neighborhood and one of the most popular Muslim preachers in the country. On many Fridays he is off speaking in another state, in Canada, or in Europe. He routinely attracts audiences of hundreds of people and annually raises hundreds of thousands of dollars for Muslim causes. Today he was preaching at home.

The crowd fell silent as Wahhaj reached the *minbar*, a small wooden platform with a carved roof. He picked up the microphone and solemnly offered prayers in Arabic and English. When he finished, he paused, looked down for a moment, and then smiled confidently. He began his homily. As a result of embracing Islam, he declared, "I'm a better husband, a better father, a better son to my parents." He extolled the religion's power to reform individuals and entire communities. He acknowledged the "long line of brothers who came out of prison" having converted behind bars. Twenty-five years earlier, drugs and crime poisoned the blocks around the mosque, he said. Then Muslims chased away the dealers and their clientele. Islam became the dominant presence on the corner of Fulton and Bedford. Five times a day the call to prayer, chanted in Arabic and amplified through loudspeakers, competes with the traffic noise. Vendors sell Islamic audiotapes from rickety folding tables on the sidewalk. Previously neglected buildings have been repaired; legitimate merchants have returned. "When Islam came, it became a better area," Wahhaj said exultantly. "I want this area to be an oasis in the midst of a desert."

As with the health of the neighborhood, he said, so it should be with the individual. Life expectancy tables show a huge gap between white and black. "Can we change it? Yes, we can." Muslims must avoid alcohol and drugs, but there was more: "Take your medication, get checkups. I'm telling you, brothers, go to the dentist. Fix your teeth. You wonder why you're not married, look at your teeth." Laughter rippled through the hall.

He shifted to the issue of earning a living. "Some brothers here used to sell drugs," he said. "It's better to be a *poor* man!" Drive a taxi, he commanded, hoist a suitcase at the airport, or pick up garbage. His cadence echoed the Baptist preachers of his youth. "This is *honorable* money!" he proclaimed. "It's *honorable* to sweep the streets of New York!"

Then, without warning, the mantra of self-improvement ceased. The imam glowered. "The more we grow in this area," he said, "the more pressure we're going to get from some segments of the community who don't want us to be successful." He named no names (but on other occasions has referred to the media, backers of Israel, and the FBI). "I believe there's going to come a time when the authorities will come after me," he said. "They will find a way." The imam's change of direction was abrupt but not surprising to anyone who had heard him preach before, either in person or on audiotapes sold on the Internet. Wahhaj frequently turns sharp rhetorical corners, moving from optimistic exhortation to darker subjects and back again.

He told his audience that his popularity, which attracts throngs to

Masjid At-Taqwa and earns him all those out-of-town speaking invitations, was viewed as a threat by certain unidentified forces. "They have to get me like they got Malcolm, like they got Martin Luther King, like they got everybody else," he said. "That's what they do. I'm warning you. Already I've seen signs that they have laid the foundation." The signs he was referring to were press reports that mentioned his testimony for the defense in a 1995 terrorism trial, which concluded with the conviction of eleven Muslims for conspiring to blow up the headquarters of the United Nations and other New York landmarks. Prosecutors, he said, had demonized him. All these years later the media were still reporting that he has been "linked" to the conspiracy. "How am I linked?" he thundered. "How am I linked? Tell me!" Reaching a crescendo, he said, "They're going to come after me, I'm telling you!" There were murmurs of affirmation. The imam said he would welcome death in the service of Allah. "If they kill me," he said, "don't be crying."

It isn't easy to fit together the pieces of Siraj Wahhaj. He is unquestionably a star in American Islam. He travels the country extolling the Quran and the Prophet Muhammad, a rare crossover luminary, an African-American popular among immigrant Muslims. "He lifts up the spirit of Muslims," according to Altaf Husain, a prominent Muslim activist of Indian descent. He summarizes Wahhaj's message as: "Have hope; we can do this together. We can contribute to America."

But to his followers in Brooklyn and elsewhere, the imam sometimes portrays America as a shadowy realm of sabotage and deceit. He has told followers that the "real terrorists" are the Federal Bureau of Investigation and the Central Intelligence Agency. He has preached that an Islamic society, in which adulterers face stoning and thieves have their hands cut off, would be superior to American democracy: "In time, this so-called democracy will crumble, and there will be nothing. And the only thing that will remain will be Islam."

This does not sound like the cleric who, in 1991, was the first Muslim ever to lead a prayer before the start of a session of the House of Representatives. Wahhaj presents different sides to different audiences. He did not rail against the FBI and CIA when in 1999 he joined other Muslim notables to dine on lamb and lentils at a State Department dinner hosted by Secretary of State Madeleine Albright.

Wahhaj denounces terrorism, but he takes great pains to remain neutral about Osama bin Laden. In one of a series of interviews he told me that the al Qaeda leader's videotaped boasts about the attacks may have been a media ruse, doctored videotape, perhaps, or even a performance staged by American-backed operatives. "I'm just not so sure I want to be one of the ones who say, 'Yeah, he did it. He's a horrible man,'" Wahhaj explained.

Do such views make Wahhaj an ominous figure? Or are they merely an emblem of a rebellious African-American style, meant to conjure images of martyred black legends? Members of the imam's following who came out of prison, some having heard his tapes behind bars, say his words and example helped lift them out of despair. Wahhaj's complicated mixed message is worth sorting out because it mirrors the opinions of many African-American Muslims, just as his spiritual journey mirrors a much larger black experience.

THE NIGHT SKY IN MECCA

Siraj Wahhaj, a Brooklyn native born in 1950, was originally named Jeffrey Kearse. At the age of seven he challenged his mother: "How come we got to go to church anyway?" She took out a leather strap and whacked the boy a couple of times, he recalled. "Now you understand why you got to go to church?" she asked. Jeffrey thereafter won an award for perfect church attendance and later taught at a Baptist Sunday school. "I enjoyed the belief in God," he told me. As a teenager he read about the Reverend Martin Luther King, Jr., and sometimes heard him speak on the radio. King seemed to fulfill the Christian ideal of sacrifice in pursuit of social justice.

Jeffrey grew up in public housing in the Brooklyn neighborhoods of Brownsville and Fort Greene. His mother was a nurse; his stepfather, a hospital dietitian. The younger of two boys, Jeffrey showed early promise as an artist, and visitors to the apartment sat for portraits in oil or watercolor. He attended a public high school in Harlem that focused on music and art and received a partial scholarship to New York University, beginning in the fall of 1968. He declared a major in math education and a minor in art, intending to become a teacher.

But before he got to college, Jeffrey's life had begun to shift course. On April 4, 1968, he was playing basketball when the news whipped through the St. John's Recreation Center: Dr. King had been shot dead. By his own account, Jeffrey hadn't suffered much direct racial discrimination. But King's killing had a jarring effect: "He was my hero. I was a Christian at the time. I went home crying." Anger previously absent from his life began to surface and simmer. On the streets of Brooklyn, black power slogans were drowning out those of nonviolent groups such as King's Southern Christian Leadership Conference. Looking back, he says, if he hadn't joined the Nation of Islam, he probably would have signed up with the Black Panthers.

At NYU he met an older student named Jerry 10X. Like other members of the Nation of Islam, Jerry had jettisoned his original surname for an *X*, marking him as an ex-Christian and ex-victim of white society. The 10 signified that he was the tenth Jerry in New York to adopt the X. Jerry took Jeffrey to prayer services and theology classes at Mosque No. 7 in Harlem, once headed by Malcolm X.

During the 1950s and 1960s, the Nation of Islam had expanded impressively, offering a defiant alternative to the Christian churches. It established mosques (7B in Queens, 7C in Brooklyn, and 7D in the Bronx) and dispatched men to the tenements and public housing towers with copies of the *Muhammad Speaks* newspaper. Nation ministers preached that "blue-eyed white devils" had stripped blacks of dignity and hypnotized them with turn-the-other-cheek stories of a pale, blond Jesus. It was time for the black man to stand up for himself and his family and create a separate black society grounded in work, worship, and self-respect.

No Nation of Islam figure had been more fiercely eloquent than Malcolm X, a reformed street hustler and ex-convict originally known as Malcolm Little. Though Malcolm had been killed in 1965, his presence was still felt among black Muslims in New York City. "Malcolm was boda-cious," Wahhaj recalled. "He was bold, courageous. Look at him talking to the white man like that! That's appealing to the African-American, when usually African-Americans are bowing down to the white man and the white power structure. Islam taught you to be afraid only of Allah."

The figure of the rebellious, charismatic preacher, a wayward man once lost and now found, was integral to the Nation of Islam. Equally important was a loathing of white society, rooted in the humiliation of white bigotry. Near the end of his life Malcolm X broke with the Nation of Islam and publicly began to distance himself from the sect's racial mythology. He made a pilgrimage to Mecca and changed his name to el-Hajj Malik el-Shabazz, a symbol of his migration toward conventional Sunni Islam. He founded an independent mosque in Harlem. In response, the Nation of Islam leadership turned on him as a traitor. "Malcolm is worthy of death," Minister Louis X, later known as Louis Farrakhan, wrote in December 1964 in *Muhammad Speaks*. Three months later, on February 21, 1965, several black Muslims shot and killed Malcolm as he gave a lecture in the Audubon Ballroom in Harlem.

The assassination of Macolm X, one of the most familiar symbols of a tumultuous era, has never been fully or credibly explained. Three men tied to the Nation of Islam were convicted of the crime and sentenced to life in prison. But for many African-Americans, Muslims in particular, the shooting became an illustration of how hostile forces—white racists, the police and FBI, and possibly Jews—would snuff out any black leader who gained a significant following.

Publicly released FBI documents show that federal agents had begun tracking Malcolm as early as 1953 and sometimes relied on informants within the Nation of Islam. The FBI and New York City police were aware of threats on his life and could have done more to protect him. But according to the historian Clayborne Carson, a leading scholar of the voluminous FBI files on Malcolm X, there isn't credible evidence that the government developed a plan to use Nation of Islam dupes to dispose of the black leader. As for Nation of Islam complicity, Carson contends that

the organization's top leaders wouldn't have had to ord
in an explicit way: "If you label somebody as an enem
then the strongest believers are going to believe that
take matters into their own hands."

In the circles in which Jeffrey Kearse, now knov
moved, Malcolm's death was a confirmation of the pow̲ ̲ ̲ ̲ viciousness
of black Islam's antagonists. The assassination three years later of Martin
Luther King, Jr., who, it turned out, was another subject of extensive FBI
monitoring, reinforced the impression that all black leaders were targets.
Malcolm and Martin were martyrs; the FBI, CIA, and police were the enemy. These were themes that were to persist in Jeffrey 12X's Islamic journey.

꿈

The sense of oppression that is deeply woven into the fabric of black Islam
in the United States goes all the way back to slave times. Among the West
Africans brought here in bondage, most during the eighteenth and nineteenth centuries, were thousands of Muslims. Berber settlements and
trans-Saharan trade had brought Islam to West Africa from Arab areas to
the north. A small number of Muslim slaves in America left narratives or
other evidence of their lives in Maryland, South Carolina, and elsewhere,
reporting that they had quietly maintained Islamic beliefs and ritual. But
most were forced by owners to embrace a submissive Christianity, and
African Islam withered in America.

African-American Muslim history restarted at the turn of the twentieth century, when Arabs were just beginning to migrate to the United
States from the faltering Ottoman Empire. During this period Muslim
missionaries from the Middle East and India discovered receptive audiences among some former American slaves and their descendants. A number of African-Americans came to see Islam as their original and true
religion. Today many black Muslims still prefer to call themselves "reverts"
to Islam, rather than converts. The faith became a means of expressing an
independent black identity in a hostile white society.

Islamic motifs surfaced in black fraternal groups that rejected Christianity because of its association with slavery. In 1913, Timothy Drew, a

Carolinian who called himself Noble Drew Ali, founded the Moorish Science Temple in Newark, New Jersey. His seminal pamphlet *The Holy Koran of the Moorish Science Temple of America* drew on the actual Quran, the Bible, and the sayings of black nationalist leader Marcus Garvey. The sect gained thousands of followers in the 1920s. Later many members shifted their allegiance to another quasi-Islamic visionary, Elijah Muhammad.

The son of Georgia slaves, Muhammad (originally Robert Poole) fell under the influence of Wallace Fard Muhammad, an immigrant Muslim peddler and missionary who preached in the early 1930s in the black slums of Detroit, a city where many Arab immigrants settled. Master Fard, as this teacher was known, mixed Islamic principles with predictions of an apocalyptic resurgence of the black race. Fard, whose precise origins and identity remain mysteries, vanished without explanation in 1934. It was left to Elijah Muhammad to build the organization that became known as the Nation of Islam. A physically frail but compelling figure, Muhammad was a riveting speaker who portrayed Fard as an incarnation of Allah and himself as Allah's chosen Messenger. He wore neatly tailored suits, bow ties, and a Turkish-style fez decorated with stars and crescent moons. Running the Nation from his Chicago headquarters, he struck a chord with hundreds of thousands of poor and working-class urban blacks by attributing their woes to white racism and prescribing self-reliance as the best response. Muhammad's most talented aide, the fiery Malcolm X, became the sect's public face until he was assassinated in 1965.

In the 1970s Jeffrey 12X spent a good deal of time at Mosque No. 7 in Harlem, then under the leadership of Louis Farrakhan, a former calypso singer once known as the Charmer. Jeffrey dropped out of NYU after a couple of years to peddle the Nation's trademark whiting fish and bean pies. He moved a thousand copies a week of *Muhammad Speaks*. College seemed irrelevant. "I'm a Muslim now; I don't need that," he thought. The Nation's idiosyncratic beliefs included the myth of Yacub, a black mad scientist who had spitefully created the evil white race. Jeffrey

12X repeated the sect's separatist lessons. "I preached it. I taught it," he acknowledged. He became a skilled orator and with Farrakhan's backing rose through the Nation's ranks in New York to become minister of Mosque No. 7C in Brooklyn.

Years later he said that the sect's primary appeal to him hadn't been its science fiction or reverence for the Messenger. "It wasn't the theology that attracted me to the Nation of Islam at all," he told me. "It was the kind of do-for-self black pride."

In 1975 the Nation was shaken by news that Elijah Muhammad had died at age seventy-seven. Jeffrey 12X and others were told the reports were "white man's trickery." Among the Messenger's supernatural qualities, his followers had been taught, was a life span that would last for many generations. But the next day officials at the Nation's Chicago headquarters admitted that Muhammad had in fact died.

Jeffrey 12X felt dazed. "I no longer believed in Elijah Muhammad as the Messenger of God," he said. "His teaching began to unravel in my mind." Like thousands of other Nation members, he began reading the Quran for the first time on his own and wondering about "real" Islam, as it was practiced in the Middle East. With the encouragement of Elijah Muhammad's son Warith Deen Muhammad, Jeffrey and others groped their way toward the traditions and beliefs of Sunni Islam. He saw himself as following an honorable path: "I was a minister in the Nation of Islam, same way Malcolm was, and the same way Malcolm left the Nation and became a Sunni Muslim, likewise I [did]." He changed his name to Siraj Wahhaj, an Arabic phrase that means "bright light." He decided he would never again paint a portrait, in deference to the orthodox Muslim teaching that depicting the human image is idolatry. For a time he headed a mosque in Brooklyn that looked to Warith Deen Muhammad for leadership. But he felt he needed to go back to the source of Islam. In 1978 he traveled to Naperville, Illinois, for religious training sponsored by a dawa organization based in Saudi Arabia.

At just the moment that Wahhaj and many other African-Americans were searching for the meaning of "true" Islam, Saudi Arabia was stepping forward to provide the answer with its worldwide proselytizing campaign. Some African-Americans received tutoring from teachers paid by Saudi groups. In Naperville, Wahhaj recalled, he joined a class of fifty African-American imams who received forty days of intense religious instruction from the Saudi dawa organization Dar-Iftar. Wahhaj was an avid student. While others relaxed in the evenings, he studied in his dormitory room until the wee hours, one classmate recalled. Wahhaj and four others from the Naperville session were chosen by the Saudis to travel to Mecca for four months of advanced training at King Abdul Aziz University. There Wahhaj was part of a class of about twenty African-American imams who studied theology, Islamic law, and Arabic. The instructors were from Sudan, India, and Egypt, he said, emphasizing that they weren't Saudis. All such religious training in the kingdom requires the blessing of Saudi authorities, and instructors typically are affiliated with one or another fundamentalist faction. Wahhaj told me that one of his teachers was Muhammad Qutb, a well-known Egyptian émigré member of the Muslim Brotherhood and the brother of Sayyid Qutb, that movement's radical ideologist.

Wahhaj described Mecca with wonderment: "Absolute awe. I was blown away." He rose at 3:00 a.m. to walk to the nearest mosque, so as to arrive before anyone else did. His hosts gave him his own key. The black desert sky was filled with stars. As dawn approached, the call to the day's first communal prayer broke the silence. Later, at the morning class, Wahhaj sat in the front row and taped every lecture. He has returned to Saudi Arabia on pilgrimage five times since, but nothing compares with that first sojourn. "I was on a spiritual high for four months," he told me.

Wahhaj insisted that he hadn't embraced the intolerant Saudi brand of Islam known as Wahhabism. Though Saudi-funded, the programs he had attended years ago were "definitely not what you would call Wahhabism," he said. At times he denies that Wahhabism even exists, saying it is merely a pejorative term created by Western enemies of Islam. Whatever label he

prefers, however, he is on shaky ground when he insists
Muslims "have never looked to Saudi Arabia for guid
African-Americans." The claim is contradicted by his ex
of thousands of other Americans, including numerous ima...
indeed sought religious guidance from Saudi institutions and Saudi-paid
teachers.

On the other hand, Wahhaj shouldn't be neatly categorized as a Wahhabi or any other type of fundamentalist. For one thing, he has friendly
relations with some black Christian clergymen and secular public officials.
Full-fledged Wahhabis would refrain from such ties. His dealings with
women outside his family, while formal, aren't as distant as those of traditional Saudi men. Some of his sermons, opinions, and past personal affiliations betray an affinity for fundamentalism. But the roots of his anger at
American society trace more directly to the condition of American blacks
than to grievances grounded in the Middle East. The Quran serves as a fil-
ter for his reactions to homegrown racial frustration. And while Wahhaj
preaches more often about the Prophet Muhammad, Malcolm X remains
as central an influence on the imam as he was during the era of "by any
means necessary."

The 1970s were a period of ferment for African-American Muslims, a
population that then numbered several hundred thousand. Elijah
Muhammad's son, Warith Deen Muhammad, disbanded the Nation of Islam and started a new movement he initially called the World Community of Islam in the West. An unassuming man very different from his
vibrant father, Warith Deen Muhammad admitted his ambivalence over
inheriting a leader's role. The younger Muhammad did, however, call on
African-American Muslims to reject racial separatism and learn the
Quran.

While Wahhaj initially signed on to Warith Deen Muhammad's new
movement, Louis Farrakhan did not. Farrakhan, Wahhaj's former teacher,
revived the old Nation of Islam and kept its base in Chicago. A mesmeriz-

.g speaker, he excoriated whites and particularly Jews. This drew media attention that helped him cultivate a reputation in the 1980s and 1990s as the spokesman for African-American Muslims and spiritual heir to Malcolm X. The irony that Farrakhan had labeled Malcolm worthy of death was lost on his followers. Gradually, illness and his attachment to the cultish quirks of the Nation of Islam diminished Farrakhan's standing as a religious guide. Contrary to the perception of most white Americans that he is the leader of black Islam, his group has shrunk in size and importance as the majority of African-American Muslims turned to Warith Deen Muhammad and other leaders.

Further complicating the picture has been the emergence of African-American Muslim groups and mosques independent of both the Nation of Islam and Warith Deen Muhammad's movement. The Mosque of Islamic Brotherhood in Harlem, for example, was founded in the late 1960s by Sheikh K. Ahmad Tawfiq, a Floridian of mixed African and Native American descent who had followed Malcolm X during his brief post–Nation of Islam phase. Tawfiq studied with the help of a scholarship at al-Azhar in Cairo. He turned the Mosque of Islamic Brotherhood into a Harlem landmark, which at its peak ran a school, health food store, tea room, and proselytizing program in New York prisons.

While some African-Americans went to Mecca or Cairo for training, others encountered Islamic teachers who arrived in this country beginning in the mid-1970s. The foreign instructors, mostly supported by stipends from the Muslim World League, a major Saudi charity, came from predominantly Muslim countries in Africa, the Middle East, and South Asia. Leaders of the Mosque of the Islamic Brotherhood supervised those receiving foreign tutoring to prevent them from embracing any form of extremism, according to Al-Hajj Talib 'Abdur-Rashid, the current imam. The mosque has endorsed "a mainstream, balanced Islamic understanding and experience that is based on a strong social justice platform," he said.

Some African-Americans in the late 1970s and 1980s moved toward fanaticism. One group became involved with Jamaat ul-Fuqra, an organization "committed to purifying Islam through violence," in the words of the

Harvard terrorism scholar Jessica Stern. Fuqra's spiritual leader is Sheikh Mubarik Ali Gilani, a Pakistani mystic. Long before most Americans had heard the word "jihad," Gilani encouraged followers to join in armed struggle to defend Islam around the world. Members of the group, whose name refers to poverty, have set up communities in California, Colorado, South Carolina, New York, and other states. Fuqra followers—their total numbers aren't known—have been convicted of fraud, murder, and small-scale bombings. The violence has apparently been aimed at Muslim rivals rather than the public at large. Gilani and American Fuqra leaders have denied allegations that the organization encourages criminal activity or terrorism.

"WHERE THE LOVE IS AT"

After returning to Brooklyn from his four months in Mecca, Siraj Wahhaj began to feel confined by his obligations to Warith Deen Muhammad, the son of Elijah Muhammad. Wahhaj chafed at what he considered the theologically incorrect approach to which the younger Muhammad clung, such as mixing Christian Bible teachings with those of the Quran. "My learning now was toward more orthodox" Islam, Wahhaj said.

Against a backdrop of Saudi proselytizing and the broader surge of Islamic fundamentalism, thousands of other black Muslims similarly embraced what was presented to them as orthodoxy. Diana Eck, a scholar of comparative religion, has observed that this move cut against the tendency of black religion in America to reject orthodox doctrine (typically, that of white Christians). After a period of experimentation with quasi-Islamic beliefs, most African-American Muslims wanted to practice an Islam that was closer to what was practiced in the Muslim world. The foreignness of Islamic tradition, with its distinctively choreographed prayer and emphasis on Arabic, became an expression of black independence.

It was over Independence Day weekend in 1981 that Wahhaj and a small group of followers broke away from Warith Deen Muhammad's organization to form Masjid At-Taqwa in Bedford-Stuyvesant. The name means "mosque of God-consciousness." At first members gathered for

Friday prayer at an apartment where furniture was moved out of the living room and into a bedroom so that twenty-five people could kneel. At the time Wahhaj and his followers learned of the dilapidated former clothing store at the corner of Fulton and Bedford, drug dealers and junkies were using it for shelter. Pedestrians foolish enough to pause for red lights risked having their watches or purses snatched. Landlords had let neighboring tenements and storefronts disintegrate. The city asked only thirty thousand dollars for the one-story property, and the Wahhaj group pieced together the money to buy it.

Wahhaj built Taqwa on a foundation combining the old Nation of Islam self-help philosophy, the defiance he so admired in Malcolm X, and the literalist approach to Islam he had embraced since his study in Mecca. He preached, and still preaches, a faith of personal responsibility and hard work. He urges former criminals to reform, and he condemns liquor, drugs, gambling, and pornography. In much the same vein as many socially conservative black Christian pastors, he rails against homosexuality: "God created Adam and Eve, not Adam and Steve!" His admirers include Muslims in the inner city, on college campuses, and at Islamic centers throughout the United States. His sermons on tape receive top billing at online Islamic stores.

Wahhaj urges a return not just to old-time values but to the strictures of Islam as it is thought to have been practiced many centuries ago in Arabia. His vision of an ideal society sometimes sounds very much at odds with modern, mainstream American life. He sermonizes on the wisdom of ancient punishments. In a characteristic portion of one talk widely available on audiotape, he runs through the penalties for three categories of sinners: people who have sex out of wedlock, thieves, and adulterers respectively. "If Allah says a hundred strikes, a hundred strikes it is," he says. "If Allah says cut off their hand, you cut off their hand. If Allah says stone them to death, through the Prophet Muhammad, then you stone them to death, because it's the obedience of Allah and his Messenger—nothing personal." (The Quran actually doesn't call for the stoning of adulterers. The punishment is the same as for sex outside marriage: a hundred lashes [24:2]. Wahhaj apparently relies on a controversial hadith, or saying of the Prophet, that has been interpreted by fundamentalist Islamic authorities as calling for stoning.)

At an Islamic conference in Orlando, Florida, I attended in the summer of 2003, he spoke at a workshop attended by a hundred African-American and immigrant women in hijab. He told them that Islam condones a man's marrying up to four wives. He tried to make this sound more palatable by noting that when the four-wife rule was introduced in seventh-century Arabia, it served as a restriction on preexisting tribal custom encouraging even more wives per husband.

On several occasions when we spoke, I asked Wahhaj why he stressed stoning adulterers and marrying multiple wives. Because of Internet sales of his tapes, such views reach the ears of untold numbers of Muslims beyond his immediate audiences. Is he advocating draconian vigilantism? Would he really prefer to see unmarried lovers lashed in the town square? And why has he preached that a society governed by ancient Islamic law would be better than America's constitutional democracy? In a recorded sermon entitled "Islam Is Better than Democracy," he says, "Allah will cause his *deen* [religion], Islam, to prevail over every kind of system, and you know what? It will happen."

The imam tried to reassure me, but only up to a point. He said he regretted the tone of his harshest comments about democracy. But his anticipation of its collapse, he said, is nothing to get nervous about. This "is similar to a Christian saying eventually God's kingdom is going to come." In the meantime he has urged audiences to become more involved in electoral politics, and the imam himself maintains friendly public relations with Brooklyn's Jewish borough president, Marty Markowitz, and other local politicians.

As for his keenness for Islamic punishments, he told me, "Obviously, in the American context, we can't cut off the hands of thieves," or whip fornicators, or stone adulterers. He does hope, though, that Americans one day will be persuaded, not coerced, to embrace Islamic law. In the meantime lauding strict penalties for sexual and other infractions sends a message of discipline and probity to his flock.

But even under Islamic law, known as *sharia*, things might not be as unforgiving as they sound, he said. Take adultery. For a conviction, the Quran requires four eyewitnesses to the offending act, not just circumstantial evidence but the sex itself. How often would that occur? Not very, he said. Moreover, the Quran warns potential accusers that if they don't have four witnesses, *they* are subject to being lashed eighty times (24:4). Once you eliminated all forms of pornography, removed sexual images from movies and television, and mandated that women cover their curves more diligently—all of which would happen in an Islamic society, he said—fewer men would think to sleep with women other than their wives. These kinds of qualifications do sometimes crop up in his sermons. But they tend to get drowned out by his strident depictions of how things were done fourteen hundred years ago.

On polygamy, interestingly, he gave less ground. The imam had nothing bad to say about multiple wives, as long as a man can follow the Islamic rule of treating his spouses equally. Wahhaj said he recognizes that a man can get only one official marriage license from city hall. But for religious purposes, he performs polygamous weddings at his mosque. "If a man can have a hundred girlfriends, and it's legal," he explained, "I don't say you can't have more than one wife."

For his part, the imam said he has just one wife, a legal secretary named Wadiyah. "I love her, and we're very, very close. She's my sweetheart," he told me. But he refused to discuss their relationship, and I was not able to interview her. Wahhaj's first marriage ended in divorce. He has eight children, ranging in age from adolescence to mid-thirties. A ninth child died of heart failure while she was in college.

At the time we spoke, the imam and his wife lived with four of their children in part of a three-family house in East Flatbush, a mostly black area. He said proudly that he had sent all his children to Islamic elementary and junior high schools. Most then went to public high schools, although two daughters were attending a Muslim high school. Another daughter, known as Sister Hujrah, who is married and in her twenties, serves as one of the imam's two secretaries. Six of his children are practicing Muslims. Referring to two daughters who aren't, the imam said wryly, "Maybe they're on a leave of absence."

~⌒

A woman worshiper at Taqwa named Eisa Nefertari Ulen offers a different perspective on the mosque and its imam. Other women I approached at Taqwa were unwilling to talk. "The sisters at Taqwa don't smile," Ulen said, smiling. She sounded neither critical nor defensive. The plain fact is that men dominate Taqwa, as they dominate almost all mosques. Far fewer women come to Friday prayers at Taqwa: no more than one for every twenty men. The women who do attend tend to dress in traditional Islamic garb; only a few men do.

Ulen spent her earliest years in Harrisburg, Pennsylvania, in a family rooted in the black bourgeoisie: funeral home owners, schoolteachers, a journalist, and a great-great-grandfather who fought in the Union army. Her father had friends in the Black Panthers, the Communist Party of the U.S.A., and the Nation of Islam, although he never called himself a Muslim. After her parents divorced, her mother took her to Maryland and raised her in the Catholic Church. Ulen taught in predominantly black Catholic schools after graduating from Sarah Lawrence, the elite women's college in suburban New York. But despite all her catechism, she had always been troubled by the existence of "so many different versions of the Bible." Which was the truth?

Islam never felt alien, given her father's interest in it. While earning a master's degree in philosophy and education at Columbia University in the mid-1990s, Ulen started attending prayers at Taqwa. "I read the Quran, and it made perfect sense to me," she said. "My big concern was giving up Jesus. Then I read a little more, and I realized I *wasn't* giving up Jesus," an honored prophet in Islam.

Ulen, now a writer and adjunct lecturer on literature at Hunter College in Manhattan, lives a more cosmopolitan life than most members of Masjid At-Taqwa. But she found a "community within the community" at the mosque, young African-American Muslims who share her interest in hip-hop music and cutting-edge poetry.

Like a growing number of Muslim women of her generation—she is in her mid-thirties—she reads the Quran in a way that highlights the essential equality between men and women. "What is in the Quran and what happens among Muslims are sometimes two very different things," she said. When she is inside a mosque, Ulen covers her hair, but not outside. Riding the subway with non-Muslim friends, she once ran into a "Taqwa brother," who loudly protested Ulen's appearance. "He just kind of fell into the chair, [saying], 'Oh, you *have* to cover.' And he started reading all this stuff from the Quran. You know, it was like"—Ulen rolled her eyes—"he was talking *at* me, not to me. It was like a little performance. He was certainly drawing attention, which, ironically enough, you're not supposed to do as a woman—draw attention to yourself. He was drawing a lot of attention to me."

Imam Wahhaj is a traditionalist when it comes to women, but Ulen still has mostly good things to say about him: His passion for Islam is contagious; his success in cleaning up his small corner of Brooklyn, uplifting. The Friday after 9/11 she went to prayers at Taqwa because it felt like a safe place. She was reassured by the imam's promise that men from the mosque were available to protect anyone who encountered threats.

Ulen praised Wahhaj for entertaining her periodic challenges to his sermons, which she has offered in private conversation. But she hasn't always found his explanations persuasive. In response to her questioning him on polygamy, he insisted that the institution actually gives a woman more choice: She can marry a man who is presently single or one who happens to be married already. This reasoning hadn't impressed her. Polygamy, she told me, may work in a tiny, remote village after half the men get wiped out in a disaster and widows need protection and sustenance. But she sees no place for it in America.

Thinking of marriage, she looked carefully among African-American Muslims but worried that a Muslim man "might want me to cover and want me to do certain things that I don't feel I want to do. I saw that as a potential source of conflict, as I saw some of my male friends become a little more into all of that stuff." She violated the prohibition on women marrying outside the faith when she wed a Christian man she met in her neighborhood.

~

Fighting drugs has been one of Masjid At-Taqwa's missions from the beginning. When the original members of the mosque bought the defunct clothing store at Bedford and Fulton, the drug dealers using the property asked if they could rent a portion to continue their business. They were told to leave.

In January 1987 a local landlord, a Palestinian Muslim, came to Wahhaj, seeking help in evicting crack dealers occupying an apartment in a nearby building. The police had been of no use, the landlord said. The imam gathered a group of followers and marched over. They banged on the door, the imam announcing loudly, "It's the Muslims. We're here to recover the property." Inside, he could hear someone say, "It's the Muslims. Don't do anything stupid."

The dealers promised to vacate, and the Muslims retreated to a car parked outside to make sure this happened. But instead of leaving, the dealers called the police, complaining that a group of armed, dangerous men were sitting in a car in front of the building. The police arrived promptly and surrounded the car. The imam and four of his followers were arrested and held in jail for three days. Police said they recovered a shotgun, a handgun, knives, and a club. Two of the Muslims were convicted of felonies. A state court dismissed the sole count against Wahhaj, misdemeanor possession of a knife.

Despite the ill will this episode generated, the Muslims and cops agreed in early 1988 to start fresh. The aim was to shut down a dozen crack houses in Bed-Stuy. After the authorities raided the locations and made arrests, squads of Muslim volunteers from Taqwa patrolled the area with walkie-talkies for forty days and nights. That period, Wahhaj noted, matched the duration of the great flood survived by Noah, a prophet recognized by Islam as well as Judaism and Christianity. It was winter and bitter cold. Women from the mosque fueled the round-the-clock effort with sandwiches, hot coffee, and tea. There were some confrontations on the street—mostly stare-downs—but eventually the crack dealers decided to relocate.

Taqwa's crack house offensive transformed the Muslims from outlaws to heroes. Senior police officials, joined by Rudolph Giuliani, then the top federal prosecutor in the city, trooped to Bedford-Stuyvesant to herald Wahhaj for his leadership. Newspapers and television stations, not just from New York but from around the country and the world, sent reporters to interview the drug-fighting Muslims. One of New York's most prominent black clerics, the Reverend Herbert Daughtry of the Pentecostal House of the Lord Church, told me that Wahhaj is "very effective, particularly within the Muslim community, and very respected in the community at large."

Today a mosque office wall crammed with framed civic commendations testifies to Wahhaj's continuing public role. Markowitz, the Brooklyn borough president, declared August 15, 2003, Siraj Wahhaj Day to celebrate a "distinguished spiritual leader" who has made "many outstanding contributions to the study and appreciation of Islam." But it was the forty days and nights battling crack "that really put Masjid At-Taqwa on the map," Wahhaj said. "The Muslims did something that was really significant to help the community."

Muscle, openly displayed, has played a role in African-American Islam since the early days of the Nation of Islam. Elijah Muhammad's Fruit of Islam security squad projected a neat but intimidating image and under Louis Farrakhan ran inner-city antidrug patrols similar to Taqwa's. Quite a few black Muslim men see Asian martial arts as a spiritual pursuit allied to Islam. Ali Abdul-Karim, a private investigator who has been a follower of Wahhaj for twenty years, runs a martial arts school he calls the Star & Crescent Ninjitsu. The presence of Abdul-Karim and his students helps deter vandalism and break-ins on the blocks near Taqwa.

Abdul-Karim also supervises Taqwa's security staff, a shifting ensemble of stern men who stand guard at mosque events. Hassan Abdul-Malik sometimes joins their ranks during Friday prayers. At other times Abdul-Malik keeps an eye on the closed-circuit TV screens in the little security office near the mosque's entrance. Unfailingly courteous, he jumps out of his chair to greet visitors and shake hands.

Not tall but built like a boulder, he was twenty-nine when we met. He sometimes wore a white turban with his black T-shirt and jeans. When I attended Friday services, he made a point of checking to make sure I was comfortable. I generally sat in a row of brown metal folding chairs for visitors and older men who couldn't manage sitting on the floor. The first few times I was greeted by my row-mates with the standard salutation, "Assalamu alaykum" (Peace be unto you), I hesitated to give the expected Arabic reply. I didn't want to create the misimpression that I was a prospective convert. But at Abdul-Malik's friendly goading, I eventually did begin answering, "Wa alaykum assalam" (And unto you, peace).

Abdul-Malik heard Imam Wahhaj preach for the first time on an audiotape he found in the library at Sing Sing, the upstate New York prison where he was serving five and a half years for robbery. Raised in both Baptist and Pentecostal churches, Abdul-Malik had once dreamed of being a policeman, but he strayed at a relatively early age, never graduating from high school. A prior felony record explained the stiff robbery sentence. All told, he served more than eight years. He lost his father while incarcerated, and that left him truly adrift.

In the dangerous, soulless life of imprisonment, Islam became a source of hope. He met other inmates who had converted, and they seemed to have the discipline he lacked. There were rules to follow, times to pray, a sense of a community, and safety. The Muslims protected their own. Muslim inmates defined themselves in opposition to white authority, but prison officials did little to interfere as long as there was order. Islam looked to a strong prophet, a desert warrior who had dark skin. Jesus, depicted as a white man, preached a forgiveness that seemed naive to some in Sing Sing. In 1996, while still locked up, Abdul-Malik declared his faith in Allah.

The topic of the Wahhaj sermon that Abdul-Malik discovered in prison was "saving yourself," and the inmate felt he needed to do just that. Wahhaj seemed to speak to him personally, addressing his dissolute past and his desire for a respectable future. "I said to myself, 'I have to get to this mosque,'" Abdul-Malik recounted. After his release he made his way to Friday prayers at Taqwa. "Everything changed when I saw him," Abdul-Malik said of Wahhaj. "I was a brand-new person." He lived in an apartment near the mosque, but Taqwa was his emotional home. He spent most of his free time there, praying, drinking tea, and chatting with other young men on the sidewalk outside. He often grazed at the table in the mosque's entryway that offered a pile of cookies and bagels to those who needed a free snack. "This is where the love is at," Abdul-Malik said.

Imam Wahhaj is "more like a father than a religious leader," the young man explained. "He led a lot of brothers to being somebody successful with a job." With the imam's backing, Abdul-Malik landed outside security assignments.

One evening Abdul-Malik was watching the door to the ballroom of the high-rise Marriott Hotel in downtown Brooklyn, where Muslims from across the country had gathered to pay tribute to Siraj Wahhaj. Other Taqwa security men scanned the audience inside. Abdul-Malik wore a new black T-shirt, and his pants were sharply creased. He said that being Muslim made him proud. The imam, he added, "represents what this religion is to us. It's respect—respect for yourself and for others. You are part of something bigger than yourself. This is bigger than the street."

THE BLIND SHEIKH

Imam Wahhaj and his followers pursue their religion in a volatile environment. First, there are the converts released from prison, not all of whom have derived the constructive lessons learned by Hassan Abdul-Malik. Prisons in New York and elsewhere have had problems with some Muslim chaplains seeking to radicalize inmates. According to an April 2004 report by the inspector general of the U.S. Department of Justice, some inmates are returning to freedom "with extreme Islamist views," a mixture of the Nation of Islam's racial hostility wrapped in the religious intolerance of fundamentalism.

Intimations of violence sometimes mingle with fears of co... Wahhaj recounted an incident from the mid-1980s, a few years after Masjid At-Taqwa started: "A Muslim came to me—it blew my mind— [and] he said, 'Hey, Imam Siraj. I know where we can get hand grenades.' My antennae went up." Wahhaj thought, "Here's a person trying to get us to do something wrong, say something wrong." The imam concluded that the man, an African-American, was "an agent provocateur," dispatched by the government to try to entrap him in a violent conspiracy. Wahhaj said he sent the man away. "People pray here, we don't ask who they are," he told me. "We don't stand at the door and say, 'Well, who are you?'"

In the early 1990s, the imam said, he met an Egyptian immigrant who attended New York–area mosques. The man aggressively pushed himself on Wahhaj, boasting of killing Israelis in the 1973 war. The Egyptian told Wahhaj he wanted to help out at Taqwa, offering at one point to redo its electrical wiring and install a security system. Suspicious, Wahhaj said no.

The cleric's wariness was justified. The man turned out to be Emad Salem, the FBI's key informant in its successful investigation of the plot to bomb the headquarters of the United Nations and other New York landmarks. It isn't clear whether Salem was working for the FBI when he approached Wahhaj. But Salem might well have been trying to insinuate himself at Taqwa, one of New York's most prominent black mosques, as part of his role as an informant. He would have had at least some basis for doing so: During the late 1980s and early 1990s the mosque opened its doors to significant players on the militant Muslim scene.

The media references to Wahhaj as someone "linked" to terrorism, about which he angrily preaches, stem from his relationships during this period. Muslims worldwide had been energized by the victory of Islamic fighters in Afghanistan over the forces of the crumbling Soviet Union. The United States had helped arm and train the triumphant *mujahideen*, but that backing had won America no loyalty among the Islamic fighters. Some militant Muslims were now fixing their sights on the United States as another infidel empire that needed to be taught a bloody lesson.

A circle of men eager for global jihad formed in the New York area. For religious guidance, they looked to Omar Abdel-Rahman, a blind Egyptian sheikh. The spiritual leader of an Egyptian terrorist organization called the Islamic Group, Abdel-Rahman had gained notoriety for providing the religious justification for the 1981 assassination of Anwar Sadat, the Egyptian president who made peace with Israel. Abdel-Rahman arrived in the United States in 1990 and began preaching in mosques in New Jersey and New York, including, on one occasion, Masjid At-Taqwa. There, speaking before about 150 men, he suggested that Muslims should rob banks to benefit Islam.

"He mentioned that here," Wahhaj recalled, "and I stopped him, and I said, 'Sheikh, no. You got brothers here, some of them came out of prison, and you're letting them know that this is permissible? I disagree with that.'" Abdel-Rahman, he said, "started laughing, and I remember him saying, 'Imam Siraj is right.' And he stopped like that."

One man who frequented Masjid At-Taqwa and also became part of the Abdel-Rahman circle was the African-American convert Clement Rodney Hampton-El. He had traveled to Afghanistan to fight with the mujahideen against the Soviets and had been wounded in the leg. Hampton-El, also known as Dr. Rasheed, worked as a hospital technician and informally dispensed medical advice. Many Muslims saw him as an "elder in the community," Wahhaj said, and admired both his adventures overseas and his generous spirit.

In February 1993 a truck bomb detonated in the parking lot beneath the World Trade Center, killing 6 people and injuring more than 1,000. The FBI investigation led to charges not only against the 4 men responsible for that attack (who were convicted and sent to prison for the rest of their lives), but also a larger network of followers of Sheikh Abdel-Rahman. The U.S. government prosecuted the blind cleric and 10 of his devotees for the broader conspiracy to bomb the United Nations Building and other landmarks in the city. The FBI figured out that 2 members of the conspiracy had ties to Masjid At-Taqwa: Hampton-El and the blind sheikh, who had lectured at the mosque. In February 1995 the government sent a letter to defense lawyers in the landmarks conspiracy case that disclosed a list of 170 people, including Wahhaj, whom prosecutors said they might name as coconspirators. Wahhaj was never indicted.

Five months later the Brooklyn imam appeared as a defense witness in the landmarks bombing conspiracy trial, held in a heavily fortified federal courtroom in lower Manhattan. Without apology, he testified that he had met Sheikh Abdel-Rahman several times and that it had been an honor to host the cleric at Taqwa. He described the blind sheikh as a "respected scholar," known for having memorized the entire Quran. "He is bold, as a strong preacher of Islam, so is respected that way," Wahhaj testified. In fact court records reveal the sheikh as a preacher of virulent hatred for the United States. In one speech, not at Taqwa, he instructed followers, "Do jihad with the sword, with the cannon, with the grenades, with the missile."

In his court testimony Wahhaj called Hampton-El "one of the most respected brothers." He added, "You always see him sitting around talking to someone, some youth, giving advice, even some imam, head of the Muslim communities, giving advice." Prosecutors presented evidence that Hampton-El provided assistance to the bombing plot by seeking to provide detonators and "clean" guns that couldn't be traced.

Wahhaj testified that he had met a third defendant, Siddig Ibrahim Siddig Ali, and that he had a favorable impression of a fourth, Ibrahim El-Gabrowny. All four of the defendants the imam discussed on the witness stand were convicted and sentenced to prison terms. Hampton-El got thirty-five years. The blind sheikh, who was also convicted by the New York jury of conspiring to assassinate Egyptian President Hosni Mubarak, was sent to prison for the rest of his life.

Years later when I confronted Wahhaj with the discrepancies between his and the jury's views of the convicted men, he waved off the entire prosecution as unjust. He suggested that there had been a government plot to trap Abdel-Rahman and his followers: "We saw Sheikh Abdel-Rahman as a man of principle. This other part that the government brought, we don't know about this. We don't know about him planning—and still are not convinced about that—planning to blow up, inspiring people to blow up." To Wahhaj, FBI allegations of any sort of conspiracy are evidence of a *government* conspiracy. He didn't seem interested in the evidence that had impressed the jury. His reference points are the assassinations of Malcolm X and Martin Luther King, Jr., events that he and many other African-American Muslims see as tied to official conspiracies.

Wahhaj periodically, and usually with great emotion, warns his followers that the government is targeting him personally. "I'm ready to die for Allah!" he has preached. "I'm ready to go to prison for Allah!" Allusions to leaders who have died while confronting hostile white forces aren't unique to blacks who are Muslim. The Reverend Al Sharpton, before he became a Democratic presidential primary candidate, built a following in New York with fiery speeches condemning the persecution of blacks. Wahhaj's oratory is similar. "If it costs me my life or my freedom, I'm going to speak out," he has preached. "I'm going to speak the truth, whether they like it or not."

Does he believe his life is actually in peril? "Of course," he told me.

So, what is one to make of Wahhaj's melodramatic speechifying and, more important, his acquaintance with infamous Muslim radicals? First, there is probably at least some basis for the imam's fears. It's likely that from time to time the FBI does dispatch informants to Masjid At-Taqwa. That's what happens if you have willingly associated with people like the blind sheikh Abdel-Rahman and his follower Hampton-El. But there is no known evidence that Wahhaj has participated or urged others to participate in terrorism.

Wahhaj's past familiarity with and continuing praise for Muslim extremists taint his reputation and detract from such accomplishments as fighting drugs, preaching personal responsibility, and building a religious institution from scratch. He seems willing to pay that price, perhaps to burnish his credentials as someone who doesn't bow to mainstream authority or white opinion. But mixing with dangerous people isn't the same as being a dangerous person.

When we evaluate all this, it is worth weighing an occasion in March 2001 when Wahhaj *assisted* the federal government in a terrorism case. He returned to federal court in Manhattan to testify in the trial of four Muslim extremists with ties to al Qaeda who were eventually convicted in the bombing of U.S. embassies in Kenya and Tanzania in 1998. One defendant sought to mitigate his involvement in the attacks by contending that he had objected beforehand to the mass killing of civilians. Called by that defendant's lawyer, Wahhaj testified that the Quran forbids the killing of innocent noncombatants under any circumstances.

The lawyer for a different defendant, in cross-examination, argued that his client had been religiously indoctrinated to think that Islam condoned blowing up American facilities to stop the "oppression" of Muslims. Confronting Wahhaj, he suggested that a declaration of jihad could justify such acts.

No, the imam testified. "Islam doesn't teach anarchy, and people can't take it upon themselves when they don't like something, even though something seems to be unjust, to get up and do that kind of violence." Surprised and pleased by this testimony, prosecutors later told the jury to heed the imam's statement.

A dedicated Wahhaj follower named Idris Abdul Wasi runs Abu Bakers, a bakery just down the street from Masjid At-Taqwa. One of the mosque's respected elders, he agrees with the imam that there are forces conspiring to smear Islam and Siraj Wahhaj. "There are elements in the media and society who are clearly enemies to Islam," Wasi told me. "They'll do anything they possibly can to turn the society against Muslims."

Wasi enjoys talking about business and has an inventive theory about one force generating the assault against Islam. He thinks manufacturers of cigarettes and alcohol have grown alarmed over the religion's ability to steer African-Americans and others away from smoking and drinking. The companies "are not going to sit back and allow that to happen," he said, and they could be the ones influencing the media to depict Islam unfavorably. He has no proof, he admitted, but still feels that "it's almost as if whenever there's a concerted effort to do something positive to uplift ourselves, there's this [opposing] effort to divert us."

A native New Yorker, Wasi sang in the choir at Bushwick Methodist

Church as a boy. But "the whole Trinity thing never really penetrated my heart or my head." This is a complaint I heard frequently from American converts to Islam, both black and white: that they couldn't make sense of the idea that the Father, Son, and Holy Ghost are all parts of one God. Wasi, now in his early fifties, saw Islam as a more logical approach to monotheism, one deity, pure and simple. He also appreciated what he saw as Islam's more clear-cut rules. He needed the discipline. "Coming up a child of the seventies, I was into the intoxicants, the lifestyle," he explained. His father, a longshoreman, drank himself to an early death. Wasi's mother was remarried to a Muslim and converted. Wasi's two younger brothers embraced Islam as well. In 1976, while a junior at John Jay College on Manhattan's West Side, Wasi followed suit. The only college graduate in his generation of his extended family, he has six children and, at the time we spoke, three grandchildren. His children were raised as Muslims, and not one drinks or smokes, he said with undisguised pride.

His business, a modest storefront, is fragrant with the aromas of the Middle East and Brooklyn, flaky baklava next to heavy yellow cheesecake. A sign instructs shoppers: THERE IS NO GOD EXCEPT ALLAH. Abu Bakers does more than peddle sweets and cake. It is one of a half dozen small businesses in the neighborhood that lease space from Taqwa. Fulton Street has come back to life over the quarter century the mosque has been on the corner. There are informal South Asian restaurants serving savory stews, a Muslim bookstore that sells Imam Wahhaj's tapes, and a grocery offering halal meat.

Almost every week, Wasi said, someone just out of prison and hanging around the mosque comes into his bakeshop, looking for a handout or a small loan. As a successful entrepreneur Wasi considers it his duty to help those who seem serious about cleaning up their lives. He dispenses financial aid and guidance on finding jobs. "In terms of African-American Muslims," he said, Islam "has turned thugs, robbers, thieves, murderers, drug dealers into productive citizens." The road back isn't easy. Drugs and liquor are readily available. Taqwa members just out of prison frequently try selling incense and body oil near subway stations, not a way to get rich. But, as Wasi said, it's better than dealing crack.

THEY ALL KNOW HIM

As popular as Siraj Wahhaj is in Bedford-Stuyvesant—Muslims and non-Muslims stop him on the street as if he were a star athlete or film celebrity—he has far more fans among immigrant Muslims and their children. Monem Salam, a Pakistani-American Muslim activist who lives in the state of Washington, told me: "If you go to immigrant mosques around the country and say the name Siraj Wahhaj, they will all know him. Why? Because he has raised money for almost every mosque." Wahhaj spends much of his time on airplanes, flying to speaking engagements that benefit other people's mosques and Islamic centers, most of them serving immigrant followings.

His breakthrough came at Muslim immigrant conferences in the Midwest in the early 1980s. He was a last-minute addition to one program headlined by the former folk rock superstar Cat Stevens, who had converted and changed his name to Yusuf Islam. Listeners eager to invite the charismatic speaker to raise money at their mosques approached Wahhaj after his religious talks. His fame spread quickly to university campuses, where he frequently addresses Muslim student groups. In contrast with some of his darker sermons at Masjid At-Taqwa and on audiotape, he generally presents an optimistic persona to younger audiences.

Many Muslims of South Asian or Middle Eastern descent still view African-American Muslims with disdain, partly because of racism and partly because the divergent practices of the Nation of Islam are still associated with all black converts. They make an exception for Wahhaj. "Imam Siraj Wahhaj has done more than any other person in the country to break those barriers down," said Monem Salam, who works for a mutual fund company specializing in investments that adhere to Islamic law.

For all the barriers Wahhaj may have broken, his own Spartan mosque hasn't benefited in any visible way. The air is stultifying in the summer, as slow-turning ceiling fans struggle against New York's humidity. The offices behind the main prayer area, including the imam's, are cramped and shabby. Wahhaj estimated Taqwa's annual budget for 2003 at only two hundred thousand dollars, extraordinarily small for a house of worship that regularly accommodates five hundred or more people for prayer. Five employees received regular salaries that year. Wahhaj said his is forty-four thousand dollars a year. (As a house of worship, Taqwa doesn't have to file tax returns.)

Some men attending Friday prayers make cash donations, but most of the bills are singles. A Kuwaiti prince gave fifty thousand dollars in the 1980s, Wahhaj said, and more recently the predominantly immigrant Islamic Society of North America made a one-time hundred-thousand-dollar gift. A mosque in Santa Clara, California, has helped out. But that's about it, he said. "My challenge here is not unlike that of Malcolm X": keeping a mosque going in a poor neighborhood while touring the country to spread the religion.

At times he sounds bitter about the disparity. He has raised, in all likelihood, millions for others, while his home mosque struggles financially. People who attend his talks at other institutions generally write checks to those institutions. His hosts pay his travel expenses, but he said that he only occasionally gets an honorarium of one or two thousand dollars. He claimed that he receives nothing from the Internet sales of his many sermons and lectures; those have been pirated and repackaged by online marketers. Despite some frustration over this situation, he has no plans to stop fund-raising for others. "That's what I do to help Muslims," he said, shrugging.

At the conference in Orlando, which drew both immigrants and African-Americans, the nonpecuniary rewards of his national stature were apparent. Everywhere he went, a small retinue followed. He received bear hugs from men and demure greetings from women. There were a dozen speakers, but his talks were the best attended. Wahhaj appeals to immigrants by stressing their religious bond with American blacks. Unlike some black imams, he doesn't berate immigrants for their racism. He eases the perhaps guilty consciences of Pakistanis and Egyptians by telling them to join hands with blacks and demand fair treatment from America. The children of immigrants respond positively to his lively encouragement to stick to their religion despite the lures of American secularism.

Wahhaj appeals to his African-American followers in part because of the respect they can see he receives from immigrants. His Arabic-language skill and his celebrity legitimize black Islam.

Wahhaj sometimes shows a dash of self-deprecating humor that sets him apart from the typically righteous prayer hall speakers. Near the beginning of one morning session in Orlando he slowly looked left and right at his audience. "I'm going to be speaking until twelve midnight," he said. "Any problem with that?"

"Go on!" someone answered, to general agreement.

JIHAD WITHOUT GUNS

In recent years Siraj Wahhaj has reevaluated his role and message, particularly in light of September 11, 2001. He has toned down some of the bristling oratory. "I do think there's definitely a different discourse after 9/11 than before," he told me. He and other prominent imams have discussed the inadvisability of portraying "we, the Muslims, against everyone else. It's not always like that." When referring to Christians and Jews, he said, he has tried to avoid the Arabic word *kafir*, a pejorative for "disbeliever." He uses the more neutral term "non-Muslim" instead. "I don't want to add to problems, and I don't want Muslims to get wrong concepts of Islam," he told me.

But he isn't ever going to discuss Islam or politics or African-American life in a way that makes white non-Muslims entirely comfortable. He remains a complex mixture: one part mainstream, one part militant; some of his inspiration drawn from Islamic fundamentalism, more from black nationalism. In his own words: "The mainstream Muslims in North America, you don't find them radical. Maybe there's a handful. I don't know. By and large, they're moderate. Militant? OK. Dress a certain kind of way? OK, yeah. You might hear some anti-American flavor a little bit, but not because they hate America, but the same way, again, our civil rights leaders spoke about the injustices of America. Then you hear it in that way, especially [from] African-Americans. If that makes us militant, then we're militant."

During one interview I raised his refusal to ascribe blame for 9/11 to Osama bin Laden and al Qaeda, almost two years after the fact. "I'm not sure if I've seen the evidence that says that they've done it," he said. "I'm not unlike so many other Muslims around the world and even in this country, decent Muslims who would never agree to something like that [9/11], who are just not sure" of bin Laden's culpability.

The imam's refusal to acknowledge bin Laden's guilt is incomprehensible to an outsider and obviously harmful to bridge-building efforts. As a Muslim leader he contributes to the impression held by many non-Muslims that people of his faith aren't entirely sorry to have seen the United States taken down a notch. Wahhaj hastens to say that he grieves for the victims of 9/11. Killing civilians, he adds, is always wrong. But granting al Qaeda the benefit of a doubt that doesn't exist undermines this message and his stature.

His approval of the term "jihad" could confuse some listeners and almost certainly would provoke suspicion among non-Muslims. In a recorded talk entitled "Blessing of Death," he tells his audience, "If ever there comes a jihad, brother, don't run from the jihad, because the sickness of the *umma* [Islamic nation] today is their fear and hatred of death. But in the old days that best generation, they loved jihad, and they loved death." Wahhaj said that his meaning was no different from that of an American president rallying troops for a just cause. "In the context of fighting a legitimate war: don't run from that," Wahhaj said. "In the context of America: our [Muslims'] jihad is not with guns, and I said that on many tapes." In a talk called "Muslims in America: Surviving After Sept. 11," he concludes: "Our fight, brothers and sisters, is not with guns and knives and bombs. That's so foolish. That's not our fight. Our fight is simply the truth."

Siraj Wahhaj has traveled a great distance since the days when he preached about "white devils" in the Nation of Islam's Mosque No. 7C. At times he now speaks the language of racial and religious respect. "It's not contradictory for me as an American to be a Muslim; nor is it for an American to be a Christian or a Jew or a Sikh or a Hindu or even an atheist, for that matter. That's what makes America what it is," he told *Saudi Aramco*

World, a magazine published by the Saudi state oil company, in the spring of 2005. The periodical, which tries to encourage warm feelings between the United States and Saudi Arabia, quotes a South Asian immigrant praising Wahhaj for his vision and calling him "a true Islamic leader."

But the sunny portrait offered by Aramco is incomplete. The truth is that African-American Islam, like immigrant Islam, lacks fully developed leaders. Wahhaj is a skillful preacher, and his life's journey offers an instructive history of the modern black Muslim experience. But that journey took him through periods of association with pernicious personalities and ideologies, some of which he declines to disavow. For all his healthy exhortations about working hard and living right, he has marginalized himself with these associations.

Most of African-American Islam has shaken off its attachment to the sect built around Elijah Muhammad. His son, Warith Deen, pointed black Muslims in a more promising direction, but he lacked the desire or will to lead an effective movement. Louis Farrakhan had charisma but put it in the service of hatred, before sliding into irrelevance. The field is open to inspiring black Muslims who can combine the call for racial justice with the humane teachings of the Quran. What is needed is someone who does that while also abandoning the rhetoric and gestures of extremism that seem irresistible to the talented imam from Bedford-Stuyvesant.

FOUR

The Feminist

The opening of the new mosque during Ramadan 2003 marked a new beginning for the Muslims of Morgantown, West Virginia. But what sort of beginning would it be?

For the men who worshiped at the mosque regularly, the spacious prayer hall, with its shining chandeliers, symbolized the growth of the local Muslim community since the days when worshipers gathered in a church basement and then a rented room across from the county jail. Traditions brought from distant lands had found an unlikely haven in the foothills of Appalachia.

Asra Nomani saw something different in the new mosque, a chance to reclaim her rightful place in Islam, a place approved, she believed, by the Prophet Muhammad himself. Earlier in the year Nomani, a thirty-eight-year-old freelance writer born in India, had made the *hajj*, the ritual pilgrimage to Islam's holiest places. In Mecca she had seen throngs of women and men worshiping together in the same crowded spaces. This was what she wanted to see in Morgantown, where her father had helped start the mosque a quarter century earlier and where women had always been excluded or kept separate during communal prayer.

The collision of these expectations turned out-of-the-way Morgantown (a three-and-a-half-hour drive northwest from Washington, D.C.) into a battlefield over women's status in Islam. Nomani, determined to praise God in the same room as men, outraged male worshipers by conducting a defiant pray-in. Rather than retreat to a special women's balcony, she simply stood behind the men. The offended worshipers—engineers, physicians, professors, and business owners—condemned her as insolent, and they made an issue of another transgression, one that would have scandalized orthodox believers of most faiths: Nomani had borne a son out of wedlock after a brief relationship with a Pakistani Muslim. Making matters worse, in the eyes of some, she wrote about her very modern love life in a book entitled *Tantrika*, which was published in 2003.

Nomani fought back, branding her antagonists fundamentalists, men who viewed modern women with contempt. As the confrontation escalated—in part because of her deft publicity skills—she became the catalyst for a broader national debate over the future of Islam in America. Back home in Morgantown, one other thing bothered Nomani. She refused to follow the requirement that women enter the new mosque through a rear door, next to the Dumpster.

THE PROPHET'S FAREWELL

Muslims are in Morgantown because of West Virginia University. They began arriving in the 1960s from Pakistan, India, and Egypt as graduate students and junior professors in technical fields. Rather than return to their homelands, some stayed. The university and its well-educated faculty and staff dominate the pleasant, hilly town of twenty-eight thousand near the Pennsylvania border in north-central West Virginia. Morgantown prides itself on being sympathetic toward racial and ethnic minorities, and few immigrants report hostility. Local liberals like to note the circumstances of West Virginia's founding: When Virginia seceded in 1861, its western counties banded together and gained admission to the Union as a free state.

The public university was established in Morgantown just after the

Civil War ended. By the early 1900s West Virginia University had put the small town at the center of the state's transformation from an economy dominated by agriculture to one focused on coal. The university trained many of the mining engineers and administrators needed by the booming extractive industries. Even with its natural resources, West Virginia has long been one of the poorest states in the nation, but Morgantown's university-affiliated population is a happy exception. In the 1970s and 1980s WVU expanded health and science complexes that have spawned local businesses in those fields and drawn more students from the Muslim world. A generic drug giant, Mylan Pharmaceuticals, has its headquarters in town, and a large federal occupational safety facility is there too. Unemployment is around 3 percent, below the national average.

On a cold Friday in February 2004 Asra Nomani took me on a tour of Morgantown, pointing out personal landmarks: the faculty apartments where her family once lived, the dorm where she had her first kiss at age nineteen, and the corner McDonald's where she drafted her "Manifesto for Equal Participation by Women." We arrived at the Islamic Center of Morgantown. "That's it," she said. "That's what the fight's about."

From its initial home near the Monongahela County jail the Muslim congregation had moved to a residential house down the block from the McDonald's. The expanding group eventually acquired a plot across the street and raised five hundred thousand dollars to build the present much-larger structure. The new mosque, dedicated in 2003, lacked the graceful forms of traditional Islamic architecture: no arches, dome, or minaret. Instead an economical three-story rectangular box supported a plain peaked roof painted deep green. On top, a modest-size crescent, also green, offered the only outward hint that Islam was practiced within. But compared with the dingy house now known as the old mosque, the new one gleamed.

Nomani approached the front door. She adjusted the gauzy cream-colored scarf covering her hair, which she wears only during prayer. Men chatting in front of the building stared at her. She softly offered the standard greeting of peace: "Assalamu alaykum." She knew them all by name and had grown up with some of them. But only one young fellow returned her greeting.

She passed through the main entrance with a line of men. "You just saw me sin," Nomani whispered, referring to her entering the front door. Her campaign of deliberately violating restrictions on women in the mosque had entered its third month. There had been loud confrontations early on, but now the men said nothing.

Nomani removed her black leather ankle boots. By climbing a narrow staircase, we reached the main prayer room, a two-story hall that could easily hold the roughly three hundred members of the congregation. (In part because of a large contingent of male graduate students from the university, men outnumber women two to one.) Light streamed in through Palladian windows. As in most mosques, there were no chairs or pews; worshipers sat on the thickly carpeted floor. Nomani walked to the back of the room, about thirty feet behind the nearest man. Where she sat, the ceiling was much lower, and there was little light. Above that area was the special women's balcony. Up front, near the raised podium where the imam stood, small boys mingled with their fathers.

The jummah service coalesced gradually. During and after the call to prayer, some of the men in front read aloud, but not in unison, from Qurans they had taken from wooden bookcases. Nomani, a petite woman with charcoal hair, sat silently, her large dark eyes closed in meditation. Her parents soon arrived, and her mother, wearing a white scarf, sat next to her in back. They were the only two women in the main hall. Her father, still a leader of the mosque, sat with the other men in front. He had Asra's toddler son in his lap.

After a while the proprietor of a local Middle Eastern grocery store rose to deliver the khutbah, or sermon. The Islamic Center lacks a professional cleric, so volunteers take turns serving as imam. The grocer, who is from Syria, announced that he would read the "Farewell Khutbah of the Prophet," which Muhammad delivered shortly before his death. As it happens, the famous sermon includes a section on relations between the sexes. The Prophet said, referring to Muslim men:

Oh, people, to you a right belongs with respect to your women and to your women a right with respect to you. It is your right that they not fraternize with anyone of whom you do not approve, as well as never to commit adultery. But if they do, then God has permitted you to isolate them within their homes and to chastise them without cruelty. But if they abide by your right, then to them belongs the right to be fed and clothed in kindness. Do treat your women well and be kind to them, for they are your partners and committed helpers. Remember that you have taken them as your wives and enjoyed their flesh only under God's trust and with His permission.

The grocer offered no context or commentary.

Men had continued to arrive, and the crowd reached about 125 people. Long rows began to form. For group prayer, Muslims stand shoulder to shoulder. Traditionally men and women form separate rows to avoid physical intimacy. Some mosques take the further step of obliging women to pray in an entirely separate room or behind a partition or up in a balcony. If they pray in the same space, men usually form the front rows, nearest to the imam, while women pray in the back. A common explanation for putting women in the back (or out of sight entirely) is that men would be aroused and distracted by the sight of women bending over during prayer, as is required of all worshipers.

The members of the Islamic Center of Morgantown raised their hands to their ears and began the series of recitations, accompanied by the bowing, kneeling, and prostrating that Muslims follow the world over. Nomani and her mother did so as well, in a two-woman line at the back of the prayer hall.

After the service Nomani noted the section on women in the "Farewell Khutbah." To me, it had sounded fairly progressive for the seventh century, although a little odd when presented without any qualification or explanation.

"There's this talk about isolating and chastising, and it's all about men controlling women, right?" Nomani said. Her voice has a hint of Valley Girl. "That's because the sermon is aimed at men. It's as if the women in the mosque are invisible."

EAST AND WEST

The name Asra means "to journey" and alludes to the Islamic story of Muhammad's mystical flight from Mecca to Jerusalem and, from there, up to heaven and back. Born in Bombay in 1965, Nomani came to the United States at the age of four. She and her older brother, Mustafa, and their parents settled in Piscataway, New Jersey. Asra's father, Zafar, was working toward his Ph.D. in the biochemistry of nutrition at Rutgers University, part of the wave of South Asian scientists, engineers, and doctors who began moving to the United States after 1965, when the country relaxed immigration restrictions for non-Europeans. Pakistan and India have suffered the same kind of talent drain to the West that has deprived Middle Eastern societies of many of their best-educated citizens.

Despite their high levels of education and material achievement, South Asian immigrants tend to be overlooked as Muslims because Americans automatically associate Islam with the Middle East. Interestingly, so do many Muslims. In mosques with mixed congregations, such as the one in Morgantown, South Asians often defer to Arabs, who recite the Quran in its original tongue and represent the lands where Islam first flourished.

Asra and her brother learned about the life of the Prophet at an informal Sunday school organized by an older Egyptian biologist. According to a favorite Nomani family story, Asra, at the age of eight, pointedly asked the gentle Egyptian teacher why there were no women prophets. He admitted he didn't know why. "He smiled and treated me with respect," Asra recalled. "There was nothing wrong with asking the question."

When Asra was ten, her father moved the family to Morgantown, where he became a professor of nutrition at West Virginia University. The Nomanis started out in a small faculty apartment and soon moved to a modest split-level house with pink aluminum siding, where they made their first Thanksgiving turkey dinner.

Asra has written movingly about the ambivalence that came with being a West Virginia girl from a restrictive foreign culture. Both Indian and Muslim tradition constrained her. After a sixth-grade square dance her parents forbade any more close encounters with boys: no dates, no mixed parties. At times she resented the rules. But she also enjoyed belonging to a group with a distinct identity and moral code. "I was grateful to have been born a Muslim," she writes in *Tantrika*. "I saw it as a privilege. Whenever I was faced with a dilemma, I asked myself whether my choice would comply with the Quran."

But as she grew older, Muslim customs seemed more and more stifling. At holiday meals, men and women gathered in separate rooms, with the male terrain always more comfortable. Men served themselves first from the steaming platters of lamb biryani and chicken masala. Women filled their plates only after the last man had been through the line. On Fridays, when the men prayed together at the mosque, Asra's brother was invited; she was not.

Asra continued to live at home when she started college at WVU, but soon her curiosity about boys overcame her sense of religious modesty. In her sophomore year she secretly began dating a blond, tobacco-chewing American in her Arabic class. The relationship inevitably came to light and caused considerable parental grief. Asra wouldn't be a virgin on her wedding night.

She stopped praying regularly and didn't participate in the Muslim Students Association chapter her father had helped start. She moved out of the family house and into an apartment with friends. She rejected her father's dream that she become a physician and threw herself instead into journalism, a pursuit that favored her habit of asking questions, sometimes past the point of being polite. Not that she gave them much choice, but Asra's parents decided to swallow their disappointment and go along with her plans. She prepared herself methodically, obtaining journalism internships in Manhattan and Washington that produced the sort of clippings that big-time newspaper editors demand of entry-level hires. A master's degree from American University added a little polish, and in 1988 she landed a job at *The Wall Street Journal*. This is how we first met; I had started at the *Journal* about a year earlier.

The visit to the Morgantown mosque on that cold February afternoon in 2004 was followed by a stealthy second reconnaissance later the same day. Asra wanted to show me the women's balcony and bathroom. Her father, conscripted to help with the mission, was not happy. "You two are secret agents," he protested in his Urdu-inflected English. "I am afraid of journalists." Professor Nomani noted mournfully that he had helped start this mosque in 1981. He still served on its board of trustees, but some of his colleagues had stopped talking to him as a result of Asra's activities. "I cannot do whatever she wants," he said of his daughter.

Asra scolded him in Urdu. The professor sighed and put on his winter coat. He insisted on taking two cars to the mosque. In his view, if there was a need to flee, splitting up might speed the escape.

Asra and I drove in my rental car. Her father strapped Asra's sixteen-month-old son, Shibli, into his car seat in Asra's SUV. At the mosque he remained outside with the baby—apparently as the lookout—while Asra and I slipped in through the front door. In our socks we tiptoed to take a look at the restrooms. The men's had a large foot basin designed for *wudu*, the mandatory ablution before prayer. The much smaller ladies' had no foot basin. "OK?" Asra whispered sharply, making sure I appreciated the discrepancy.

From there, we crept up the back stairs that women were supposed to use to get to the balcony, a carpeted space that might fit forty or fifty adults. A half wall, chest high on Nomani, made it impossible to see down to the main prayer hall from a sitting position. "Now you get it," Nomani whispered. With a commando's silent nod, she signaled that it was time to leave. There were a handful of men reading the Quran in the main hall, and she didn't want to be detected. Back downstairs and out the front: the getaway was clean.

In the early 1990s, when Nomani and I were colleagues in the Washington bureau of *The Wall Street Journal*, we had only a polite office relationship.

It was a surprise when the boss suggested I take her out for a Coke and some cheering up. Unbeknownst to me, there was a group effort to help her shake off some "personal difficulties."

She explained that she came from a traditional Indian family. Her parents had arranged her older brother's marriage to a young woman from India. Asra had been pressured to marry in the same fashion. There had even been some talk in India of her being paired with a cousin. Then, one day, out of nowhere, a classmate from graduate school had called. Omar was a Muslim from Pakistan, now working at the World Bank in Washington. He knew how to pronounce her name ("Us-ruh," instead of the Americanized "Ass-rah"). They went to the movies and ate tandoori chicken. She had had non-Muslim boyfriends since college, among them a surfer from California and a country music fan who gave her flowers. But with Omar, she felt she was completing a circle, returning to the culture of her parents.

In the space of months she and Omar were engaged. His family insisted the wedding take place in Islamabad, and before she knew it, Nomani found herself decorated like a traditional Pakistani bride: pink lipstick, heavy black eyeliner, rows of gold necklaces, and a gold brocade *dupatta*, or scarf, draped over her head. Whenever she tried to speak, her in-laws-to-be told her that a bride should be silent. Omar wore a silver turban and flower garlands. During the ceremony they sat in separate rooms, and at the conclusion of the three-day affair her husband's father instructed her that as a Muslim and a Pakistani she should now speak only Urdu.

Nomani had sought a bridge to her heritage. What she got were in-laws who expected her to behave like a self-effacing Pakistani wife. Worse, she said, her husband turned out to be a knot of emotional unavailability. They returned to Washington, but within several months the marriage collapsed. She had been attracted to him as an idea, not a flesh-and-blood man. In the end it was Omar's father who called her to confirm the divorce.

Daniel Pearl helped Nomani bounce back. He was a new addition to the Washington bureau, a handsome fiddle player with a knack for whimsical feature stories. He introduced her to her first beer at a Dupont Circle dive called the Big Hunt. Until age thirty, she had respected the Muslim prohibition of alcohol. Her friendship with Pearl remained platonic, but it deepened, in part because they shared a sense of never quite being in step with Washington's politically obsessed culture.

Pearl went overseas for the paper in the late 1990s. Nomani moved to New York to be with the latest in a series of ill-suited companions. As her search for romance foundered, she gravitated toward writing about the topic for the *Journal*. She chronicled the rise in thong underwear sales and the demise of wedding night sex. In December 1998 the paper published on its front page a story of hers under the headline "Naked Ambition: Tantra May Be Old, But It Has Generated a Hot Modern Market." The article described "scores of upstart concerns cashing in big on the hottest new wrinkle in America's 'feel good' industry—the teachings of Tantra, an ancient and sexually inclined subset of Hinduism and Buddhism." Her cheeky writing style disguised a serious interest in Tantra, which she saw as a possible connection to her roots in South Asia, where her Hindu ancestors had converted to Islam. Once more she was trying to bridge East and West. She landed a book contract to write about Tantra, left the *Journal*, and made Morgantown her base of operations.

As Nomani traveled in Asia doing research for her book, her attention gradually shifted from ancient Hindu sexual practices to modern Muslim life. She visited relatives in India and Pakistan who were caught up in the Islamic revivalism sweeping the Muslim world. She spent time with a favorite cousin in India whose husband forbade her to show her face to any man outside the family. He preached incessantly about his devotion to God, hatred of America, and disgust over Jews—all common themes among South Asian Muslims, she found. In Pakistan she stayed with an uncle and aunt who used a hand counter to tally their prayers, on the theory that frequency heightens piety. When the uncle left to pray at the mosque, he locked the women inside the house.

But behind closed doors in that house, Nomani's feisty paternal grandmother conducted an inner life according to her own dictates. Dadi, as Asra called the tiny old woman, had driven a car alone back in the 1950s—a rare assertion of independence. Her granddaughter learned that surrounded by a rising tide of fundamentalism, Dadi persisted in following an eclectic array of practices aimed at clearing the mind and soul. She did Hindu yoga, as well as Sufi meditation. The grandmother told a story about feeding sugar to an ant, illustrating the beauty of kindness to all God's creatures. For her searching granddaughter, the old woman offered a sense of spiritual hope.

On September, 11, 2001, Nomani was back in Morgantown. She was working as a volunteer that morning at the elementary school her brother's children attended. The school staff panicked when an Arab man approached the office. It turned out he was picking up his child early, as many other parents did that day. Asra went home and put on a headscarf. By marking herself as a Muslim woman, she wanted to remind her neighbors that Muslims weren't all terrorists.

By the end of September she had returned to Pakistan, seeking to write about why so much resentment against America had accumulated among Muslims. In a series of articles for the online magazine *Salon*, she offered grim portraits of angry middle-class Pakistanis who blamed America for all their discontents. Her most memorable subjects were a clique of condescending women who idolized the Taliban and compared Western women to the hut of a poor man: "Anyone can walk in any time of the day or night."

Living on her own as a freelance journalist, Nomani met a good-looking younger man with a number-crunching job in Karachi's financial district. He took her home to meet his family, even though as a divorced woman born in India she was far from a typical Pakistani parent's idea of a desirable prospect. Still, before long he spoke of marriage, and Nomani fell in love. Could she finally connect East and West? On a beach on the Arabian

Sea, she and her suitor committed *zina*, the Islamic sin of sex out of wedlock. The women of the Taliban admiration society would have felt vindicated.

In late January 2002, Daniel Pearl and his wife, Mariane, a French journalist, arrived in Karachi to stay with Nomani in the villa she had rented. Then based in Bombay, Pearl had arranged to interview a controversial Muslim cleric. Mariane, who was pregnant with their child, had her own assignment. The next afternoon Pearl left for his interview, never to return. Nomani's house became headquarters of the search for the missing reporter. After an endless month the terrible news arrived. Pearl's kidnappers had made him say, "I am a Jew," and then beheaded him.

In the midst of this chaos, Nomani discovered she was pregnant. Although her Pakistani boyfriend earlier had spoken of marriage, he now announced that he didn't want a baby and stopped seeing her. Nomani was dumbfounded. Her parents, already rattled by Asra's proximity to the Pearl affair, now received the jolting news of the pregnancy. Sajida Nomani at first wanted to know how her roving reporter daughter would care for an infant. But grandmotherly instincts kicked in quickly, and Sajida told Asra the baby would always have a family in Morgantown. Asra's father, Zafar, e-mailed her three words: "I love you."

Asra came home but struggled to recover from the combination of Pearl's death and her Pakistani boyfriend's abandonment. He suggested by telephone that she get an abortion, which she angrily refused to do. Her escape from grief came with the birth on October 16, 2002, of a baby boy. She named him Shibli, after a revered Nomani ancestor and Islamic scholar. She gave him the middle name Daneel, a variation on Daniel.

IN THE SHADE OF ISLAM

The Muslims of Morgantown decided to open their new mosque during Ramadan 2003, the holy ninth month of the Islamic lunar calendar, when the observant fast from dawn to dusk. Wearing a headscarf, Nomani approached the building on the first day of prayers. The birth of Shibli had caused her to rethink her place among her hometown's Muslims. She wanted to raise the boy in Morgantown, where she had the love and babysitting backup of an extended family. Becoming a mother also reaffirmed her sense of herself as a Muslim, even though she didn't follow the orthodox rules. She realized she wanted to raise Shibli as a Muslim too.

But Nomani had doubts about what it meant to be a believer. Was Islam bound up with the intolerance she had observed among relatives in Pakistan and India, with the hatred that had killed Danny Pearl? She concluded that no, those were perversions of Islam. The essence of the religion was the compassion she saw in her parents.

Nomani reached for the green metal door of the new mosque and prepared to open a new phase of her life.

"Sister, please, the back entrance!" A mosque elder pointed to where other women were headed.

In the converted house across the street where they used to worship, women had used a separate entrance and prayed in a separate room. But Nomani had assumed—she later couldn't say why, exactly—that in the new building women would be able to enter with men. Before she could sort this out, her momentum had carried her past the unwelcoming sentry and through the front door. She walked to the left, through the community room, and to the back stairs, where she ascended two flights to the women's balcony. She had heard about the balcony, but this was her first look at it. There were about twenty other women up there, with at least as many small children, many of them fussing. To communicate with the men downstairs, women sent notes carried by little boys. Nomani couldn't see the prayer leader and felt cut off from the service. This wasn't right.

For the first week of Ramadan she didn't speak up. She went around to the back and climbed the stairs to the balcony. When she was younger, she hadn't gone to the mosque much because she never felt welcome. Now she worried that she would be seen as a carpetbagger if she protested the segregation by sex. Still, it infuriated her—not least because up in the balcony women were even more physically removed than they had been in the old mosque.

During the early days of Ramadan she happened to watch a documentary film titled *Muhammad: Legacy of a Prophet*. It combined profiles of assimilated American Muslims—a firefighter, a nurse, a congressional staff member—with an admiring account of the Prophet's life. Moved, Nomani e-mailed one of the producers, a Muslim convert named Michael Wolfe. She told him about her chagrin over the women's balcony. She also described the celebratory dinners that broke the fast that week. The men ate in the comfortable, brightly illuminated new mosque. Across the street the women and children ate in the shabby old mosque, sitting on plastic trash bags spread across a dirty floor. As she watched the portrayal of the Prophet Muhammad's life, Nomani wrote to Wolfe, "I wanted to weep thinking about the sorry state of the Muslim community today." But she vowed that the Nomanis would "pray beside each other as we did earlier this year in two of the holiest mosques in Islam, in Mecca and Jerusalem. Our mystical night journey will continue to Morgantown."

Several powerful memories flowed together like tributaries to form the resolve that carried Nomani into the main prayer hall. There was the memory from childhood of the second-class treatment Muslim women received. There was her impulsive marriage, with the oppressive ceremony in Islamabad. There were her relatives in Pakistan and India, with their obsessive concern about women's sexuality. There was the fundamentalism that hardened into violence in so much of the Muslim world.

There was also the hajj. In February 2003 the Nomanis of Morgantown had traveled en masse to Mecca to participate in the great annual pilgrimage that is one of the five basic requirements of Islam. Asra, who brought three-month-old Shibli with her to Saudi Arabia, was overwhelmed by the immensity of the crowds—two million people in all—and the palpable sense of shared devotion. She was struck that in Meccan mosques, at the heart of Islamic orthodoxy, men and women prayed in adjacent lines and in close proximity. Conditions were more restrictive back in Morgantown. "To me, there was something seriously wrong with that," Nomani said. Her mother agreed: "That's the holiest of places, and when we were there, we prayed side by side, two groups—men here and women here—not even in the back." It was in Mecca that the idea was planted in Asra's mind that one day her family would pray as a group in their hometown.

Lugging (and nursing) an infant made the hot, dusty trips from one sacred site to another even more taxing for Asra than for most other pilgrims. Her burden was eased by the affection Shibli elicited from strangers. But the warmth came tinged with bitterness. In Mecca, as in other places governed by Islamic law, Nomani was in theory a criminal; Shibli was the undeniable evidence.

Eight months later, during Ramadan in Morgantown, these memories— of segregation since childhood, of Islamic fanaticism, of the hajj—all came together. After one Friday prayer session some women asked for a microphone so that a would-be convert could make her required declaration of faith that "there is no god but God, and Muhammad is the messenger of God." The man in charge of the microphone refused. "A woman's voice is not to be heard in the mosque," he explained. Boys and men routinely used the microphone for all kinds of mundane announcements. But on this holy night the woman embracing Islam spoke on the balcony, without amplification, while men talked below, oblivious to her devotion.

That same day members of the Muslim Students Association from the university were distributing at the mosque copies of a booklet entitled *Women in the Shade of Islam*. Published by Saudi Arabia's Islamic Propagation Office, the booklet has chapters on women's rights and "misconceptions" about women in Islam. One subsection is about beating wives. It offers extended commentary on a passage of the Quran that states: "And as for those women whose ill-will you have reason to fear, admonish them [first]; then leave them alone in bed; then beat them; and if thereupon they pay you heed, do not seek to harm them" (4:34).

It's possible to interpret this offensive-seeming verse in a benign way. The reader might note that it suggests physical force only as a final option, after nonviolent punishment has failed. In pre-Islamic Arabia, where women were treated as chattel, this instruction might have constituted a humane reform. The reader might also take into account hadith that report that the Prophet Muhammad condemned wife beating. Islamic scholars are virtually unanimous in depicting the Prophet as a respectful and loving husband to his multiple wives. Strange as it may seem, the enduring teaching of the wife-beating verse could be understood as a call for improved treatment of women.

But the Saudi-published *Women in the Shade of Islam* doesn't allow for an enlightened reading. It *encourages* hitting some wives. The booklet states that force can be used, only "without hurting, breaking a bone, [or] leaving blue or black marks on the body." It goes on to assert that psychologists have determined that beating is particularly effective with two types of women, those who try to "run the affairs of their husbands by pushing them around, commanding them, giving them orders" and those "submissive or subdued women" who become "more attracted to and admiring" of their husbands when beaten. (Fundamentalist literature available to American Muslims goes far beyond misogyny. Freedom House, a watchdog group in Washington, D.C., sent Arabic-proficient researchers into fifteen major American mosques across the country in late 2003. The survey—which Muslim groups denounced as unscientific and unfair— found that all fifteen stocked publications produced or funded by Saudis that were hostile to Jews, Christians, and the United States. A representative tract available at the large King Fahd Mosque in suburban Los Angeles, which was built with Saudi money, described America, the adoptive home of the institution's worshipers, as the "abode of the infidel." It instructed: "Be dissociated from the infidels; hate them for their religion; leave them; never rely on them for support; do not admire them; and always oppose them in every way according to the Islamic law.")

Appalled to find advice on hitting women being distributed in her hometown mosque, Nomani became even more determined to change the sexist tone of the Islamic Center of Morgantown. She raised the question of praying in the main hall with her mother. Sajida rarely went to the mosque at all, for the very reason that she didn't like the disrespect women faced. "This is just the way it is," she told her daughter.

Asra said she didn't care about "the way it is." She was going to pray in the main hall, and soon. Sajida silently wished Asra would focus on finding a husband.

As a founder and member of the board of trustees Zafar Nomani, Asra's father, had been intimately involved in the planning and construction of the new mosque. His wife didn't even know one was in the works. "He never discussed it with me," Sajida Nomani confessed over tea in Asra's house, where Shibli's plastic toys carpeted the living room. "One day," Sajida continued, "I went to drop somebody, one of the kids, and I said, 'What's this standing over here, this new mosque?'"

Sajida's father died when she was a small girl in India. Her mother sent her to live with a wealthy cousin who could afford to pay for a good education. Sajida's main memory of childhood is of missing her mother. She attended a British-run convent school—even devout Muslims in India sought the prestige associated with Christian British institutions—and then a home economics college in Bombay. Her cousin's family was religiously conservative, and in public she always wore a burka. "Head to toe, you had to wear a black thing with little holes you can see through—mesh," she told me.

Her family arranged for her marriage in Bombay to an idealistic young scientist she had never met, Zafar Nomani. After the ceremony they took a train to Hyderabad, India, his home city. Her new mother-in-law, a strong-willed and modern woman by Indian standards, met them at the station. The older lady, Asra's grandmother Dadi, looked at Sajida's long black burka and yelled, "Take it off!" Before the new bride could react, her mother-in-law stripped her of the garment. "I felt exactly as if I was naked," Sajida recalled.

The move to America was difficult. For the first two years her very young children stayed behind with relatives, while she and her graduate student husband saved money. "That was a very, very hard time for me," she said. For the next thirty-five years Zafar often worked late into the night, doing research and guiding students. His main outside interest was religion, the mosque. "I'm so conditioned from growing up, it doesn't bother me" to be excluded from communal religious life, she said. That was a world for men. "I would rather pray at home."

She raised her children and occasionally sold imported Indian clothes supplied by her brother, who was in the garment business in New York. At his urging, she opened a small store in 1981 on Morgantown's High Street, the main thoroughfare. "People just went crazy," she recalled, still sounding surprised. She played Indian music, and students would dance amid the merchandise. Indian cotton skirts, nose rings, and Hindu statuettes became hot sellers in the hills of West Virginia. Sajida Nomani, who grew up a shy Muslim girl in a burka, became an exotic local character.

Now in her late sixties, Sajida wears her long gray-streaked hair straight down her back. She dresses in loose shirts and dark slacks. Asked what "women's liberation" means to her, she said, "It is one of the reasons why I like this country—that women and men can do whatever they want to. Back in India, I would not have had a business of my own." No other woman in her family had worked outside the home. "I don't miss India at all," she said. Still, she resisted her daughter's idea of fighting the mosque. "I thought we would never win. I said, 'Just forget it.' But when she wants to do something, she does it."

While she mused about her family praying together in Morgantown, Asra gave her father and the rest of the mosque's board notice that change was coming. The warning took the form of her "Manifesto for Equal Participation by Women," a kind of bill of rights for Muslim women: to enter the mosque on equal footing, pray in the same room, and even play a role in its leadership. Nomani handed the manifesto to her father just as Ramadan was beginning and asked him to present it to his four fellow board members for adoption. "His whole thing was that women have to speak up, women have to come forward, women have to participate," she said. So she was speaking up.

As a boy growing up in the Indian city of Wardha, Zafar Nomani was given a book containing short biographies of the prophets and their teachings: "Ibrahim, Musa, Esa, Muhammad." He recited them for me carefully, using the Arabic versions for Abraham, Moses, and Jesus. "Every word I took to my heart, contemplating, meditating." He also read about the Buddha and rejection of material attachments. Mohandas Gandhi had an ashram near Wardha, and the Nomani family sometimes picnicked there. Zafar would climb a tree to see the great man speak.

His father moved them to the larger city of Hyderabad, where his law practice flourished. But Zafar didn't forget the faces of starving children in the countryside during famine times in the 1940s. He earned a degree in agriculture and, in his first job, spent two years working at a rural experimental station with three colleagues: a Hindu, a Christian, and a fellow Muslim. At night in their cramped bungalow, they heard tigers in the jungle. The four young scientists formed an interfaith mutual admiration society. At some level Zafar Nomani came to believe that there is only one, universal religion. "*Everybody* has to answer before God on the Day of Judgment for your *deeds!*" He is a small, bald man who speaks at length and with emotion, his index finger pointed toward heaven. "Lifetime *accountability*," he said, forms the centerpiece of Islam.

Zafar specialized in nutrition. He was an early advocate of not obsessing about fat intake and examined the role of carbohydrates and overall energy consumption—"*pre*-Dr. Atkins!" In 1994 he founded the *International Journal of Ramadan Fasting Research*, a publication that explores how Muslims should manage their diets during the holy month.

He invested much of his time in nurturing Islam on campus and at the mosque. "I have been fighting for women's causes from day one," he said, "but I was not that successful." Part of the problem is that many Muslim women don't seem to want to play an active role in religious organizations. "My wife says women are conditioned not to pray at mosque, and this is correct," he said. He conceded that Asra had forced his hand on the question of women's access to the new mosque. But once he had thought about it, he agreed that there was no need for a separate entrance. He also thought women should pray with the men in one hall. Nothing in the Quran said otherwise.

MUHAMMAD'S EXAMPLE

For ten days Asra had been praying with the rest of the women in the balcony of the Morgantown mosque. On November 6, 2003, a Thursday, her family joined her in taking the step she had played and replayed in her mind: praying in the main hall. She had recruited them one by one. Her mother had doubts but eventually overcame them. Asra feared her father would try to stop the adventure, but he agreed too. Her beloved niece and nephew, Safiyyah, twelve, and Samir, ten, were an easy sell. Safiyyah brought her school backpack, crammed with books, snacks, and other supplies, in case events required a long encampment.

In the early morning the five of them, along with Asra's year-old son, Shibli, bundled up in her arms, slipped in through the mosque's front door. Shoes were shed, and the Nomanis, female and male, entered the main prayer hall together. Up front a small group of men were praying. The Nomanis parked about twenty feet behind them. Samir stayed with the women. Professor Nomani took Shibli and went to sit closer to the other men. Inevitably one of the men turned around. "Sister, please!" he said to Asra. "Please leave. It is better for women upstairs."

"Thank you, brother," Asra said. "I'm happy praying here."

Harsh words followed and then a threat to close the mosque. The men berated Asra for violating their rules.

"How are you behaving like this in a mosque?" Asra's mother, Sajida, demanded of the hostile men. Her family defense reflex was strong. Accusation led to counteraccusation. The Nomanis remained for the prayer and then for a short time afterward, to show they weren't being chased out. Then Sajida said, "OK, let's go."

Despite the enmity, Asra felt triumphant. Of her antagonists, she said later, "I knew I was interrupting their prayer, I guess. It was my day to do this."

The next day the mosque's board of trustees passed a resolution establishing that the front door and main hall were "solely" for the use of men. The vote was 4–1, with Professor Nomani offering an emotional dissent. "My daughter has returned to Islam," he said. "Welcome her." The other four told him not to worry. The "Manifesto for Equal Participation by Women" went nowhere, of course. During subsequent board meetings the trustees continued to brush off Professor Nomani and defend the policy of women praying in the balcony.

Asra went every day to the mosque, sometimes with her mother. She meditated and prayed in the main hall. Men stared but typically said nothing. The board of trustees ignored her written request for a meeting.

Professor Nomani, meanwhile, became an unwelcome presence at communal prayer. Old friends questioned his sanity. But the Nomanis stuck together. On Eid ul Fitr, the holiday marking the end of Ramadan, the professor gave Asra a present, her own copy of the key to the mosque's front door.

Asra intensified the confrontation in late December 2003. She lodged a discrimination complaint against the board members of the Islamic Center of Morgantown—including, for form's sake, her father—with the Council on American-Islamic Relations, the most visible Muslim civil rights group in the country. "Formal and informal policies have created a hostile environment towards women's presence and participation in the mosque," she wrote. A senior CAIR official told her by telephone that the group doesn't get involved in internal mosque disputes. That official, Ibrahim Hooper, subsequently told me that he contacted a leader of the Morgantown mosque to urge informally that Nomani be allowed to pray in the main hall.

While women are participating in more and more aspects of American life that were once off-limits to them, CAIR's own research shows that separation of the sexes in American Islam has actually increased. A survey the group published in 2001 found that 66 percent of American mosques employed a curtain, partition, or separate room to seclude women. That figure had *risen* from 52 percent in 1994, apparently a reflection of the arrival of more immigrants influenced by Islamic fundamentalism.

The Quran doesn't dictate where women ought to pray. When Muslims discuss the woman's place in the mosque, they usually turn to hadith describing the example of the Prophet Muhammad. But the problem with these historical accounts is that they sometimes contradict one another. One hadith has the Prophet saying that women shouldn't be stopped from attending mosque. But another quotes him as advising that it's better for women to pray at home. Nomani embraced the first and tried, not very persuasively, to shrug off the second. Inadvertently she illustrated the peril of relying on ancient authorities when arguing for reform.

Whatever Muhammad preferred, there are numerous historical reports that he prayed in the same area with women in his mosque in Medina. A number of hadith also indicate that women played an active role in early Islamic religious life. They questioned Muhammad about his revelations, and he willingly taught them. After the Prophet died, his favorite wife, Aisha, became an important figure in the transmission of his teachings to others. Still, when invoking the danger of men being aroused by women prostrating in prayer, many Muslims recite a hadith in which the Prophet is reported to have said that in the mosque men belong in the front rows and women in the back.

Zafar Nomani was prone to lecturing that Islam brought great improvement in the lives of women. "Who gave rights to women fourteen hundred years ago? Do you know?" he asked me. "Islam! Right of inheritance? Islam! Who gave for the first time a right to divorce the husband? Islam has given the right. Right to remarry? Islam. Islam *started* women's rights!"

This is all more or less correct, according to scholars. When it was introduced, the religion of Islam elevated women's status. It banned the common tribal practice of female infanticide and abolished the idea that women were mere possessions. But ancient Muslim culture never treated women as equal to men or anything close to it. Neither, for that matter, did ancient Jewish or Christian culture. Rules some Muslims enforce on veiling and secluding women lack firm grounding in the Quran, but they have been common practice in much of the Islamic world for many centuries.

Modern Islamic scholars, like their counterparts in Judaism and Christianity, have had to employ imaginative rules of interpretation to navigate around anachronistic precepts in their scriptures. In Islam, these include women's testimony being assigned only half the weight of men's, men being allowed to marry outside the faith while women are not, and the condoning of polygamy.

～

Nomani drew outside attention to the controversy in Morgantown with an article she wrote about it for *The Washington Post* near the end of 2003. West Virginia's largest newspaper, *The Charleston Gazette*, followed up with a supportive editorial entitled "Woman's Place: Taking a Stand for Equality." Morgantown's local paper, *The Dominion Post*, offered similarly sympathetic coverage.

As word of her actions spread, Nomani became part of a nascent debate over American women in Islam. For several years a handful of liberal Muslim activists and scholars had spoken against mistreatment of women in predominantly Islamic societies. These critics focused on "honor killings" of unmarried mothers and forced veiling and seclusion. Only recently had such scrutiny turned to the treatment of American Muslim women. The collection of scholarly essays published in 2003 under the title *Progressive Muslims* attracted attention on some university campuses by urging a reexamination of Islamic teachings that men should dominate women.

A Web site called Muslim WakeUp! endorsed Nomani's cause and predicted, "The days of women being relegated to the attic and being forced to use the back entrance by the Dumpster are numbered." The site reprinted Nomani's *Washington Post* article, igniting emotional online reactions. "This is exactly what we require: ordinary people to take initiative and challenge the unhealthy existing norms," said one Muslim WakeUp! reader. "Asra, more power to you."

Others disagreed. "ARE YOU YAHOODI [Jewish]?" one man wrote. "THAT IS THE LAST TIME I COME HERE. YOU ARE NOT AN ISLAMIC SITE." Most of the negative responses focused not on the main issue of women's access to the mosque but on Nomani's passing mention that she had conceived a child while unmarried. "I fully agree with the points made in the article," said one man. But "the author is the last person on earth that should be complaining. She is morally and spiritually devoid of any system of ethics . . . In the small reference to the 'out of wedlock' child, she showed no remorse or guilt." Some participants noted with disgust that in her book *Tantrika*, she discussed her interest in Tantric sex. A writer using the moniker Reason wrote, "To me, she is a pagan-cow worshiper pretending to be Muslim. She is just an opinionated cheap woman-for-pleasure."

At the Islamic Center of Morgantown frustration levels were rising. During a Friday evening study group in mid-January 2004 Asra sat several steps away from a group of about eight men, including her beleaguered father. Once again she received a sharp order to move.

"Brother, I have an Islamic right to remain here and participate in this study session," she replied.

"You are arrogant and stubborn," she was told.

Zafar Nomani stepped in and said that just the previous evening he had visited the Islamic Center of Pittsburgh, where women joined men in study and prayer in the same room.

In that case, someone suggested, Asra ought to pray in Pittsburgh.

When Professor Nomani tried to speak again, one man yelled at him, "You're an idiot! Look at the daughter you raised!"

The local *Dominion Post* recounted the spat, including Asra's description of her opponents "spewing personal insults and wildly gesticulating." The paper also quoted her as saying, "Sometimes I have sat at the mosque by myself, the men filing inside, and I have wondered if some man would throw acid on my face in anger for my presence."

In principle Hazem Bata, a young leader in the Morgantown mosque, agreed that women should be treated with more respect. But he also thought that Nomani fought dirty. He resented her innuendo that Mus-

lims in Morgantown kept assertive women in line by threatening disfig-
urement. "That might be something that happens back in India, where
she's from," he said angrily, "but that's the only thing that people got out
of that article: oh, my God, Muslim men throw acid in the faces of
women!" (Asra later conceded to me that the acid comment was "unfair"
but insisted that it reflected real fears she and other Muslim women felt.)

Bata, who has a neatly trimmed goatee and a formal manner, said that
he had reached out to Nomani. He called her, and they met at a local café,
where they spoke politely for more than two hours. "You might have
some legitimate points," he told her, "but even if you do, you're going to
alienate everybody—those who are with you and those who are against
you—with the writing." If she toned things down, he said, she might get
most of what she wanted.

But Nomani wouldn't promise to tone things down. "She was not willing to compromise or budge or do anything," Bata said later. "She wanted
things done *this* way, and she wanted them done *now*."

He thought she had exposed the Morgantown mosque to unjust
ridicule from non-Muslims. Some older men did care about preserving
old ways. They were reinforced by some of the recently arrived immigrant students. But many others, including Bata, an attorney of Egyptian
descent who grew up mostly in America, didn't object to women coming
in the front door and praying in the back of the main hall.

His wife, Rayhana Rahim, a doctoral student in pharmacology, also
sympathized to a degree with Nomani. In the late 1990s Rayhana and her
older sister, who are of Afghan descent, became the first female officers
of the Muslim Students Association at WVU. Rayhana gave most of the
credit to a man, Zafar Nomani, Asra's father and at the time the faculty
adviser to the MSA. Professor Nomani had simply declared that it was
time for women to help lead the organization.

Some male members from the Middle East were aghast at the prospect of women leading any public endeavor. The MSA at West Virginia
University, like many of its counterparts on some four hundred campuses
across the country, shifted demographically during the 1990s, as propor-
tionally more immigrant students from the Middle East joined those from

South Asia. WVU enrolled a total of three students from Egypt and Saudi Arabia in the fall of 1993; by 2003 that number had grown to fifty-five. At many schools the influx from the Middle East reflected increased recruiting of students whose prosperous families or governments paid full tuition. Some of the Middle Eastern engineering and computer science students espoused fundamentalist strains of Islam and often sought to tilt MSAs and local mosques toward their strict understanding of the religion.

Rayhana recalled lecturing her literalist critics that they could do as they pleased at home or at the mosque, but on campus they would have to be more open-minded about women. "This is not the same culture as back in Egypt or wherever you're from," she said she told them, and Professor Nomani backed her up. But beyond securing their right to serve as officers of the MSA, the Rahim sisters didn't try to change much, Rayhana conceded.

Like her husband, she had sat down with Nomani for a talk. Rayhana agreed that it wasn't fair that the women's bathroom was less well equipped than the men's. But she said to Nomani, "I want to know how you really feel, whether this is for publicity or whether this is a genuine effort to turn the community around."

Nomani said she wanted broader awareness, not just in Morgantown. "I want the rest of the world to know."

"To know what?" Rayhana demanded. Nomani, she said, didn't have a clear answer. ("To know that some women are standing up for their Islamic rights," Nomani later told me she had responded.)

Nomani baffled the Batas. But in truth their perspective was also a little difficult to sort out. They agreed that women deserved better treatment but insisted that the Morgantown mosque had always been a male institution. Men are "highly encouraged" to pray at the mosque, Hazem pointed out. For women, he said, it is considered optional.

Rayhana thought that the women's balcony was unnecessary, but she didn't feel that strongly about it. She had warm memories of the old mosque, even though at holiday times men occupied all the space, forcing women to carry their prayer rugs to a nearby park or hotel ballroom.

These days, she said, there seemed to be much less interest among the women in communal religious activities. Rayhana, for one, had two young children and was finishing her doctorate. "There's just not enough time right now to go," she said. She didn't get to the new mosque until months after it had opened. "I went through the back [door] because I wanted to be alone and see the women, and then I came down and saw the men also. No one said, 'Oh, my God, there's a woman in front of me.' No one said anything.

"It's not mandatory for the women to go," she added, echoing her husband. "Most of them would like to go someplace nice, like a nice restaurant, to get together, instead of the mosque."

The Nomanis took a break from the mosque battle one evening in February to attend the annual Most Beautiful Baby Contest at Morgantown's Mountaineer Mall. At the contest, put on by a company called New Star Discovery Inc., parents paid to enter their small children in categories like "Best Head Shot" and "Prettiest Eyes." The odds of taking home a cheap plastic trophy improved the more categories one entered. Asra put down eighty dollars, close to the maximum. Contestants were led or carried across a rickety stage. Shibli wore a tiny black leather motorcycle jacket with a little silver chain attached to the shoulder. On one pass he pointed at the judges like a rock star acknowledging his fans. In short order, he amassed three trophies and then a fourth as the overall champ among boys fifteen to twenty-three months. Professor Nomani announced he was taking the triumphant group of Shibli backers to the Peking House for dinner.

Over lo mein and chicken with mixed vegetables, twelve-year-old Safiyyah, Asra's precocious niece, discussed which boys in her class were "really hot." That led to the question of whether Safiyyah's mother, Azeem, would ever allow her to date.

"No!" Azeem declared.

Safiyyah, a Queen Latifah fan who wears purple eye shadow, observed that the adults had just been joking about her younger brother, Samir, receiving phone calls from girls. "Hmm, what do you call that," Safiyyah asked, "a double standard?"

Zafar Nomani enjoyed the merriment, but his mind drifted back to the mosque. Members of the board had been telephoning him. "You must stop her," they said, referring to Asra. "She is using you, embarrassing you."

"I say, 'Once she is eighteen, she has her own mind. She goes to college, becomes a journalist; she is her own person. *You* talk to her.'"

A WOMAN'S HONOR

It looked as if Nomani were making progress at the mosque. She continued to pray in the main hall, entering the building through the front door. Mosque elders sent her an e-mail, saying, "Sister, the Board of Trustees wants to reassure you that no discriminatory policy will be implemented in the Islamic Center of Morgantown." Combined with her being tacitly permitted to pray where she chose, the statement was an incremental victory. Equally encouraging, Nomani thought she had found an ally outside her family: an American convert named Christine Arja.

An attorney in her late twenties, Arja had grown up in Michigan, puzzled by religion. A good deal of that puzzlement, she told me, stemmed from her father's membership in an eccentric Christian sect whose ideas she often had trouble understanding. During college she explored Islam and found it simpler and clearer than Christianity. She became a Muslim and shortly thereafter married a Lebanese Muslim physician whose career took them to the Morgantown area. Like Nomani, she had been turned away from the front door of the new mosque. "I was like, you've *got* to be kidding me," Arja recalled. After that she sometimes prayed with Nomani in the main hall, and in the spring of 2004 the pair wrote and distributed a pamphlet aimed at local Muslims entitled *Break the Silence*. They recommended seminars on raising Muslim kids; a diaper-changing table; and *wudu*, or ritual washing, facilities for the women. They also demanded that women be included in mosque leadership.

Arja had reservations, though. While she respected Nomani's idealism, she worried that her public campaign would hurt the image of Muslims. Also, Arja found that Nomani "had a little bit of an air of being more worldly than some people you meet here in Morgantown—how she talked and the things she would talk about."

✺

Even as she and her new collaborator were ironing out their platform, Nomani was looking beyond women's rights. She turned her attention to the blunt intolerance of some of the sermons given at Friday services. In April 2004 a Muslim Students Association member gave a khutbah and said, according to notes Nomani took, "To love the Prophet is to hate the ones who hate him." Elaborating, the young man, an immigrant from the Middle East, said that "the most wonderful example of love" could be seen in the story of a man who killed two close relatives when they opposed the Prophet Muhammad. "Stay far away from those who are enemies of Islam," he lectured.

Nomani interpreted this rhetoric as endorsing hatred of non-Muslims. "I left the mosque Friday sick to my stomach," she wrote in an e-mail.

Two weeks later Hany Ammar, a computer science professor from Egypt and one of the more influential members of the Islamic Center, gave a sermon warning that the West is filled with "immoral people" on "the dark path." When he arrived in Morgantown in 1990, Professor Ammar told me on another occasion, he had been disgusted by the neighborhood around the mosque, then just a rented room. "We were surrounded by bars. We heard music from bars" during prayer, he said, an expression of revulsion crossing his bearded face. To him, the new mosque symbolized the ability of the town's Muslim professors, physicians, and engineers to create a holy sanctuary. "This was a big event for us. We were thrilled," he said. "Then comes Sister Asra, and she denied us this happiness."

In his khutbah Ammar, a large middle-aged man who wears a white knitted skullcap, warned that Islam suffers when Muslims emulate Americans. With "blind copying of the West, our rights, honors, and dignities will be violated," he said. He discouraged "imitating of kuffar," a disparaging term for non-Muslims. "The Western culture is like a mirage," he said.

Ammar and his wife, Mona, had had plenty of opportunity to observe life in the "mirage" since arriving in America twenty-five years earlier. They had raised five children here. While he lectured his fellow Muslims to keep their distance from nonbelievers, Hany Ammar did business with kuffar at the Pentagon and NASA, which have underwritten his research. Later, when I asked him to clarify the message of his sermon, he said: "We should be proud of our Islamic heritage. Sayings of the Prophet show you don't think about other cultures. You don't take from other cultures to patch up your own culture. You should not imitate others. Be proud of your culture and stay within that."

On April 16 Nomani launched a new broadside, a complaint addressed to CAIR and other national Muslim groups, accusing the mosque of sponsoring sermons that encouraged listeners "to 'hate' and communicated statements dangerous to the fabric of American society, American law, and the Muslim community."

This escalation caught Christine Arja by surprise. She too disapproved of some of the sermons delivered at the mosque. But her approach differed from Nomani's. Arja didn't view the foreign-born speakers as dangerous. She wanted to persuade them to be more open-minded. "I don't think, sometimes, they realize exactly what they're saying," she said.

The day after the complaint to CAIR Arja sent Nomani an e-mail ending their brief alliance. "Your actions have gotten everyone so up in arms that in all fairness, you can't expect someone to be leaping for joy or opportunities to talk to you . . . I don't want my children to be totally assimilated into western cultural ways," she continued. "I don't want Noor and Zaynah growing up to resemble Britney Spears, or using drugs in their teens and a zillion other things."

One warm spring evening in the midst of the controversy, Hany Ammar assembled six active members of the mosque for a group discussion. Five men and I sat around folding tables arranged in a U shape. Christine Arja, the only woman present, sat at a separate table, ten feet from the nearest man. She wore a headscarf and a beige raincoat that she kept buttoned to her neck. At first things were friendly, as a gracious young man named Ahmed served strong, sweet tea in Styrofoam cups.

Then the mood shifted. Ammar, to whom the others deferred, explained that "Sister Asra" appeared to be working on behalf of a "neoconservative" plot to recruit and promote "moderate" Muslims, by which he meant fraudulent Muslims, as a way of undermining real believers. "I think this is *exactly* what she intends," another man said. Ammar said Nomani might be in league with Daniel Pipes, a prolific columnist and author who rails against what he calls "militant Islam." This elicited nods from the others.

Hazem Bata, sitting across from me, offered a less conspiratorial assessment. "You can't measure what we do with your own gauge, just as you can't measure meters with a yardstick. Don't judge it by American standards." He compared Muslim practices to those of Orthodox Jews who separate men from women during communal prayer. "In the U.S., separation reminds us of slavery, segregation, separate but equal," Bata continued. "But it's not an insult to women at all in Islam to be separate from men . . . I don't think Ms. Nomani was judging what went on in the mosque by an Islamic gauge. She was using her own gauge." He didn't leave it there. "I don't think she has a pure intention behind any of her articles," he said. "She is establishing a foundation of popularity for herself."

"There's a lot of people who say, 'Make her stay away,'" Ammar said. "There's a mosque in Pittsburgh. Maybe she would be happy there."

Ammar spoke for the mosque hierarchy in late April, when he sent a long memo to CAIR and the other national Muslim groups, replying to Nomani's allegations. He denied that anyone preached hatred in Morgantown. "Further, we strongly disavow acts of hate and speech directed at inciting or invoking hate toward any group or individual." As for the MSA member's sermon advocating hatred of those who hate Muhammad, he suggested that the speaker might have used an imperfect translation from an Arabic text. "The sermon was directed at acts or practices deemed detestable by God, not at hate towards any group of people," Ammar wrote. "The use of the word 'hate' may be compared with the word detestable or severe dislike, and may have been chosen in the difficulty in translating between Arabic and English." Ammar didn't explain why using the word "detest" rather than "hate" would have made a difference.

He accused Nomani of taking things "out of context," and he warned that she was disseminating "false information about the teachings of Islam that will open opportunities for attacks on Islam and Muslims." He also complained that members of the community "are troubled that their individual state of worship and reflection during our Friday sermons is interrupted by the sound of Ms. Nomani writing notes and flipping pieces of paper as she attempts to record every word of the speaker."

About a week later another MSA member, Ahmed El-Sherbeeny, gave the Friday sermon at the Morgantown mosque. The engineering graduate student, the same Ahmed who had graciously served tea during my group interview of mosque leaders, offered some thoughts on the topic of women. "A woman's honor lies in her chastity and modesty," he declared. "When she loses this, she is worthless." He offered as an example the story of a Muslim man who had sex with a Muslim woman, then refused to marry her because she was no longer a virgin. "She didn't deserve his respect," El-Sherbeeny said.

Nomani, again taking notes near the back of the prayer hall, felt as though the sermon were directed at her. El-Sherbeeny said that women's "sensitive nature" explained certain dictates of Islamic law. Wives don't have the same rights as their husbands to seek divorce because "Allah created women sensitive and emotional, especially during her menstrual period," the grad student said. This same sensitivity justified the traditional Islamic requirement that to counter a single male witness in a legal proceeding, there need to be two female witnesses. The rule doesn't "belittle" women, "as is claimed by the enemies of Islam," he added.

Later, in response to my questions, he elaborated in an e-mail: "Islam is a superior religion in terms of giving Muslim women rights and honoring them, something that I had hoped (but did not expect) would get through to Asra Nomani and her kind." Nomani, he explained, was demanding the wrong sort of rights. "To her, for example, a Muslim woman has the right to a sexual relationship with whomever she wants, whenever she wants—something rejected clearly by Islam and most other religions."

In private El-Sherbeeny was courteous and soft-spoken, other members of the mosque said. Five times a day, beginning at dawn, he hurried to the mosque to chant the ritual call to prayer. He wore a special wristwatch alarm that reminded him at the appointed times. On campus he helped lead the MSA, promoting upbeat events like Discover Islam Week.

But at the mosque he revealed a bleak view of outsiders. "In general, we see the inferiority of women outside Islam," he said in his sermon. Muslim women should not be "deceived" by the West, especially the practice of women going out to work. El-Sherbeeny's wife wore a full facial veil and a long gown when she left her home. Presumably she didn't wear any fragrance because her husband preached that "any woman who wears perfume so men can smell her, it is as if she has advocated adultery."

At times Nomani wavered, telling her mother she feared she was only making enemies. "I'm not afraid," Sajida replied. The older woman had summoned courage from a reservoir she hadn't known she possessed. "If you fear Allah, you won't fear anybody," she said.

As Asra thought about all that had happened, anger replaced anxiety. Distinctions blurred between the intolerance she had encountered in Karachi and attitudes at the Islamic Center of Morgantown. "I hate them. I hate them," she said at a weaker moment, her enemies seeming legion. She stepped up her attack, this time on the opinion page of *The New York Times*. In an article titled "Hate at the Local Mosque," her focus shifted from where women prayed to what men said in sermons. She recounted the talk of hating those who hate the Prophet. "Americans need not look elsewhere to hear hate-filled rhetoric preached by fundamentalists. It resounds in our own back yards," she asserted. Her father had just quit the board of trustees. He was "tired of complicity," Asra wrote. "If tolerant and inclusive Islam can't express itself in small corners like Morgantown," she concluded, "where on this earth can the real beauty of Islam flourish?"

Awareness of what was going on in Morgantown was spreading. The *Pittsburgh Post-Gazette*, the region's biggest newspaper, sent a pair of reporters to cover the May 7 election at the mosque. Men were quoted as disdaining Nomani's objections. "We're not hateful people," one member told the *Post-Gazette*. "She's trying to use the community as a bridge to fame." El-Sherbeeny, the engineering grad student who had sermonized on the worthlessness of nonvirgins, told the paper, "She doesn't seem to have anything better to do than to fight her fellow Muslims." He told the paper that Nomani had misunderstood the meaning of his sermon on women. "Women are to be cared for and supported financially and physically as wives and daughters and sisters," he said. "And women have a responsibility to preserve their chastity and their honor." The paper reported that El-Sherbeeny "realized his sermon would strike a sensitive nerve with Nomani, a single mother. But her problem isn't so much what he called her 'great sin,' but what he perceives as a lack of repentance."

Despite the defiance, there were signs that Nomani's campaign was having an effect on the mosque. When the votes had been counted for the new executive committee, two of the nine winners were the moderate-minded Hazem Bata and Christine Arja. Arja was the first woman ever elected to help run the mosque. Nomani said that influential male members of the congregation had backed Arja as a public relations move. That may have been so, but Arja's election still created an important precedent.

Internal disillusionment with mosques isn't limited to Morgantown. Many American Muslims, and not just women, are growing disenchanted with their places of worship and the people who run them, according to Omid Safi, an Islamic scholar at Colgate University and the editor of *Progressive Muslims*, the 2003 essay collection. He explained that "Morgantown" had become shorthand for female dissatisfaction within Muslim communities. A majority of Muslims forty or younger, he said, are repelled not just by the treatment of women but also by the all too common disdain toward non-Muslims and American culture. The grandson of an Iranian ayatollah, Safi quit attending a traditional mosque in upstate New York after 9/11, in part because the immigrant imam there was so dismissive of non-Muslims. Safi instead pursued his spiritual life privately, with friends and family.

Ahmed Nassef, the editor in chief of the Web site Muslim WakeUp!, agreed with Safi and called the situation "a major crisis in American Islam." The problem, according to Nassef, a former marketing executive who came from Egypt as a young child, is that Muslims who see American culture as evil tend to dominate American mosques. This alienates more open-minded and assimilated Muslims who often don't speak up. Nassef and Safi independently told me that the influx of male students from the Middle East has encouraged mosques to embrace harsh fundamentalism. Muslims who have lived longer in America, including converts, often defer to recent immigrants who are seen as understanding "authentic" Islam—that practiced in the region that gave birth to the religion. Obvious symptoms of this phenomenon, Nassef has written on his Web site, are "the rabid misogynistic policies common in most mosques, such as limited access to main prayer halls or bans on women serving on mosque boards."

DAUGHTERS OF HAJAR

As she received encouragement from people like Omid Safi and Ahmed Nassef, Nomani broadened her vision of the campaign. She got in touch with other Muslim women around the country whose writing or activism she admired. Nomani invited five of these women to come to Morgantown in June 2004 to help her start a "historic new women's rights group." They called it Daughters of Hajar, a reference to Abraham's second wife, who gave birth to Ishmael, ancestor of the Arab tribe that produced the Prophet Muhammad.

Publicity about her actions had brought Nomani a strange sort of local fame. Non-Muslims—neighbors, ex-teachers, and former classmates—stopped on the street to congratulate her, even though most of them didn't understand what exactly she had accomplished. Even little Shibli seemed to sense something unusual. He chose these several days to learn to put his hands to his ears, in imitation of the beginning of prayer and say what his mother and grandmother insisted was "Allahu akbar."

Over lunch one afternoon at a Tex-Mex restaurant, Sajida said that she worried about her daughter. "She is obsessed with the mosque. No eating, no sleep, just the mosque."

Asra had her laptop out on the table, next to a chicken enchilada. She was sending e-mail via a wireless connection while talking on her mobile phone. The Associated Press and local reporters planned coverage of the Daughters of Hajar. A documentary film crew had come to town to do something for public television.

Nomani received a call from another member of the mosque, who warned her that Hazem Bata and others were working on a petition to ban her. "Why does he hate me so much?" Nomani asked her mother when she got off the phone. She recounted how she had told Hazem months earlier that her actions would benefit his wife. "She's a casualty," Nomani had said. "She doesn't come to the mosque anymore. She doesn't participate. She doesn't try." That's not at all how Rayhana Bata saw herself, of course.

The conversation shifted abruptly back to how much warm support the Nomanis had received from their many non-Muslim friends. Asra showed me e-mail from evangelical Christians who compared her with the Virgin Mary and Shibli with the baby Jesus. For the first time in hours her mother's worried expression gave way to an amused smile.

The next morning the Daughters of Hajar gathered at Dorsey's Knob, the highest point in town. They perched awkwardly on a large boulder while the four-person documentary film crew scrambled to find artsy shots. The Muslim women discussed their plans for a protest march to the mosque and the need to keep their message punchy but substantive. It soon emerged that Nomani's out-of-town guests didn't realize that she and her mother were already entering through the mosque's front door and praying in the main hall. What, then, were the Daughters of Hajar demanding? Answer: they would celebrate the *progress* in Morgantown and call on other mosques to follow suit.

As the march kicked off, a press corps of twelve (including me) now outnumbered the Daughters of Hajar. Mohja Kahf, a literature professor at the University of Arkansas, led a prayer in Arabic and English: "Oh, God, grant before me light, and behind me light." The marchers wore bright pinks, blues, and golds. Placards announced verses from the Quran about speaking truth and upholding equity. A policeman stopped traffic at an intersection, and the procession made its way past the Christian Student Fellowship building.

The reception at the mosque was less than warm, but the Daughters of Hajar used the front door and entered the main hall without interference. The sermon, delivered by a graduate student, stressed the importance of ceremony. "Deliberate disregard of ritual obligations," the speaker said, "is destructive of the very foundations of religion." Looking directly at the Daughters, he recited the hadith about men praying in front and women in back. Nomani and her allies, heads covered, offered their entreaties to God.

Outside, after the service, Christine Arja told reporters that Nomani had been allowed to pray in the main hall for six months now. In a sense, the Islamic Center of Morgantown was tacitly acknowledging that Nomani had won: Women were officially tolerated in the main hall and presumably could use the front door to get there. But Arja wasn't making a friendly overture. Nomani, she said, "does not represent the majority views of the women in this community, who feel like they're being read their feminist rights in Islam like a *Miranda* warning." Arja correctly noted that the Daughters of Hajar weren't challenging the basic rule against men and women praying side by side. "It's puzzling to us," Arja said, "that she keeps publicizing and propagandizing this event when it's been resolved for a long time."

Not far away Sajida Nomani was telling local Channel 12's camera, "I'm glad that the movement has started. My daughter, Asra, has gone through a lot to bring about that change, and now that she has such beautiful friends to help her, I'm pretty sure that we will succeed." By Morgantown standards, this was a media circus, complete with backed-up traffic and rubbernecking pedestrians. It all would be on the evening news, starring Asra Nomani.

Christine Arja and Hazem Bata looked on disapprovingly. Fuming, Arja said to Bata, "That's it. She's gone."

Zafar Nomani shadowed his daughter throughout the eventful day, looking after Shibli. He rarely went to the mosque for prayers anymore, preferring to drop off family members and then sit in the McDonald's on the corner, drinking coffee by himself. His faith in God hadn't faltered, but he couldn't face men he now considered *former* friends. In his view, his family had been punished for Asra's openness about being a single mother. That angered him. "It is between her and God—period!" Asra "has done something wrong, sinned in the past," he said. But his loyalty ran to family. He reassured his daughter: "Don't think you're a failure—no." A woman had been elected to the executive committee. The mosque had caved on allowing women in the main hall. There was greater openness, more *accountability*—the very core of the religion, in his view.

As for himself, the professor said, "I know my relationship with God. If I am at peace, why should I care who says what?" Was he at peace, though? Once when we were driving in his minivan, he blurted, "These men at the mosque tell me I give the mosque a bad name, my family gives the mosque a bad name." He slammed both hands on the steering wheel. "Ach! Bull*shit*! I'm fed up."

The Daughters of Hajar weekend continued the evening of the march, as seventy-five local people, most of them Christians, gathered in a lovely old house affiliated with the Morgantown Public Library to hear a program entitled "A New Generation of American Muslim Women Speak." The event was underwritten by Donn Marshall, a Morgantown contemporary of Nomani's. On 9/11, Marshall lost his wife, Shelley, who had worked at the Pentagon. "I'd like to thank Asra, a classmate of mine from Suncrest Junior High, Morgantown High, all through those years, because I'm almost forty years old and she still calls me dude," he told the audience, smiling. "This weekend in Morgantown the good women are doing something," he continued, in a more serious tone. "You'll find not a religion of hatred, but one that stresses justice and charity."

Each of the Daughters then rose in turn to offer a sample from her writing or a short speech. Nomani explained more about Hajar: "The Quran says that as an act of faith in God, Abraham left Hajar and their son Ishmael at a place where the holy city of Mecca now stands. Hajar became a symbol of will, faith, and fortitude." Nomani also read a portion from her forthcoming book on the hajj, *Standing Alone in Mecca*. The dominant image she painted was that of a single mother in the grip of spiritual pain: "I am in Mecca, a criminal in this land for having given birth without a wedding band on my finger."

The showstopper was Mohja Kahf, the literature professor from Arkansas, who read from her feminist Islamic poetry. In "Among the Midianites," she depicted Moses as a head turner on a Harley-Davidson who attracted the attention of a pair of maiden sisters:

> He parts the uncouth crowd like butter
> and says in his sexy Sean Connery growl,
> "Let the ladies through,"
> gesturing with his sunglasses up the street
> to where the two sisters' little Geo is parked
> So much for Moses keeping a low profile
> among the Midianites . . .

Kahf next recited a poem called "Khadija Gets Her Groove Back," about Muhammad's first wife, a wealthy widow who hired him to run her caravans and asked him to marry her. The narrator is Khadija's sassy hair-dresser:

> So Khadija comes in to get her cornrows done
> She's all DKNY with padded shoulders,
> the Madame C. J. Walker of her day,
> founder and ceo of Khadija Enterprises,
> prez of SCARAB (Seventh Century
> Arab Businesswomen). I do her hair
> all the time, mmm-hmm, and lately
> she has this shine. Girlfriend, Khadija,
> how is that new man working out,
> the one you hired from the temp agency?

There was a stirring in the back of the room. "That's enough! You're making fun of the Prophet!" The speaker was a middle-aged woman in hijab and a long lime green gown.

Kahf looked startled. "It's joyous and not making fun at all," she responded.

"I don't think you are a good Muslim," the heckler said in an Arab accent. "I think the angels are cursing you now."

Kahf, who was born in Syria and wears hijab, invited the woman to listen to the poem, saying, "It's a beautiful description of the Prophet."

"You are making *fun* of the Prophet," the woman said, but eventually she sat down.

In the poem, the hairdresser recounts Khadija's response to the question about how the new man, Muhammad, was "working out":

> Like a brocade cloak
> that envelops its wearer
> Like a caravan heavy with the treasure of Byzantium
> when it is first spotted entering the town
> and you have been expecting it for a long, long time,

she says to me,

oh honey,

he is working out

just fine

Hearty applause followed. When Nomani closed the program, she nodded toward the heckler and said, "I'm actually very glad that you spoke, Mona, and that we heard the voice of silence." Nomani's gentle tone belied her condemnation of the older woman. "Each one of us, in the quiet of our nights, hears that voice of silence, and it works. It does silence us oftentimes."

Mona was Mona Ammar, wife of Hany Ammar, the president of the newly elected executive committee of the Islamic Center of Morgantown. She was not through either. During a question and answer period, she demanded rhetorically, "What is the meaning of Islam?" Her answer: "Submission. You are submitting to Allah's rule. I don't think there is any courage or bravery in breaking the rules. I think the courage is in abiding." A younger woman, also in conservative Muslim dress and sitting next to Ammar, nodded.

A former college instructor of communication theory, Ammar told me she had arranged with Nomani to have tea a couple of months earlier, to try to sort things out. "I asked her, 'Why don't you devote that energy to something worthwhile, something important?' I don't know what drives her to this. To get attention? I don't know."

Kahf, the poet, told the audience that segregation in mosques was growing more extreme. In Fayetteville, Arkansas, where she lived, she had been told there was no room for women to pray at all, and this after she had taught Sunday school and cleaned bathrooms at the mosque.

The Morgantown residents listened closely, heads swiveling to follow the back-and-forth. A middle-aged Muslim neighbor of the Nomanis wanted to know whether the Daughters of Hajar approved of sex out of wedlock.

Skirting the question, Nomani said that men shouldn't be forgotten in this equation, including her son's father. "I'm taking responsibility for that which I did, and I will not live with shame for it," she said. "I will not hide in a corner and pretend it didn't happen."

～

She certainly didn't hide. Nomani took her campaign to Muslim conferences around the country. Then she and several of the other Daughters of Hajar reassembled in Manhattan with a far more audacious challenge to the Islamic status quo. Nomani arranged for a woman to lead a gathering of men and women in Friday prayers.

The idea, akin to a woman's presiding over a Roman Catholic Mass, shocked many Muslims, as Nomani knew it would. It also drew reporters and television cameras from as far away as Chicago and Qatar. Nomani timed the controversy to coincide with the release of her new book about going on the hajj and promoting women's rights within Islam. The woman-led prayer session was a stop on what she called the Muslim Women's Freedom Tour, which doubled as her national book promotion tour. Sustaining the echo of the black civil rights movement, she announced in one of her press releases, "Muslim women are moving from the back of the mosque to the front of the mosque."

The Quran doesn't directly address whether women can act as imam and lead prayer. Women have been known to lead other women in private services. But fourteen hundred years of Islamic tradition point to men as the leaders of mixed congregations. Nomani now set her sights far beyond the issue of space in the mosque and took aim at the hallowed institution of the male imam.

Working with Ahmed Nassef, head of the progressive Web site Muslim WakeUp!, she recruited Amina Wadud, a scholar at Virginia Commonwealth University, to lead the prayers in New York. Wadud, an African-American convert, interprets the Quran as commanding equality of the sexes. She agreed to put her belief into action. Nomani and Nassef spread the word on the Internet, announcing the unusual gathering and that three mosques in New York City had refused to host it. A downtown art gallery withdrew its offer of space after receiving a bomb threat. Imams denounced the idea as blasphemous and a publicity stunt. The Assembly of Muslim Jurists in America issued a fatwa saying that participants would have their prayers "nullified."

Finally, Nomani and her allies arranged to hold their prayer ceremony in a Gothic stone chapel affiliated with the Episcopal Cathedral of St. John the Divine, just south of Harlem. About thirty men joined sixty women at the service, together only slightly outnumbering a pushy international press corps. The New York Police Department sent twenty officers and a helmeted SWAT team with automatic rifles. Outside the chapel a dozen Muslim protesters waved signs. One said, MIXED-GENDER PRAYER TODAY: HELLFIRE TOMORROW. An angry young man told reporters, "If this was an Islamic state, this woman [Wadud] would be hanged, she would be killed, she would be diced into pieces."

Inside, Nomani, dressed in a bubble-gum-pink blazer and matching Timberland boots, welcomed the worshipers as cameras flashed. The menace reflected in the protesters' language was no trivial matter, however. An earlier Internet attack on Nomani had carried the subject heading "Death to Asra." At the prayer ceremony a large private security guard shadowed her every step.

Wadud, the somewhat overwhelmed prayer leader, wore a lavender paisley robe and headscarf that concealed all but the oval of her face. She referred to herself as "a lonely academic" and explained in her sermon that the Quran teaches that men and women "are always on a line of horizontal reciprocity." She spoke nervously, apologizing when she lost her place. Nomani spent part of the sermon in the back of the enormous room, talking on her mobile phone, ironing out security arrangements. Meanwhile a PR man handed reporters flyers about her book.

Women sat mostly to Wadud's left, men to her right. But in the middle there was no separation of the sexes. Men prayed next to women, and a few men even ended up praying *behind* women—all without incident. Nomani, when she took her seat, chose the front row, a position she said she had never tried before. She vowed to organize similar woman-led services in Boston, San Francisco, and Washington, D.C. "This is our faith too," she said afterward. The delighted expressions of the women and men who congratulated her indicated that they agreed.

A LINE OF HER OWN

Back in Morgantown, out of the spotlight, one could get a more representative snapshot of the state of American Islam than that offered by the extraordinary woman-led prayer service in New York. As a result of Nomani's scrutiny, Friday sermons at the Islamic Center of Morgantown became less harsh, at least for a time. The executive committee took the unusual step of banning Ahmed El-Sherbeeny, the Egyptian grad student who had preached about "worthless" nonvirgins, from delivering sermons or leading prayer. He was punished for a talk in which he argued that God forbade believers from loving or caring for nonbelievers. While labeling this message "inappropriate," the mosque leadership said in a public notice that El-Sherbeeny would continue calling the faithful to prayer.

El-Sherbeeny defended his sermon, saying it was drawn from Islamic scripture, medieval scholarship, and a Web site based in Saudi Arabia. The Saudi Web site, El-Sherbeeny argued in an e-mail to other Muslims, made clear the position of Islam: "One of the most important fundamentals of our religion is to love and be loyal to Islam and the Muslims, and to hate and renounce the disbelievers." In 2005 he was allowed to resume leading prayer at the mosque. Nomani's effect was already fading, El-Sherbeeny told me, citing a verse from the Quran that he translated as "For the scum disappears like froth cast out; while that which is for the good of mankind remains on the earth" (13:17).

But El-Sherbeeny was incorrect. Nomani's agitation had uncorked all sorts of tension at the Islamic Center of Morgantown. There was a loud confrontation, and threats to call the police, over whether a women's religious study group had permission to meet in the mosque. Nomani had nothing directly to do with the spat or with another one concerning a potluck dinner at which it had been agreed that men and women would share the mosque's community room, albeit on opposite sides of the buffet table. Some men objected that the arrangement encouraged too much intimacy.

Christine Arja resigned from the executive committee, in large part because of the acrimony. She now believed that Nomani had been correct all along. The clashes over the study group and the potluck left Arja enraged. "Women will no longer stand for or tolerate the indignities that have been perpetrated on them for so long by the hands and actions of men claiming to be Muslim," she wrote in a furious e-mail to mosque leaders. "I now honestly believe that our community needed a wakeup call." She apologized separately to Nomani "for any anger or frustration I have directed toward you in the past. I think that it came from a place of being too optimistic with our community and thinking that other strategies could work."

Hazem and Rayhana Bata disagreed. They maintained that mosque leaders, not Nomani, deserved the credit for allowing women to use the front door and the main hall. "It was those silent efforts that we made that really benefited the community," Hazem said. "In the meantime we didn't destroy the image of the community."

During Ramadan a year after Nomani began her push in Morgantown, a guest imam preached about the benefits of fasting. He said the symbolic sacrifice builds up *taqwa*, or consciousness of God. Taqwa protects against the "temptations of this society," he explained, singling out "naked women," drugs, alcohol, and lotteries. He repeated the litany a few minutes later, speaking urgently but without animus toward any group or religion.

Nomani was the lone woman in the main hall. She wore dark slacks and a navy hooded sweatshirt. She had the hood up, covering her hair, in technical compliance with tradition. She looked like an adolescent boy. The time came for the communal prayer. The men in front of Nomani organized themselves into long lines, young sons squeezing in next to their fathers and older brothers. Nomani took a step back, straightened her posture, and prepared to pray in a line of her own.

FIVE

The Mystics

The journey that led Victor Krambo to Islam and Sufism began in the late summer of 1971. On the day he arrived for his freshman year at Southern Methodist University in Dallas, antiwar protesters held a big rally and then stormed the administration building. It was dizzying for the son of a conservative German Catholic family from the suburbs of Chicago. Jarred by new ideas, Krambo felt his father's Republican certainties slip away. He had stopped going to church before college and now looked into Eastern philosophy. He grew his hair long and smoked a lot of marijuana.

After graduating with a journalism degree, he got involved with an alternative theater company in a converted Dallas warehouse. There he met Sheryl Lovelace. She had grown up in Kansas City and like Krambo attended a conservative Methodist college. Upon graduation, she too stepped into the cultural hurricane sweeping young America. "We were all, like, questioning everything," she recalled years later. She and Krambo began living together. They took a three-month motorcycle trip to Alaska. At the warehouse they put on Bertolt Brecht plays.

Krambo first learned about Islam from an adventurer named Russell, a former Southern Baptist who used his college loan money to travel in the East and returned to Dallas a Muslim convert. What really impressed him were Russell's descriptions of the Prophet Muhammad's compassion and mercy. Krambo hadn't been consciously looking for a new faith, but he did feel adrift. "It's a subliminal need in everybody's life: some direction, some set of guidelines that one can use to get through this very confusing life," he recalled. In a small mosque in Irving, Texas, he became a Muslim at the age of twenty-six.

When he called home to Chicago with the news, his mother became hysterical. His grandmother wanted to know why he was rubbing his face in the dirt "like the rest of those heathens." But his gruff father responded without alarm. "The only thing I know about Muslims is they cut off the hands of thieves," he said to his son. "Sounds like a good idea to me."

SEEING GOD EVERYWHERE

Equipped with only a meager understanding of his new religion, the young convert decided to adopt an Arabic name as a symbol of his seriousness. He chose Abdul Kabir, which means "servant of (Allah), the Vast," and thereafter called himself Abdul Kabir Krambo. Having thus committed himself to Islam, he made some unsettling discoveries. In contrast with his open-minded friend Russell, many of the immigrant Muslims he met in Dallas held what he considered to be "very negative attitudes, dividing the world into 'us' and 'them.'" They lectured him about living unmarried with a woman. They routinely castigated Jews and Christians. They demanded to know when he was going to try to convert his parents—a notion he found ludicrous.

One day an uninvited delegation of veiled Muslim women visited Sheryl at home to deliver the message that her sleeping arrangements condemned her to eternal hellfire. This appalled her. What had Victor become involved with? "I was like, 'Well, OK, I'm outta here!'" She took off for New Mexico, where she lived for a while at a spiritual retreat offering residents a medley of faiths: Muslim prayer on Fridays, Jewish services on Saturdays, and Christian worship on Sundays. In between there was Buddhist meditation.

Unwilling to lose Sheryl, and not very enthusiastic about Muslims issuing moral edicts, Abdul Kabir followed her to New Mexico. They patched things up and got married in what he later called "an old-fashioned hippie wedding." Two children followed. With money tight, the family moved into a three-room adobe house that lacked running water. There weren't many jobs, and life was hard. Domestic relations frayed. Eventually Abdul Kabir moved out. With no clear plan for the future, he went back to Chicago, where there was construction work.

In Chicago he looked for an approach to Islam different from the harsh, judgmental thinking he had encountered in Dallas. He visited various mosques and participated in small prayer circles that met in people's homes. One of his new acquaintances was a convert from Judaism named Abdul Haqq Sazonoff, a jovial bearded man steeped in borscht belt humor and Sufism. The Sufi path immediately appealed to Krambo, who had read about Buddhism and meditation back in his college days. Sufism cuts across sect lines to include both Sunnis and Shiites who focus on "purifying the heart." Employing a vocabulary similar to that of contemporary New Age disciplines, Sufis emulate a master, or sheikh, and practice a form of group meditation known as *zikr*, which is sometimes silent and other times raucously vocal. Turkey's whirling dervishes are Sufis, as was their inspiration, Rumi, the thirteenth-century poet of divine love. Sufism's spirituality and ecumenism have made it the most common avenue of conversion to Islam among white Americans such as Krambo and his new friend Sazonoff. Unlike the racial and class turmoil that lie behind many African-American conversions, the white move to Islam, which claims far smaller numbers, often reflects a more inner-directed search.

Hungry for a discipline that would shape his amorphous life, Krambo immersed himself in Sufism. He performed zikr for hours at a time, repeating formulations of the name of Allah as a remembrance of the divine and a means of clearing mind and soul of selfish concerns. "I had suddenly fallen into the monk's life," he recalled. "It was intense."

"You were kind of weird," his wife said.

"I was experiencing this sense of the interconnectedness of every-thing," Abdul Kabir explained. The omnipresence of God and the need to think and act as if always in the presence of God are central Sufi concepts. "The divine, Allah almighty, can speak to you with anything in His creation, if you are paying attention. It was like, a bird lands on my windowsill, it had tremendous significance for me. Nothing seemed accidental. Any per-son, a bum on the street or a casual acquaintance, could say something which had deep and significant meaning because I was listening at this deep level." He saw God in everything. "If you become aware of that pres-ence, it's an overwhelming thing," he said. "It tends to bring you to your knees and make you tremble."

Abdul Haqq Sazonoff belonged to a branch of the Naqshbandi order, one of the best-known Sufi groups in the world. He told Krambo about his spiritual leader, a renowned mystic and holy man named Muhammad Nazim Adil al-Haqqani. Grand Sheikh Nazim lived in Cyprus and visited London every year to meet European and American followers. He was a man of extraordinary perception, Krambo was told. He saw into your soul. Curious, Krambo went to London to see Nazim in 1979. "When I fi-nally laid eyes on him, my heart breathed a big sigh," he said. "I felt im-mediately I had reached a place of safety and trust that are desperately needed." He also realized Sufism did not require round-the-clock mania. "You might say I was able to put my burden down there."

The grand sheikh sat for hours in a mosque in central London, telling stories about the lives of the Prophet and lesser Muslim saints whom the Naqshbandi believe inherited a glimmer of Muhammad's divine light. He gave advice on marriage, careers, and children. He preached adherence to Sunni ritual but complete acceptance of other faiths. Krambo was over-whelmed. Nazim "absolutely doesn't care what a person calls himself," he told me. "What he cares about is his sincerity, his truthfulness, the com-passion he carries in his heart. He says, 'You look for your brothers every-where.'" Krambo refers to this as "the primordial religion": loving the one God and treating others as you would have them treat you. "This is what the Prophet Muhammad taught because this is what every prophet taught. How can you have a disagreement with your Jewish brothers or your Christian brothers? They relate to this prophet or that prophet or this description or that description. The essence of that is identical. You pare all that away, it's the same. It's one."

"So, he came back a changed man," his wife said.

The Krambos started over in New Mexico. Abdul Kabir had made *bayah* to Grand Sheikh Nazim, a formal declaration of fealty, and Sheryl's interest in Islam gradually increased. While she teases her husband about his "weird" inner experiences, her own account has a distinctly other-worldly cast. After hearing Abdul Kabir's avid descriptions of Nazim, she began encountering the holy man, she told me, though these weren't physical or even conscious encounters. "It was after several very powerful dreams," in which Nazim appeared and spoke to her, she explained, "that I made my bayah with him, before I even met him."

A SHEIKH FOR AMERICA

The Krambos moved northwest, eventually settling in 1990 outside Yuba City, California, fifty miles north of Sacramento. They could afford to buy a small house there, and Abdul Kabir found a demand for his electrician's skills. That year Grand Sheikh Nazim gave his blessing for another migration, one covering a greater geographic and cultural distance. He said that God had signaled that his son-in-law and deputy, Muhammad Hisham Kabbani, should move from Lebanon to the United States. He would become the spiritual leader of the Naqshbandi in this country.

Coming into Kabbani's presence is like stepping back to the eighteenth century. A man of modest height and rounded shoulders, he wears flowing robes of the finest quality and a tall white turban with a green felt tip. His expansive and silky white beard reaches to his abdomen. He sometimes carries a silver-handled walking stick. From across a room he looks like an illustration from a rare old book about the Ottoman Empire. Up close his surprisingly smooth skin and often impish expression make him seem younger than his years, now approaching sixty.

Kabbani's more committed followers consider him, as they do his teacher and mentor Grand Sheikh Nazim, a living saint possessed of miraculous powers. In public a retinue of at least several followers always trails him. People continually seek his blessing and ask him to ease physical ailments, from backaches to cancer, with a touch of his hand and a prayer. When he stops to use a public restroom, someone is there to hold his turban and cane.

One cold January morning in 2004 when I visited the sheikh at his headquarters mosque in Burton, Michigan, a score of his followers crowded into his office. The sheikh and I sat side by side in large modern chairs, with his disciples at our feet. The men wore turbans or skullcaps in a range of colors. All the women covered their hair. Some in attendance bowed and tried to kiss Kabbani's hand. He shooed them away, but not so emphatically as to stop others from trying. This weekend about a hundred followers from out of town had joined the community of several dozen families that live in the vicinity to celebrate Eid ul Adha, the holiday marking the end of the hajj period.

A young African-American man from Memphis dressed in brown robes had given me a framed verse from the Quran and asked that I offer it to the sheikh as a gift "from his students." I did so, awkwardly, given that I didn't really know any of these people.

The sheikh frowned and shouted, "*Not* my students!"

Had I violated Sufi etiquette? Others in the room looked equally confused.

The sheikh smiled. "They are my *teachers*, all my teachers. That one, that one, that one!" he said, pointing around the room. Relieved laughter greeted his little joke.

Seated in front of Kabbani and me were young physicians of Arab and South Asian descent and several white American converts with impressive beards, including Abdul Kabir Krambo, who had flown in from California. There were immigrants from Bosnia, Turkey, and West Africa. Sheikh Kabbani introduced a man in a maroon *kufi* as the "most famous gastroenterologist in New Jersey." This man was sitting next to his wife, also a physician, the sheikh explained, and their two college-age children, one on the way to law school, the other to medical school. For a spiritual man, the sheikh is acutely aware of social and professional status. Fund-raising forms distributed that weekend asked for a minimum contribution of eight hundred dollars.

The sheikh's office had many of the contents one would expect: leather-bound Qurans propped open on decoratively carved wooden stands, shelves crammed with Islamic scholarly volumes, and framed calligraphy of the ninety-nine qualities associated with Allah. There were also some surprising artifacts, none more so than the signed, official portrait of President George W. Bush in a dark business suit and bright yellow tie. Blown up nearly to life size, the Bush photo had a heavy gold-colored frame, into the corner of which was tucked the menu from a White House Ramadan dinner that Kabbani had attended in October 2003.

Before I could ask about the president's incongruous image, the sheikh produced another official White House photo, this one an eight-by-ten-inch shot of Laura Bush with Emine Erdogan, the visiting wife of the prime minister of Turkey. The president's staff had just sent the picture along with a thank-you note, after seeking Kabbani's advice on what kind of gift to give the Turkish first lady. The sheikh had recommended poetry by Rumi, and that had apparently gone over very well. "They come to me for help," a pleased Kabbani said of the White House. His followers whispered in admiration.

Over that long weekend in Michigan the sheikh reminisced about how he had come to America.

The Kabbanis are regionally prominent in religion and business. The sheikh's father led a Lebanese equivalent of the chamber of commerce and was active in textiles and building. "Like Rockefellers, we are that kind of family in Lebanon, very well known," the sheikh told me. But the Kabbanis had religious capital as well. One of the sheikh's uncles oversaw the national association of Muslim scholars. Another uncle was Lebanon's mufti, or top Sunni religious authority. Hisham Kabbani, the seventh of eight children, grew up in a mansion where his father hosted international religious conclaves. The large, airy house echoed with prayer and learned talk about Islam. One of the guests was Nazim Adil al-Haqqani of the

Naqshbandi order, then in preparation to become a grand sheikh. From an early age Hisham Kabbani was impressed by the otherworldly Nazim and by the spiritual teachings of Sufism.

His father encouraged young Hisham to study and travel with Sheikh Nazim. They frequently visited the grand sheikh of the order, who lived in Damascus, where Hisham studied Islamic jurisprudence. But as a boy and young man Hisham also led a vigorous secular life. He attended French- and English-language secondary schools and then earned a degree in chemistry from the American University in Beirut. He obtained a medical degree from a university in Belgium. For amusement, he and his brothers competed in road rallies, and there were always several shiny sports cars parked at the Kabbani mansion. There is no shame in privilege, Kabbani explained. Many people "think Sufism means having patches in your pants. That is not correct." Still, he "never missed one prayer" and felt drawn to the spiritual realm. "It's not something you can take from reading books," he said. "It's something they pour in your heart. You feel it. So when you speak, it comes. It's energy."

Kabbani tells a story about Grand Sheikh Nazim that is typical of the miracle tales Sufis enjoy. In 1971 Nazim paid the Kabbani family an unexpected visit. He said to Hisham, then twenty-five, "I have been told by the Prophet to come to you today because your father is going to die." The father was old but thought to be in good health. Nazim said he would die at the stroke of 7:00 p.m. He instructed the Kabbanis to call relatives so everyone could see the father one last time. Five minutes before the appointed hour Nazim went to the elder Kabbani's room. The father greeted the holy man but then was stricken, crying out, "My heart, my heart!" At 7:00 p.m. exactly, Sheikh Kabbani says, his father expired.

After his travels around the Muslim world and study in Damascus, Hisham Kabbani eventually received permission to teach Islamic spiritualism, meaning that he had become a sheikh in his own right. In a union that bound two influential families, he married the grand sheikh's daughter Hajjah Nazihe Adil. In the late 1970s Lebanon's civil war prompted some of the Kabbani brothers to move to Saudi Arabia, where for a time Hisham managed a large hospital the family helped build in Jeddah. In the

1980s he oversaw construction of high-rise buildings elsewhere in the Middle East, all the while continuing to teach Sufism.

In 1990 Kabbani received word while in Singapore on a business trip that he had mail back home from the American Embassy. An older brother had applied for visas on behalf of the entire family, and Hisham's name had come up. After fifteen years of civil war Lebanon was still unstable. Kabbani had visited the United States before, and several of his brothers had attended American universities, but he hadn't planned on relocating. He asked his mentor what to do about the visa offer. Grand Sheikh Nazim, characteristically laconic, said, "Since God sent it, you go. Go!"

So he went.

The duration of Kabbani's move to the United States and the precise scope of his mission weren't clear at first. He had a wife and two children, and they eventually joined him. But the divine sign delivered by the Lebanese postal service hadn't included details on his agenda.

Certainly one goal was to bolster the thin Naqshbandi ranks in this country. Sufis and quasi Sufis of various descriptions had practiced in America for decades. Hazrat Inayat Khan, a famous sheikh and musician from India, spread Sufi ideas early in the twentieth century, and his son, Pir Vilayat Inayat Khan, gained popularity among New Age devotees, relatively few of them Muslim. In Philadelphia a community grew up around another teacher, Guru Bawa Muhaiyaddeen, who offered a mélange of Sufi and Hindu teachings. In New Mexico, California, and Illinois, the Krambos and others like them had associated themselves from afar with Grand Sheikh Nazim, a Sunni who stressed that Sufism grew only from an authentic Islamic foundation. Now, in Kabbani, the Naqshbandi of America were to have a classically trained resident sheikh to lead them.

Sufism, Kabbani teaches, provides a guided path for developing the inner spirit, rather than emphasize mere dos and don'ts. Sufis conceive of three stages along this path. The most basic is *islam*, which means "submission" or "correct ritual actions." Sufis share these essentials, also referred to as the five pillars, with all other Muslims: the declaration of faith, prayer, charity, fasting, and pilgrimage.

The next level is *iman*, which means "faith" or "correct beliefs." Many Muslims never bother with iman, thinking the five pillars sufficient. Iman suggests six aspects of faith: belief in God, His angels, His books, and His prophets; in the Last Day; and in the imperative toward good rather than evil. If islam is the frame of a spiritual home, iman is the carved wooden furniture one puts inside, Kabbani explains. Muslims must accept all of God's books and prophets, including those of Christians and Jews, he says. Muslims shouldn't hold themselves above non-Muslims.

The third and innermost dimension of the faith is *ihsan*, which means "virtue" and refers to living and worshiping God "as if you are seeing Him," Kabbani explains. Muslims don't depict God or imagine they can see Him in something like human form. But achieving ihsan means being conscious of God's presence—Buddhists call this mindfulness—and acting with constant love for Him and His work. In the words of the Quran, "Wherever you turn, there is the face of God" (2:115). Ihsan entails purification. "You cannot come with dirt inside, conspiracy inside your heart, or cheating with other individuals," the sheikh says. Ihsan, "the highest level of perfection," requires a relentless personal "struggle against the ego, the bad desires of the self."

Sufis see intimations of their practices and beliefs in accounts of the Prophet Muhammad's life—in other words, from the beginning of Islam. Muslims hostile to Sufism describe it as a set of superstitions and deviant customs that cropped up hundreds of years after the prophetic period. Sufis insist that any later developments reflect the legitimate accumulation of wisdom.

Today scholars generally agree that Sufism had surfaced as a discernible movement by the early eighth century, when small circles of ascetic Muslims began rejecting the increasing worldliness of Islamic society. The word "Sufi" is derived from *suf*, which means "wool" in Arabic and probably refers to the rough woolen garments the ascetics wore. Some Sufis became known for an exuberance and ardor that other Muslims interpreted as irreverence and that sometimes had fatal consequences. The mystic Al-Husayn ibn Mansur al-Hallaj was executed in 922 in Baghdad for teachings that seemed to identify himself with God. Sufis interpret al-Hallaj as having meant only that God infuses man with divine love.

Sufis seek to experience God's presence by means of zikr, the meditative repetition of names for the divine or other holy phrases. Through extended group zikr sessions, some Sufis achieve elevated states of consciousness. This can take the physical form of a slow, trancelike dance made famous by the whirling dervishes of Turkey, who wear tall hats and full skirts that billow as they slowly spin. The Naqshbandi aren't particularly known for turning, but on two occasions I did witness Turkish followers of Sheikh Kabbani rise from a zikr group, step forward to kiss his hand, and begin to rotate as if being moved by a force outside their bodies. Gradually they extended their arms in the graceful manner of ballet dancers and continued to spin for more than fifteen minutes, while others chanted God's name and kept time on shallow drums. Some of those spinning eventually collapsed, severely dizzy and disoriented, but others sat down calmly.

For Abdul Kabir Krambo, who doesn't whirl, the purpose of zikr is "to absorb the detritus floating around in your mind and your heart. When we say, 'Allah,' when we say the word with our tongue, we also have to think of that divine presence, which is with us always, but we're just forgetful of, unmindful of it. The zikr, for me, is a way of clearing distractions out of the heart."

Formal Sufi orders had appeared by the thirteenth century, a period of turmoil in Islam, during which Mongol armies invaded from the East. The Naqshbandi order was founded in the fourteenth century by a mystic who lived in what is now Uzbekistan. The word "Naqshband" refers to one who embroiders cloth, and on a metaphoric level the name came to be interpreted as describing the imprinting of the divine upon the human heart. The Naqshbandi, who were highly mobile, expanded into Persian lands and what is now Afghanistan and then into India and China. The order also spread to the West, into the Ottoman Empire and the Balkans. Today various Naqshbandi branches claim a total of two million followers, including large populations in Indonesia and Malaysia, where Sheikh Kabbani has preached to crowds of tens of thousands of people. There are thousands of committed Naqshbandi adherents in the United States, although determining a precise number is difficult since many Sufis don't affiliate with a mosque. Other Sufi orders also have American contingents.

For centuries Sufis have helped spread Islam, often by building cloisters, lodges, and schools. While pious members of some orders removed themselves from society, others plunged into politics and even warfare. Sufis forged close ties to some Mongol princes, to the ruling classes in Mogul India, and to Ottoman sultans. In the nineteenth century Naqshbandi fighters in Sumatra resisted the Dutch and battled the Russians in the Caucasus. During the Soviet era Naqshbandi and other Sufis struggled to maintain underground spiritual communities in the face of Communist efforts to stamp out religion. In Afghanistan in the 1980s Sufi orders helped organize Muslim resistance to Soviet occupation.

Sheikh Kabbani's first stop upon arriving in the United States in 1990 was Jersey City, New Jersey, where he stayed with relatives. Visiting a neighborhood mosque as an ordinary worshiper, he discovered something surprising. "I was sitting listening to the services on Friday . . . I begin to hear things that even in the Middle East I never heard: hate and destruction and killings and fire speeches and a style of denouncing of the spiritual side of Islam . . . I felt a danger. If that is allowed to grow, that is going to have a great impact on the Muslims," Kabbani continued. "It's a school of thought, like—what you say?—a *combatant* school of thought, a school of thought that does not accept anyone else except themselves: either you are the same as we are, or we consider you an unbeliever."

Things did not improve when, the following week, he attended a different New Jersey mosque. A young Egyptian imam denounced the celebration of the Prophet's birthday, a traditional holiday, known as Mawlid al-Nabi, that is particularly popular with Sufis. Kabbani recalled the imam's preaching, "Anyone celebrating the Prophet's birthday will go to hellfire" for emulating Christians in their adoration of Jesus.

After two weeks Islam in America didn't seem very promising to the Lebanese spiritualist. He considered packing up and getting on the next plane back to Beirut. "Why I have to put myself in that kind of problem?" he wondered. "I don't want. I will leave."

What Kabbani discovered in American mosques in the 1990s was the same thing that Professor Khaled Abou El Fadl found during the same period and that feminist Asra Nomani encountered a decade later, a form of Islam shaped by the fundamentalism that has inundated the Middle East and Asia since the 1970s. Broadly, that fundamentalism came from two sources—modernist revivalism and Wahhabism—both of which condemned Sufism.

Modernist revival movements, such as the Muslim Brotherhood, which started in Egypt in the 1920s, sought to fend off Western influence and respond to the malaise of the Muslim world by re-creating an idealized Islamic society. This theocratic society would embrace scientific and technical advancement but otherwise reject all things non-Muslim and secular. The Muslim Brothers painted Sufism as the crude religion of the uneducated and a reason for the lagging condition of Arab and other predominantly Muslim countries. In particular, the Brotherhood condemned Sufism's historical tendency to absorb local customs as fostering superstition and idol worship.

Overlapping and often melding with modernist revivalism has been Wahhabism, the intolerant literalism emanating from Saudi Arabia and spread worldwide by that kingdom's oil money. The idealized Islamic society Wahhabis yearn for wouldn't include Sufis or other "innovators." In the name of fighting idolatry, Saudi Wahhabis obsessively destroy Sufi tombs and shrines. Many mosques built since the 1970s in the United States and around the world have received Saudi funding, and many of the imams who preach in those mosques received Saudi-supported tutelage.

As a result, Wahhabi hatred for Sufis echoes in many Muslim American prayer halls.

These were the echoes that Sheikh Kabbani heard when he came to America. He well knew from his extensive travels in the Middle East and Asia about antagonism toward Sufis. But he hadn't realized it had reached the United States.

Though discouraged, he decided to stay in America and broaden his focus. He cautiously looked for mosques where Sufis were welcome and helped launch several new mosques and Islamic centers. At the same time, he began barnstorming New Age America, a colorful array of holistic centers, healing retreats, and hippie bookstores. He gave talks at Hindu and Sikh temples and spoke at churches interested in "interfaith dialogue."

He settled in the early 1990s near New Age–friendly San Francisco. He also bought a sprawling rural retreat in Fenton, Michigan, known among his followers as the Farm. "God's favor on us, my father was very rich," the sheikh told me. "He died, but still we have a lot of properties." He later moved his base to the Farm and in 2001 opened a headquarters mosque in nearby Burton, a town adjacent to the dilapidated city of Flint.

Kabbani reached out effortlessly to non-Muslims. One of his favorite opening lines is: "Our Prophet said that human beings—he didn't say just Muslims—are equal like the teeth of a comb." He offered Islamic authenticity combined with a friendly soft sell. "I began to build a good relationship," he explained, "not recruiting their people, no, explaining and teaching there is a meeting point where all of us meet and an end of the road that all of us like to reach it, which is spirituality."

The attachment to a teacher or master is one of the most controversial aspects of Sufism, eliciting the accusation from other Muslims that Sufis worship mortals along with God. On a more practical level, the gurulike relationship creates an inherent danger of exploitation. But the Naqshbandi, like other Sufis, believe there is no avoiding this risk. Kabbani, in his book *The Naqshbandi Sufi Way*, points to the verse in the Quran that states, "Fear God and accompany trustworthy people" (9:119). Trustworthiness in this sense includes wisdom about the divine and about human psychology. Without an honorable and wise master, Kabbani explains, would-be Sufis could stray toward pseudospirituality, as has happened more than a few times over the centuries.

Abdul Kabir Krambo, who is not a wealthy man, regularly travels hundreds and sometimes thousands of miles to pray and meditate in close proximity to his spiritual teachers. "When I'm sitting with Grand Sheikh Nazim or Sheikh Hisham, I'm thinking it's the closest thing in experience to [that of] the companions of the Prophet Muhammad, the type of experience they had . . . or the companions of Christ or the companions of Moses had," he told me. "This is a taste of that reality, and everything else in terms of religion pales in comparison to that."

The sheikh also serves a functional role in the daily lives of close followers. While I visited Kabbani and his wife at their home on the Farm in Michigan, he received a steady stream of phone calls from people all over the country, wanting to know his opinion on questions of child custody, selling a family corporation, and contributing medical equipment to charity. He listened carefully in each case and then issued a crisp answer: Yes, sell. No, don't surrender custody. Receipts—*always* get receipts for in-kind contributions. To answer such questions, he explained to me, it is sometimes necessary to consult the Quran and pray, but not always.

The versatile presence of the sheikh certainly provides part of Sufism's allure for some disaffected Muslims, like Hedieh Mirahmadi. She grew up in a wealthy and not very observant Shiite Iranian-American family in Beverly Hills. As a single lawyer in the early 1990s she felt a void in her life and turned back to Islam. But leaders of the large Los Angeles mosque where she sought solace seemed consumed by competitive and jealous urges, she said: " 'The Jews have power; we need to get power. The Americans have power; we need to get power.' I didn't understand that paradigm."

Her older brother had met Sheikh Kabbani and announced that he had found spiritual direction for the first time in his life. Hedieh agreed to meet the Lebanese cleric. Days before the encounter, Mirahmadi told me, she had an intense dream in which Fatima, the Prophet Muhammad's beloved daughter, ushered her into a large white tent: "'Welcome to my son's home,' Fatima said in the dream, referring to Sheikh Hisham. 'We've been waiting for you a long time.' It was phenomenally powerful."

When the real-life meeting came, Kabbani entered the room, and Mirahmadi, then twenty-five years old, passed out cold. "Looked straight at him and fell over," she said. When she regained consciousness, she began crying, overcome with a feeling of love for a white-bearded man she had never met before.

Kabbani smiled at her and said in a fatherly tone, "Oh, Fatima is always looking out for you, isn't she?" As far as an amazed Mirahmadi was concerned, the sheikh knew all about her dream. "It was just instantly knowing I was exactly where I should be," she recalled. She eventually went to work for the sheikh as his main representative in Washington, D.C. Her older brother also joined Kabbani's inner circle.

In one of his more unlikely ministerial and recruiting missions, Sheikh Kabbani for a time became a well-known figure on the streets of South Central Los Angeles. He helped fund food drives and provided other aid to poor black families. The wealthy Mirahmadi family organized some of these efforts. During the mid-1990s the sheikh occasionally turned up in South Central to shake hands and comfort young people, some of whom decided to convert to Islam. These activities brought Kabbani into contact with Bo Taylor, a former gang member turned antiviolence activist. By Taylor's count, the sheikh converted to Islam no fewer than five hundred young men from the street. "We love him," Taylor told the *Los Angeles Times*. "Here's this man coming from the Middle East and offering assistance to people in the community who don't even know him—which is more than I can say for a lot of people who live here."

Kabbani's enthusiasm for spreading spiritualism led him to become an unwitting participant in a Los Angeles tabloid celebrity farce. In May 1996 he was invited by Muslim students to speak at El Camino College. Kabbani brought a surprise guest, O. J. Simpson. Acquitted the previous year in the murder of Nicole Brown Simpson and Ron Goldman, the former football legend was there as part of a campaign to polish his tarnished image. According to the *Los Angeles Times*, Kabbani told the college audience that the pair had met after a mutual friend told the sheikh he had seen a Quran in Simpson's house.

"I guess the sheikh was worried about my soul," Simpson quipped. He went on to say that it was the media's fault that his reputation needed repair.

A few weeks later Kabbani attended a fund-raising event at Simpson's Brentwood home, the *Los Angeles Times* reported. Simpson announced he wanted to help with Bo Taylor's antiviolence initiative. The sheikh said years later that he didn't regret his brief relationship with the fallen celebrity. "In Christianity, in Judaism, or in any faith," Kabbani explained, "you cannot say we don't meet with this one or that one when our meeting might help people in their path of self-realization and repentance."

Kabbani's ministering to the gang set petered out in the late 1990s, as he focused on the more ambitious goal of establishing himself as a Muslim leader with national heft. But the larger endeavor hit obstacle after obstacle. When he sought to speak at Islamic conferences, the door often slammed in his face. When he showed up anyway, typically with an entourage, the greeting from organizers was chilly. Booths the Naqshbandi rented to distribute literature at Muslim gatherings were shut down. On one occasion conference organizers had a stubborn Kabbani follower arrested, although no charges were pressed.

Hurt and angered, Kabbani fired back at those who excluded him and demeaned Sufism. In articles, in speeches, and, beginning in the mid-1990s, on the Internet, he labeled his opponents Wahhabis. He was the first major Muslim leader in the United States to make a public issue of Wahhabism, a term most Americans encountered only after 9/11. Kabbani said that he sought to save American Islam from an inevitable backlash against Islamic fundamentalism. "I want Muslims in America to know that if we continue with the Wahhabi thinking, the Wahhabi ideology, we are going to a disastrous end," he said. "This is not a political stand; it is life or death."

On another level, this was also a turf war. Kabbani ran into resistance from established Muslim leaders in America who didn't welcome a new competitor, especially one with a regal manner. Explaining the rivalry, Sulayman Nyang, an Islamic studies scholar at Howard University in Washington, D.C., told *The New York Times*, "America is a big magnifying mirror, and [Muslim American leaders] compete for access to it, because it projects you internationally and makes you look big." Kabbani staged national conferences of his own in 1996 and 1998 that attracted large audiences and delegations of muftis from Central Asia, Turkey, and the Balkans. He launched a glossy magazine and opened a Washington office he called the Islamic Supreme Council of America, a grandiose name that irritated other Muslim groups.

Kabbani began to receive favorable press. *The Washington Post* called him a spokesman for "the silent majority of mainstream Muslims in the United States." At the August 1998 Naqshbandi-backed conference in the capital, he set aside his planned remarks to denounce the al Qaeda bombings of the American embassies in Kenya and Tanzania that had occurred that very day. "We are American, and our children are American," Kabbani told the *Post*. "We want integration, not segregation. We as Muslim Americans extend our hand to Jews, Christians, Hindus, and Buddhists living on this earth."

Other Muslim leaders might mourn the human casualties of particular acts of Islamic terrorism or talk about becoming part of the fabric of American society, but until 9/11 few embraced American patriotism with Kabbani's zeal. Further, when it came to Israel, some of these leaders and organizations made excuses for terrorists who attacked Jewish citizens. Some warned that America would face divine punishment for its role in the Middle East.

To be sure, these leaders and others, including Siraj Wahhaj, the popular African-American imam from Brooklyn, toned down their rhetoric after the attacks on the World Trade Center and Pentagon. And Kabbani's broad-brush labeling of Muslims with whom he disagreed as Wahhabis may not have been the most precise description. But the larger point is that years before the 2001 terrorist attacks, the Sufi sheikh called others of his religion to account for their strident rhetoric, and they didn't like it.

Detractors struck back. His conferences drew bomb threats. He received telephone death threats at his home, prompting a fruitless FBI investigation. An English-language Muslim Web site called IslamicWeb.com carried a virtual library of works with titles like *The Naqshbandi Tariqat Unveiled* and *The Great Naqshbandi Hoax*. One compendium, *Sufism—The Deviated Path*, offered a list of denunciations and this supplication: "May Allah disfigure the appearance of Kabbani as he has disfigured the views and statements of the Salafis [fundamentalists] in order to demonize them in front of the common folk."

By the late 1990s Kabbani's campaign to boost his image and air out some of American Islam's dirty laundry had come to the attention of official Washington. The sheikh and his top aides offered advice to the White House national security staff and lawmakers on Capitol Hill. Kabbani had his picture taken several times with President Clinton. The sheikh didn't shape policy in any noticeable way, but he added an unconventional Muslim voice to the debate over the Middle East. While he called for creation of a Palestinian state, he firmly criticized Palestinian terrorist groups. He opposed the American-backed United Nations sanctions on Iraq because in his view, they only made life worse for innocent Iraqis. But he argued that the United States should help depose Saddam Hussein, a position shared by few other Sunni Muslims.

In January 1999 the State Department invited Kabbani to speak at a public forum entitled "The Evolution of Extremism: A Viable Threat to U.S. National Security." The event would powerfully rile Muslim circles. In a rambling lecture, Kabbani said it "is completely wrong" to view Islam or most Muslims as extremist. "The authentic, traditional voice of Islam," he said, "is moderation and tolerance and love—loving and to be loved—and living in peace with all other faiths and religions." But a current of extremism coursed through Islam, he said, tracing its origins to Wahhabism. This current, which he argued contradicted the benevolent lessons of the Prophet Muhammad, had spawned bin Laden and al Qaeda. On the basis of the sheikh's personal contacts in Central Asia, he warned that al Qaeda was seeking to acquire nuclear weapons from the former Soviet republics. "We want to tell people to be careful, that something major might hit quickly," Kabbani said.

At the time this might have sounded alarmist to listeners who hadn't paid attention to bin Laden's threats and to al Qaeda's increasingly ambitious attacks, such as embassy bombings in Africa that killed 224 people. After 9/11 Kabbani sounded prescient, even though he had focused on the danger of loose nuclear warheads, rather than hijacked passenger jets.

Turning to the domestic scene, Kabbani cautioned that Muslim charities in the United States that claimed to be collecting donations for humanitarian aid were instead sending most of the money to militants for buying weapons or other supplies. On this topic too, the sheikh was ahead of the curve. After 9/11 the U.S. government came to the same conclusion and shut down several of the best-known Muslim charities in America because of their alleged ties to al Qaeda and Hamas.

Kabbani went further, condemning unnamed Muslim organizations in America as "extremist" and saying they had taken over local mosques. "The ideology of extremism has been spread to 80 percent of the American Muslim population," he said. Muslim university students presented a special danger. "If the nuclear atomic warheads reach these universities," he added, "you don't know what these students are going to do, because their way of thinking is brainwashed, limited, and narrow-minded."

Kabbani's State Department talk mixed prophetic analysis with raw hyperbole. Extremism, at least at a rhetorical level, does infect many mosques, but the 80 percent figure is debatable. The sheikh later clarified that he meant that 80 percent of American mosques had been "introduced to" extremist ideology, not that four out of five Muslims had embraced it. But his loose language at the State Department allowed anti-Islam polemicists to quote the 80 percent figure without noting Kabbani's premise that ordinary Muslims generally didn't deserve blame. His

suggestion that Muslim firebrands on campus were on the verge of obtaining nuclear weapons was, to put it politely, unsupported by evidence.

The speech received little public attention until some of the largest
Muslim American groups used it as an opportunity to strike back at a man
they viewed as an annoying upstart. "With heavy hearts," eight of these
organizations jointly and publicly demanded in February 1999 that Kabbani retract his statements at the State Department and apologize. The
groups said he had put all American Muslims at risk by painting them as a
peril to society.

Kabbani refused. He stressed repeatedly that American Muslims as a
group posed no threat. His main target was their leadership, the people
who had shut him out. Those rivals now intensified their efforts to isolate
him. Muslim businesses and professionals stopped buying advertising in
his *Muslim Magazine*, which soon ceased publication. Islamic conference
panelists walked out if they learned he was on the bill, and Naqshbandi
members were turned away from several mosques.

A MOSQUE BURNS

In 1990, the year the Krambos settled in Yuba City, there wasn't even a hint
of the storm that would swirl around the Naqshbandi. Abdul Kabir Krambo,
a long-distance student of Grand Sheikh Nazim, became a fervent follower
of his newly arrived representative, Sheikh Kabbani. Kabbani in turn val-
ued a connection in an area of California with a Pakistani-American population familiar with Sufism.

Rural Sutter County had been swept up in the mid-nineteenth-century
gold rush, after which settlers developed the area's rich farmland. Immigrants from British India, drawn by the availability of agricultural work, began arriving at the turn of the twentieth century. Today the county boasts
vast stretches of arbors and emerald rice fields, interrupted every so often by
two-lane roads and small towns. It also offers rich variety in religion. Hindu
and Sikh temples cater to the large population of Indian descent. Practically
every stripe of Christian church competes for parishioners. In the early 1990s

Muslims, mostly Pakistani immigrants, began organizing to build a mosque. Until then they had prayed in a converted garage and on Fridays driven an hour south to Sacramento to attend jummah services there.

Abdul Kabir was hired to help with the construction of the new mosque a few hundred yards down rural Tierra Buena Road from where he and his family lived. Soon he was directing the project and was asked to join the board of directors. "I was the token white guy," he said. The minaret and dome had been erected by the summer of 1994, and the nearly completed Islamic Center of Yuba City was being used for prayer.

On September 1 Abdul Kabir Krambo and a small group of fellow Sufis stayed at the mosque after the evening prayer and did zikr until about 10:30 p.m. Passing drivers during the next thirty minutes noticed nothing unusual. By 11:30 p.m. the mosque was burning.

Firefighters arrived promptly, but the intensity of the flames made it difficult to get close. Within an hour the building lay in ruins. The authorities determined later that rolled-up carpeting and rugs had been soaked with a flammable fluid, indicating arson. Investigators questioned many people, including Krambo and others who had done zikr that night, but no arrests were made. As far as the authorities were concerned, the incident was a mystery. For many evenings after the fire Krambo, shaken by the event, sat on his porch, a shotgun at the ready. He feared there would be more violence. Fortunately, there wasn't.

The Islamic Circle of North America, the largest American Muslim group catering primarily to South Asian immigrants, quickly seized on the burning of the Yuba City mosque as an emblem of anti-Muslim persecution—and a way to raise cash. The ICNA sent a fact-finding committee to examine the situation and launched a national fund-raising drive. The group asked in a four-page brochure in 1994 that donations be sent to a Defense of Islam Fund, care of ICNA headquarters in New York. The group said that through its publications and broadcasts, it planned "to develop a decisive system to respond to the anti-Muslim hysteria in the U.S."

After the fire the ICNA sent just two checks totaling six thousand dollars to the Islamic Center of Yuba City, according to Krambo and other members of the mosque board. Because of the apparent scope of the fund-raising drive, they suspected that much more had been raised but had no proof. The board members sent the ICNA a series of letters, asking for an accounting of the fund-raising drive. They said the ICNA offered no response (and the group didn't respond to my inquiries).

Krambo and his colleagues turned to Sheikh Kabbani for help. He provided part of his donor mailing list, from which the Islamic Center of Yuba City raised about $150,000 over a couple of years. Combined with a generous insurance settlement, that sum was enough to get the mosque rebuilt, a process finally completed in 2002. Today the stately minaret and curving dome of the large building rise above rows of walnut and plum trees, which seem to march in perfect alignment toward craggy mountains on each side of the valley.

Within weeks of the reopening, the elders of the Islamic Center of Yuba City faced a fresh challenge. A pair of newcomers to the area, young professional men with families, began asserting themselves within the mosque. They interrupted prayer sessions to demand that the mosque distance itself from Sufism and end such practices as the distinctive Sufi tributes to the Prophet Muhammad. They demanded on other occasions that the community cut its ties to Sheikh Kabbani, whom they portrayed as seeking nefarious influence in Yuba City. They also helped form a competing organization, which unilaterally announced that it would launch a full-time Islamic school. The mosque already ran a small Sunday school, and Krambo and his allies worried that a full-time parochial school would encourage cultural isolation.

Then e-mail, letters, and flyers began circulating that accused various mosque leaders of dealing in "liquor, pork, and gambling" or of being drunks or ex-convicts. One flyer, dated June 10, 2003, and surreptitiously distributed at the mosque and in shopping areas in town, was headlined "Muslim Community Hijacked in Yuba City, CA." The flyer lashed out at "the Zionist fake Shaykh [*sic*] Hisham Kabbani's (curse upon him) cult." It asserted, "On September 1, 1994, before midnight Krambo along with his cult members after performing cult worship, set the mosque on fire."

Heated confrontations broke out at the mosque, and the police were summoned on several occasions. The outsiders "created a sea of chaos," Krambo said. Fellow board member Abdul Hamid Bath agreed: "All of a sudden this devil came into our community." The newcomers, who, like Bath and most of the other worshipers, were of Pakistani descent, won over the recently installed Pakistani imam. The board eventually fired the imam. Rank-and-file members of the congregation—mostly "simple people," Bath said, "who don't care who's in charge"—were perplexed by the feuding. Attendance dwindled; weekly donations fell off.

Khalid Chaudhry, one of the new arrivals who helped provoke the controversy, told me that he had only one concern, what he called the "criminal cult" devoted to Kabbani. A community college economics instructor in his early forties, he explained that he had moved to Yuba City from Chicago with his physician wife and two small children. He said they wanted to live in warmer weather and had heard about the Yuba City arson and the rebuilding of the mosque. But what he found, he said, "is not real Islam. This is a cult of a man," meaning Kabbani. "This board of directors, they are not good Muslims. The practices are not good Islam." Chaudhry, who came to the United States as a graduate student, at first denied having had anything to do with the accusatory flyer and other attacks. But then he said of the flyer, "Ninety-nine percent of that is accurate," and he repeated the accusation, for which he had no evidence, that Krambo and other Sufis had "arsoned the mosque."

Unproved conspiracy theory met with unsupported conjecture. Krambo and Bath in their darker moments wondered if the string of unlucky events, beginning with the arson years earlier, had been part of a plan: a campaign to prey on a Sufi-influenced community, raise money on its misfortune, and then, when it showed signs of surviving, undermine it by means of outside saboteurs. Bath doesn't have proof, but he suspects Chaudhry and his main comrade "were professionally trained to come over and disrupt our community."

With police failing to name a suspect, it's impossible to determine now who started the fire. But Sheikh Kabbani has done nothing to discourage theorizing about the enemies of Sufism. In a lecture to four hundred

people at the Islamic Center of Yuba City in 2003, he portrayed the struggle there as part of a larger battle against fundamentalist forces. "They
have conspired to take our mosques in America in order to create an ideology," he said. "These wild animals want to come in and destroy human-
ity as a whole, and not only that, but discredit Islam."

Khalid Chaudhry dismissed Kabbani as a government stooge. "He is
financed by the CIA," Chaudhry told me. He denied any role in any sort
of conspiracy. "I want to preserve my religion and values and be part of
American society too." He and the other man accused of instigating conflict have since left the Yuba City area. Chaudhry said he did so to keep his
children clear of the strife.

The battle left lasting wounds. Khalid Saeed, a former president of the
Yuba City mosque, said over tea in the living room of his large home that
he was thoroughly disillusioned and rarely attended communal prayer
anymore. His grandfather, a member of the first small wave of Indian immigrant rural laborers, had arrived in California in 1905 to pick fruit. The
family had thrived over the years and accumulated wealth and many acres
of fruit trees. Saeed had contributed the five acres on which the mosque
was built.

He had met Kabbani and found him to be "a nice person," Saeed said.
But he didn't trust the man. The sheikh, he said, was "very well connected. He does most of his talks in the upper levels of government."
Saeed blamed Kabbani, acting through his agent, Krambo, for all the dis-
sension in Yuba City. The sheikh, Saeed said, "was trying to get everybody
to follow him the way he wants them. To me, he seemed like he was trying to form a cult." Muslims shouldn't rely on a spiritual guide to explain
the meaning or practice of Islam, Saeed said. "There is one Quran," he insisted, "only one Quran, and only one interpretation of it."

One February evening Abdul Kabir Krambo invited me to join the zikr circle at the Islamic Center of Yuba City. Before leaving for the mosque, he
led his family and some friends from out of town, other white converts,
in the *maghrib* prayer in the Krambos' dimly lit living room. Amid the

couches, coffee table, television, bookshelves, piano, and easy chairs, there wasn't much space for kneeling, but no one seemed to mind. In addition to the Krambos, the worshipers included a banker in a gold-green Indian-style tunic, his traditionally dressed wife, and a software engineer who wore a plaid shirt and a multipocketed photographer's vest. The Krambos' fish tank glowed fluorescent green in the semidarkness, as Abdul Kabir murmured in Arabic.

After maghrib, twenty men and five women assembled at the Islamic Center. Seven of the men were Pakistani immigrants, including Abdul Hamid Bath, Abdul Kabir's friend and fellow board member. The Pakistanis sat together, forming a third of the circle. The women sat separately from the men, but a carved wooden partition that marked off the women's area for communal prayer was now open in front. The software engineer, Ali Jensen, led the proceedings.

Beware any religion based on form and rules, Jensen said, or one that harps on nonbelievers. God accepts into heaven all those who remember Him, but also those who live virtuous lives, even if they aren't believers. "The religion is love," he said. "That is why we remember God and His Prophet—because of love, always love."

Jensen began chanting, "La ilaha ill Allah" (There is no god but God), and the others followed, roughly in unison. Every several minutes Jensen changed the cadence and wording slightly, but he always returned to the name of God and qualities describing Him: *Rahman*, the Merciful, and *Raheem*, the Compassionate. Some participants rocked back and forth in time with the words. Abdul Kabir Krambo's fair-haired granddaughter wobbled cheerfully between the men's circle and the women. "Allahu akbar, Allahu akbar," the adults chanted.

On another evening Abdul Kabir pulled out one of his volumes of Rumi to make a point. Rahma and her daughter-in-law, Nureen, had served a delicious lamb stew and were now clearing the dishes. Jalal ad-Din ar-Rumi, who lived from 1207 to 1273, is best known for the passion of his tributes to love, divine and human. But Rumi imparted social commentary as well, and Abdul Kabir thought this passage from "Religious Controversy," a personal favorite, illustrated a deft blending of themes. "'The blind religious are in a dilemma, for the champions on either side stand firm,'" he read.

> Each party is delighted with its own path.
> Love alone can end their quarrel.
> Love alone comes to the rescue when you cry for help against their
> arguments.

Muslims should melt their differences in the heat of what Rumi elsewhere refers to as "burning, burning love," Abdul Kabir said. Too many Muslims, he continued, misunderstand Sufism's elevation of the Prophet Muhammad to superguru status as the forbidden worship of a mortal. Sufis appeal to Muhammad to "intercede" on their behalf before God on Judgment Day. Some seek the intercession of dead Muslim saints and even living holy men.

Krambo's son, Ahmed, who sat across from me, said evidence of intolerance even cropped up in Islamic children's books. One he had recently bought from a mail-order company for his two-year-old daughter, Khadija, had seemed like an ordinary fable about a smug spider that discovered its web wasn't as strong in the wind as it thought. Then the book took this turn, which Ahmed read aloud: "Likewise, the false gods from whom people seek help are like the weak house of the spider. Therefore, we must turn to Allah alone to seek his help. No one other than Allah is worth worshipping."

"You go in these mosques, and all they do is talk about idolatry and unbelievers," Ahmed said. "Then you find it in their books, the little kid books."

"These are for two- to six-year-olds," his mother interjected. "At that age they don't even know who Allah is. How are they going to understand what idolatry is?"

Rahma, a tall woman who wears long, patterned skirts and covers her hair when in public, had thought carefully about how to inculcate Islamic values. Until a few years earlier some of the Pakistani-American families around Yuba City were driving their children to a mosque in Sacramento for Sunday religious classes. But some of the teachers in Sacramento told the Yuba City kids they were going to hellfire because their parents were polytheists, meaning Sufis. Rahma encouraged the mothers of these children to start a small Sunday school in Yuba City. The idea took off once the rebuilt mosque was completed in 2002. Rahma's own children were grown by then, but she agreed to help run the informal school.

One task Rahma took upon herself was ordering religious books from Astrolabe Islamic Media, a major English-language catalog company. High on her list was *Riyad-us-Saliheen* (*Gardens of the Righteous*), a collection of hadith, or sayings and actions attributed to the Prophet. Muslims have studied the collection for hundreds of years. But when Rahma skimmed some pages of the leather-bound two-volume English edition, she noticed something troubling: The Riyadh-based publisher, Darussalam, had inserted a good deal of bracketed language into the hadith text and tacked on extensive commentary. Practically everywhere she looked, she found the word "jihad," plus footnotes that interpreted that charged word as physical fighting or holy war, rather than as personal or spiritual struggle.

Rahma showed me an example from the opening pages, where the reader finds this awkwardly translated admonition ascribed to Muhammad: "There is no emigration after the conquest (of Makkah) but only Jihad [(striving and fighting in the cause of Allah) will continue] and intention. So if you are summoned to fight, go forth."

The historical context for this obscure-sounding pronouncement was that the hostility of the people of Mecca had compelled the early followers of Muhammad to flee to Medina. But once the Muslims had gained strength and returned to take over Mecca, the obligation to emigrate ceased. The Saudi publisher added copious commentary, including the idea that the hadith commands Muslims not to live in any "land of infidels." Proximity to infidels reduces Muslims' readiness for "striving and fighting in the way of Allah," the text stated. This keenness for religious battle "must be kept always alive so that the Muslims may respond at once to the call of Jihad whenever the need for it arises anywhere."

Rahma, who years earlier had read another translation of *Gardens of the Righteous*, didn't recall so much emphasis on conflict. She dug out the older edition, published by Curzon Press in London in 1975. The translator of this version emphasizes that in the context of this prophetic saying, "jihad" means "spiritual striving," not "physical fighting." Sadly, though, the Saudi-published volume is the one widely available in the United States. "Why is there any surprise," she asked, "that those who are reading and studying these new toxic editions, which mask themselves as sources of knowledge for Muslims, end up in radical, political, militant groups?"

Rahma's children, Ahmed and his younger sister, Jamila, now in their twenties, were brought up on different fare. "I remember all the stories you used to tell me about the sheikhs and the Prophet," Ahmed said when the conversation turned to his childhood. He had been with his father and other men and boys in the basement of Sheikh Kabbani's former house near San Francisco when he announced that he wanted to make bayah with the sheikh. He was only twelve, young for this important step. His father asked him, "Hey, are you sure about this?" Ahmed said that he was. "I got a feeling that that's where I needed to be, that was a step I needed to take," the son recalled.

Ahmed didn't enter public school until fifth grade; before then his mother taught him at home. Once enrolled, he said, "I started changing my clothes, cutting my hair, and showering." As years went by, the changes took on a different cast. "I started using drugs. I started dressing differently. I started acting differently, completely differently from the way that I had lived as a younger person." When he was sixteen, he told his father that if he stayed in school, he feared he would get into serious trouble. He asked for permission to leave school and work on Sheikh Kabbani's rural estate in Michigan. A number of Naqshbandi members, mostly young men, lived in outbuildings, trailers, and tents. They tended farm animals, prayed their five prayers, and did zikr.

With his father's consent, Ahmed moved to Michigan. Around the time Ahmed turned seventeen, the sheikh suggested he start thinking about getting engaged. The Naqshbandi, like most observant Muslims, discourage premarital sex. Fortuitously, an old Naqshbandi friend happened to call Abdul Kabir to discuss whether their children might make a suitable couple. Ahmed showed little interest—until he saw a picture of Nureen, then fifteen. She was (and is) tall and stunningly beautiful. The teenagers hit it off and soon wed in a religious ceremony presided over by Sheikh Kabbani. After Nureen turned sixteen, they got legally married, and soon they had two daughters.

Ahmed, Nureen, and their daughters live in a separate wing of the one-story house that Abdul Kabir expanded to accommodate his father, who spent the last year of his life there. The crucifixes the old man put up have been removed, as have the gin and scotch he kept in the cupboard. When his father died, Abdul Kabir personally washed and shrouded the body according to Islamic tradition. He thinks the cantankerous Catholic would have enjoyed the idea of being ushered out in such an unlikely way.

The Krambos believe in living as an extended family. "If there are people praying," Ahmed explained, "it makes it easier, instead of having to muster that strength, every day, over and over and over again. If they already have it, I can feed off of that enthusiasm and knowledge." Ahmed, a slender, bearded young man, said that all his close friends are Naqshbandi. "At this point in my life, to stay away from those things that tempted me earlier, I don't associate too much or at all with anybody who is interested in proving themselves," he said. Among the Naqshbandi, "you might have a kid bring a joint to zikr and run off into the woods and do it, but it's a pretty rare thing."

"You're known by the company you keep," his mother said for reinforcement. "We're really blessed with a lot of very high-quality people."

Ahmed works most days with his dad, repairing and installing electrical systems for homeowners and small businesses. Social gatherings at the Krambo home usually involve the entire extended family and revolve around zikr or other religious events. Men gather in the living room, while the women talk and cook in the kitchen. Some of the younger men wear turbans and traditional tunics. Periodically one of them will take out his miswak and rub his teeth. Male friends refer to each other in a joshing way as "sheikh," responding to a request to pass the chicken curry, for example, with "As you wish, sheikh, as you wish." For all their attention to old ways, many Naqshbandi are big fans of science fiction, especially the *Star Wars* movies, which involve spiritual masters and inner struggles between good and evil.

Even Sheikh Kabbani appreciates the pedagogic potential of popular culture. It was suggested to him during the course of a 1994 interview that "Material Girl," the early hit song by Madonna, reflected the deterioration of Western values. Kabbani demurred. "You have to be both material and spiritual," he said, according to Montreal's *Gazette* newspaper. "Sufis can give people joy in their spiritual life," the sheikh said. "Well, Madonna is giving people a kind of joy in their material life. You cannot say she is wrong. Sufis don't object and criticize. They are accepting everything. That's why, when my children are looking at Madonna on MTV, I say, 'Let me come and look also!'" Given her more recent interest in Kabbalah, or Jewish mysticism, Madonna no doubt would welcome the sheikh's curiosity.

INDEPENDENCE DAY

When Sheikh Kabbani is at home in Fenton, Michigan, he presides over prayer and zikr at As-Siddiq Mosque and Islamic Center, a former Episcopal church now adorned with metallic onion-shaped domes. The long wooden pews have been pushed to the side of the main hall. Carpets and prayer rugs of crimson, green, and gold cover the floor. Up a flight of stairs is a women's balcony with a Plexiglas half wall to allow the women to see below. During some services women drift down from the balcony to sit in the back of the prayer hall.

One Friday afternoon the sheikh delivered a jummah sermon on the theme of diversity. Islam, he said, is "a perfect religion brought to us by a perfect person, the Prophet Muhammad." But there had been other great prophets, he said, including Moses and Jesus. Paraphrasing the Quran, the sheikh declared, "If Allah wanted everyone to be the same, he would have made them the same." The congregation of about a hundred included American-born and immigrant, black and white. The day-to-day imam, who leads prayer in the sheikh's absence, is a gentle African immigrant named Sahib Mahmoud.

None of the prophets coerced anyone in matters of faith, Kabbani told his followers. He shifted to the voice of Moses, who in this rendition sounded something like an elderly New York Jew: "If you like, you like, and you take it. I'm going." Then the sheikh offered a brief impersonation of Jesus, who sounded a lot like Moses: "If you like, you take it." Finally Muhammad, again in the same voice: "If you like, you take it . . . I'm going to Medina."

For immigrants to America, Kabbani had a finger-wagging reminder: "When you migrate, it means you are establishing a relationship with the country that hosted you. They give you all kind of privileges. You come against them, that is treason." He paraphrased another verse from the Quran: "Obey Allah, obey Prophet, obey those in authority." Obedience to temporal power plays a large role in his preaching. "If you obey those who are in authority, you will be happy, or else you are in problems, and Allah created us to be happy, not to have problems," he said in another sermon. "Those who disobey the authority, they end up in jail. You disobey the Prophet, you disobey Allah, you end up in a different jail."

The sheikh acted on his teachings. When President Clinton was in the White House, Kabbani put a photo of the two of them on the cover of his magazine, together with a cameo image of Hillary Clinton, kerchief over her hair, during a visit to the Middle East. In a signed preelection editorial in 2000, Kabbani lavishly praised Bill Clinton's remarks at a White House reception honoring Muslim leaders. "Discord and ill feelings [among the Muslims] dissolved like salt in water, and it became a sweet event, the likes of honey, which each person thirsted to taste."

After the Republicans swept into power, Kabbani attended similar events hosted by George W. Bush. "The president is a very spiritual person, a very loving and caring person. He liked me, and I liked him," the sheikh told *Insight* magazine. Kabbani had audiences with State Department and defense officials. "We consult with him to learn about the world of Islam," a senior Bush Pentagon official told me in February 2004. "We don't know a lot, unfortunately."

When it really counted, however, the Bush team didn't listen to Kabbani. A backer of the Iraq invasion in 2003, he urged American officials to reach out early to Sunni clerics in Baghdad who have Sufi leanings. These clerics, he explained, could serve as intermediaries to the larger Sunni minority that had enjoyed privileged status under Saddam and could become dangerous after his demise. The idea was never really tested. Once Baghdad fell, he said, the Americans didn't move quickly enough to cultivate the Iraqi Sunni-Sufis before the anti-American insurgency threw the country into chaos, and Kabbani's allies fled Iraq.

On the Friday before the July Fourth weekend in 2004 I accompanied Abdul Kabir Krambo to a post-jummah lunch served by his Pakistani-born friend Abdul Hamid Bath. About twenty men and boys gathered in a small, unfurnished building used for communal events. Steaming trays of spicy goat, chicken, and lamb, sweet yellow rice, salad, and piquant yogurt dressing soon arrived. (The women who had cooked the feast were nowhere in evidence.) Outside, goats nibbled on grass in unwitting preparation for their role at a future gathering.

A shy, gracious host, Bath owns a convenience store and belongs to a large Sufi family well known in the area. He said that the Pakistani community appreciates having the Krambos involved at the Islamic Center. Abdul Kabir has strong opinions, but he has helped steer the mosque through trying times. Bath said that he and Abdul Kabir agree that extremism "is a big problem" among American Muslims. "We've lost that concept of what Islam is really about: a peace-loving religion," Bath said. "Also respecting the country you live in," his brother Shafique chimed in. "This country is feeding you. You need to be loyal to this country. People are forgetting this."

This consensus doesn't mean the Baths and Krambo see eye to eye on everything. As we were waiting for lunch that Friday afternoon, Krambo sought support for his plan for a small fireworks display in the mosque parking lot on Sunday evening, the Fourth. The Pakistanis objected that while they were as patriotic as anyone else, they didn't like the idea of this secular celebration near their house of worship.

"In Pakistan we don't do this at the mosque," Abdul Hamid said. "Fireworks on Independence Day, yes, but not at mosque."

Krambo, his voice rising angrily, said the mosque needed to reach out more to non-Muslims and be "a part of the larger society."

"Mosque is prayer, Quran, zikr," an older Pakistani farmer wearing a red and white-checked turban said angrily.

"Paul, what do you think?" Abdul Hamid Bath asked, turning to me. "Do churches have fireworks at the church?"

I said I was Jewish, but for what it was worth, my mother always warned that fireworks could put your eye out.

Bath took this as my siding with him. "Yes, you see," he said to Krambo, "you want to do fireworks, do them yourself."

The pungent aromas from the lunch buffet began to draw attention, and the argument dissipated. "I've got a few flaws," Krambo told me afterward, "especially that short temper sometimes." He was ashamed that at the age of fifty, his internal battle against certain baser instincts continued.

The next morning Krambo set off on his electrician's rounds, his green prayer cap replaced by a blue baseball hat that bears the name of his little company, All Electric. Crossing over the Feather River in his pickup truck, wooden Islamic prayer beads swinging from the rearview mirror, he mentioned that the neighboring city of Marysville is known for its impressive July Fourth celebration. (Fireworks apparently were still on his mind.) The problem with the Marysville event, he continued, was that it attracted bikers, and a lot of celebrants would be drunk by nightfall. "My wife wears a scarf," he said. "That could be a problem if there's an excess of patriotism." A semiprivate celebration at the mosque would avoid such dangers.

The Naqshbandi take a stoic view of anti-Muslim bias. In that, as in so many other things, they emulate their sheikh. Kabbani dismisses the topic as a distraction. He believes the complaint that Muslims get singled out at airports is overblown. If anything, he said, he finds it strange to see non-Muslim American mothers with small children getting thoroughly searched when he usually receives only routine scrutiny. "If there was discrimination, I would be the one who is searched," Kabbani said.

That is not to say that he has never felt abused. Immediately after 9/11 President Bush invited Kabbani and other Muslim leaders to appear with him at a prayer service at the National Cathedral in Washington. Afterward officials advised the sheikh that given the confusion at airports, he might do better to drive home to Michigan. Wearing his usual outfit, he was subjected to obscene gestures by occupants of other cars on the Pennsylvania Turnpike, and a police officer pulled over his car, saying he was checking out something "fishy." But Kabbani shrugged off the episode.

Krambo pulled into the parking lot of a gas station and grocery store owned by an old friend and customer. The sign over the cash register featured a replica of a Smith & Wesson revolver and warned, "We don't call 911." The store owner came out and gave Krambo a bear hug. "This is a beautiful guy," he said of Krambo, who was already out of earshot, unloading a ladder from his truck. Krambo had been solicitous when the store owner's family went through difficult times. "He says he's a Muslim, OK," the store owner said softly, "but he's one of the best Christians I know."

Later, while Abdul Kabir made a quick trip to a hardware store to pick up a high-pressure sodium lamp, his cellular phone rang. It was Sheikh Kabbani calling from Michigan. Krambo's daughter, Jamila, was visiting there. She had announced that she wanted to stay and work in the Naqshbandi administrative office. Kabbani was calling to ask her father's permission.

Like her brother, Jamila had married young, in her case, at eighteen, to a groom of the same age. Sheikh Kabbani came to Yuba City in 2003 to perform the wedding under a large white tent in the Krambos' yard. But the union lasted only six months. Jamila then thought about getting an accounting degree or becoming a marine biologist, but she hadn't taken any of the usual steps toward those disparate goals. The arrangement in Michigan offered room and board but no salary. The sheikh's organization would pay for Jamila to take some business courses at a nearby college.

Jamila got on the phone with her father. In a supportive voice, Abdul Kabir asked if this was what she really wanted. When she said yes, he concluded cheerfully, "Well, OK then." A side benefit, he told me later, would be the wider array of young Naqshbandi men Jamila could meet in Michigan. Sure enough, she soon met one and married for a second time.

Independence Day arrived with a perfect blue sky in the Sacramento Valley. The Krambos invited over friends for halal hamburgers and hot dogs. Children splashed in the swimming pool. Parents scooped ice cream. Birds sang in the fruit trees.

This wasn't an exclusively Naqshbandi gathering. One guest, Robert Wachman, an earnest former Peace Corps volunteer in Nepal, had befriended Abdul Kabir after hiring him to repair an electronic menorah used by the small local Jewish congregation. Wachman had been to the Islamic Center of Yuba City to hear Sheikh Kabbani speak. He gathered from Kabbani that Muslims weren't out to get Jews. Wachman, who teaches English as a second language at Yuba Community College, found that reassuring. After 9/11 he and Krambo organized a series of interfaith meetings in the area with the assistance of a Presbyterian minister. It was only a small gesture, Wachman said, but you do what you can do.

Standing at his smoky grill, Krambo mused that he probably had more in common with Wachman than with some Muslims. "It's critical, central to the religion, really, to figure out how to live at peace with other people, people of other faiths," he said. "That's central to Sheikh Hisham's teaching. That means if there are things you can't agree on, you see whether they can be set aside so the focus can stay on those things you *do* agree on. I see this as the American way. In a big country with a lot of different groups, we try to live and let live, not force our ideas on everyone else." In that spirit, more or less, a compromise had been reached on the fireworks question. Krambo could have his celebration in the mosque parking lot, but he shouldn't expect the Bath family or other Pakistani-Americans to attend.

After the early-evening prayer a group of about fifteen people, most of them Krambos and their friends, assembled in front of the mosque. Wachman brought his teenage son. Several Pakistani-American worshipers leaving the prayer hall scowled as they walked past, but they kept moving toward their cars. A man from Afghanistan and his small wide-eyed boy stayed to watch.

The sky turned black and starry. Ahmed Krambo began lighting bottle rockets. Swirling and whistling, other offerings exploded in shiny bursts of silver to the "ooohs" and "wows!" of the spectators. A question arose about the legality of the unlicensed affair, but the consensus was that the police would smile on such innocent festivities. Abdul Kabir and his son brought out the heavy artillery: projectiles that lurched skyward and five seconds later made a satisfying thump, throwing off canopies of red, white, and blue that for a moment illuminated the minaret and dome of the Yuba City mosque.

SIX

The Webmaster

In the days after September 11, 2001, Moscow, Idaho, mourned with the rest of the country, and wherever people turned in the rural university town, there was Sami Omar al-Hussayen. The tall, bearded graduate student from Saudi Arabia led fellow Muslims as they joined an emotional candlelight vigil for the dead. He helped organize a blood drive for survivors. On behalf of the small mosque in town, he issued a press release saying that Muslims in Moscow "condemn in the strongest terms possible what are apparently vicious acts of terrorism against innocent citizens." Classmates and professors at the University of Idaho, where al-Hussayen was seeking a Ph.D. in computer science, applauded these thoughtful responses. Here was a visitor proud of his Muslim identity but comfortable putting his children in American public school and taking them to Chuck E. Cheese's for pizza.

So people in Moscow were astonished in February 2003 when word spread that FBI agents had arrived before dawn at al-Hussayen's home near campus, rousted him from bed, and taken him away in handcuffs. They carted off his computers and financial records. Female agents interrogated his startled Saudi wife, Maha. As unmarked government sedans circled the campus, scores of investigators fanned out to question members of the Muslim Students Association. "They come to our house in the morning, and they try to scare us," another Saudi graduate student told the university's student newspaper. "I am really very, very scared these days."

Al-Hussayen was charged with "material support" of terrorism. Prosecutors alleged that since the late 1990s his academic and public persona had been a cover for a secret career stoking Islamic fanaticism. The government said that from his out-of-the-way perch in northwest Idaho, he had helped set up and supervise Arabic-language Web sites that spewed violent anti-American views and encouraged suicide bombings. Just four months before the 9/11 attacks one of these sites carried an edict by a Muslim religious scholar justifying the crashing of hijacked airplanes into buildings.

Twelve Idaho citizens, most of whom, it became apparent during jury selection, didn't know a single Muslim, would have to decide al-Hussayen's real identity. Was he the mild-mannered campus leader or the dangerous promoter of "extreme jihad"? Or was there a third alternative? Could it have been that in his ordinary face-to-face dealings in Moscow, al-Hussayen was indeed the kind soul his American friends admired, while on a more abstract level, he held, or at least tolerated, views that most Americans would find abhorrent—namely, a deep loathing of Jews and Israel and a high regard for the ideology, if not all the violent tactics, of Islamic holy war?

Neither side in the courtroom battle titled *United States of America v. Sami Omar al-Hussayen* would hear of middle ground. The government accused al-Hussayen of violating part of the controversial USA Patriot Act barring the provision of "expert advice" to terrorists—in al-Hussayen's case, advice about computers and the Internet. His online enterprises motivated people to kill innocent civilians, prosecutors argued. In their view, he served the same cause as Osama bin Laden and deserved to spend fifteen years or more in prison.

Jailed while waiting for his trial, al-Hussayen maintained that he opposed all forms of terrorism. The values of "justice and human rights that the American people believe in" were his values too, he declared in an on-line open letter. His defense lawyer compared the Saudi student with a magazine editor who publishes a range of views without necessarily en-dorsing all of them. Even if al-Hussayen did believe the objectionable opinions on the Web sites he tended—that Jews, "the brothers of mon-keys and pigs," deserved to be slaughtered, for example, and that jihad was justified to stop the Israeli and American conspiracy to take over the Middle East—the lawyer argued that those beliefs fell under the protec-tion of the First Amendment's free speech clause.

There is ample reason to be troubled by the ideas al-Hussayen helped disseminate. They conceivably could open the door to violence. He repre-sents the paradox of Muslim student immigrants: they are eager to take advantage of America's openness and its educational and economic op-portunities, but many are intensely hostile to U.S. government policies—sometimes to the point of sympathizing with the country's enemies. Does that make the immigrant Muslims a threat, or does allowing their at-titudes and actions illustrate the flexibility of a great democracy? In al-Hussayen's case, did the government overreact? Where should prosecutors draw the line? His trial became a critical test of how far the authorities can take the domestic antiterrorism fight.

Beyond questions of criminal liability, there remains the issue of what Americans of all backgrounds ought to think of someone whose Muslim beliefs and loyalties inspire him to circulate praise of mass killing. The group for whom this has the greatest and most immediate consequences is young Muslim activists. But the dilemma should concern everyone who favors both free speech and security.

BIG MAN ON CAMPUS

On January 23, 2003, the FBI intercepted a telephone call Sami Omar al-Hussayen received from a cousin in Saudi Arabia named Abu Riyad. After an exchange of traditional Arab greetings and family news, Abu Riyad asked al-Hussayen when he would complete his Ph.D.

"Allah willing, I will be done by the end of this semester."

"May Allah help you succeed, and make matters easier and bring you back safely."

The conversation was a mix of banter and serious talk. Al-Hussayen recounted a family camping trip by the Pacific Ocean. His wife, Maha, had asked their three young boys how they felt about leaving the United States, where they had spent most of their lives. "The kids replied that Saudi Arabia is nice, but does it have a camp for camping?" al-Hussayen said, chuckling.

He switched subjects. "Abu Riyad, are you aware of tomorrow's lecture?" The title was "The Intifada and the New Tartars," al-Hussayen said. "It will be on the Internet." He mentioned the Web site where users could click to hear an audio broadcast, and he urged his cousin to listen.

The intifada of the lecture's title was the armed Palestinian uprising that began in 2000 and featured suicide bombings of Israeli civilians. The "Tartars" referred to Mongol armies that overran much of the Islamic Empire in the thirteenth century. The "*New* Tartars," according to the lecturer, Sheikh Safar al-Hawali, of Saudi Arabia, were the Americans. The United States, according to al-Hawali, was dead set on "imposing the Jewish supremacy" over the entire Middle East.

Al-Hawali's radicalizing influence on young Arabs has earned him the title Awakening Sheikh. With American forces gathering in early 2003 to invade Iraq, he urged his Internet listeners to view that impending conflict as part of a larger campaign to conquer all Islam for the benefit of U.S. economic interests and "the Zion, the Jewish project." The "blessed Intifada," al-Hawali said, was Islam's hope for turning the tables. "Terrorism acts [have] planted an atmosphere of fear and panic" among Jews, he said approvingly. Of Muslims wishing to aid the Palestinians, he said, "Whoever prepares to fight will fight." The man who doesn't grab an AK-47 or strap on a belt of explosives should "make every effort with his pen, with his writings, with his riyal, his dollar, his dinar." Muslims, al-Hawali told listeners, paraphrasing an ancient Islamic text, must "fight the Jews until the trees and the stones speak and would say, 'Oh, Muslim, Allah-worshiper, this is a Jew. Come and kill him.'"

From his enthusiasm on the phone about the al-Hawali lecture, it was clear al-Hussayen was a fan of the sheikh's. In fact he had used his computer skills to help make the audio version of the intifada talk available worldwide on the Internet.

↜ ↝

Al-Hussayen grew up in a well-to-do family in Riyadh. They weren't rich on the scale of the Saudi royal clan, but there were trips abroad and a vacation home on the Persian Gulf. Sami's six siblings include doctors and senior Saudi government bureaucrats. As teenagers Sami and his older brother, Abdul, traveled to Britain to polish their English. They also accompanied their father, a top official in the Saudi Education Ministry, on trips to the United States that included detours to amusement parks and historic sites. Back home, Sami attended King Saud University and closely followed Middle East politics. After the Iraqi invasion of Kuwait in 1990, he and a friend drove to the Saudi-Kuwaiti border to assist refugees fleeing Saddam Hussein's forces. They spent a week there, distributing food and water to shaken Kuwaitis. In 1992 al-Hussayen married a kindergarten teacher named Maha, and they soon started a family.

Oil rich but poor in institutions of secular higher education, Saudi Arabia pays for qualified students to obtain graduate-level training abroad. Al-Hussayen began his overseas education at Ball State University in Muncie, Indiana, in 1994. After earning a master's degree there, he moved to Southern Methodist University in Dallas and then, in 1998, applied to transfer to the University of Idaho, which has a solid computer science program. Idaho said yes, so in 1999 al-Hussayen, then thirty, moved to Moscow.

The town of twenty-two thousand is the hub of a region of fertile hills called the Palouse, named for a local band of Native Americans. White settlers arrived in the area in the 1870s, and the hamlet that became Moscow took shape after the railroad came through a dozen years later. The town's name is something of a mystery, as there is no evidence that it refers directly to the Russian city. Idaho gained statehood in 1890, and Moscow was chosen as the site for a land-grant school. While agriculture—wheat, lentils, and dry peas—remains the area's primary economic engine, the university gradually transformed Moscow into a regional cultural center. Today jazz, theater, and visual arts all are available in generous supply. The town provides a small enclave for political liberals in an otherwise highly conservative state. There is a bohemian bookstore–coffee shop on Main Street, and a local entrepreneur named MaryJane Butters publishes *MaryJanesFarm*, a nationally circulated magazine on "simple solutions for everyday organic." More than five hundred foreign students enroll every semester at the university out of a total of thirteen thousand. Idaho for many years has recruited abroad, both to bring diversity to its remote campus and to bolster tuition revenue. Moscow residents take pride in making the visitors feel comfortable, although the al-Hussayen arrest caused some to think twice.

A Pakistani immigrant named S. M. Ghazanfar sees himself as a beneficiary of the area's hospitality. He arrived in 1958 to attend Washington State University in Pullman, Washington, just eight miles from Moscow. Beginning with the equivalent of only a tenth-grade education, he obtained a Ph.D. in economics and moved over to teach at the University of Idaho. He raised a family and became chairman of the university's economics department. In his late sixties and retired from teaching, he continues to write about the influence of medieval Islamic social and economic thought on later European scholarship. The lesson to be learned about Muslims and the West isn't purely historical, in his view. "There is continuity, damn it! We are not strangers," he told me, his voice rising. "Most assuredly, our heritage is Judeo-Christian *and* Islamic."

He recalled how Muslim students for decades—just a handful at first, later dozens each year—had quietly made their way to the American Northwest. In the 1960s and 1970s most came from Pakistan and India; more Middle Easterners began turning up in the 1980s and 1990s. After praying for years in borrowed church basements and student union rooms, local Muslims raised funds to buy a small house in Moscow that was converted to a mosque. Later a larger Islamic center was built in Pullman "with substantial funding from Saudi sources," Ghazanfar said. Between the two large universities, the local Muslim population swelled to three hundred, most of them transient students.

Ghazanfar, a friendly man who insists on being called Ghazi, paused when asked how attitudes among Muslim students had changed over the decades. Some of the Arab students, especially the Saudis, were more religiously austere than the Pakistanis and Indians, he said. "I sometimes would be a bit critical. The literalism of some goes too far in my judgment. At times I have been uncomfortable with some sermons" delivered by immigrant students. They "think I am too moderate, too liberal," he said. "I react: 'You're coming from a different world.'"

In the last several years Ghazanfar had noticed more Middle Eastern students pursuing degrees in the social sciences, rather than engineering and other technical fields. He approved of this development and hoped that by branching out, these students would learn to be more flexible thinkers. He didn't know al-Hussayen well but said that the Saudi was known as "nice, polite, articulate, and outgoing."

Al-Hussayen may have been outgoing, but his wife, Maha, observed the traditional constraints on Saudi women. In Moscow she rarely ventured out in public without her husband. When in the presence of men outside her family, she wore a concealing gown, with a head covering and facial veil that left only her eyes showing. She generally didn't initiate conversation with unfamiliar men and never shook a man's hand in greeting. When at home with her boys, she would have the eight-year-old, Muhanad, answer a knock on the door, in case the visitor was a man. The al-Hussayens lived in a complex of small town houses for married students and their families. Maha didn't drive, so her husband ferried her to and from the WinCo supermarket and the strip malls that flank Moscow's modest downtown.

By contrast, the al-Hussayen boys—Muhanad, Tameem, five, and Ziad, two—seemed entirely at home in American culture. They zipped around on skateboards and spoke perfect English. Sami coached the older boys in a municipal soccer league and sometimes volunteered as a parent aide in their public school. On weekends he took the boys out for pizza and to the Islamic Center of Moscow, the little mosque in a converted residential house downtown.

University administrators were aware of Sami because he was less shy than the other dozen or so Saudi graduate students, who mostly kept to themselves. He volunteered to serve on a committee that advised the university president on questions of diversity and human rights. Raul Sanchez, the administrator who led the committee, befriended al-Hussayen and, at the Saudi's invitation, visited the mosque. Sanchez, a father of two boys, was struck by how the adoring al-Hussayen children hung on their father's lanky frame while he, with a patient smile, tried to carry on an adult conversation.

Most of the al-Hussayens' expenses were covered by the thirty to forty thousand dollars a year the Saudi government doled out for Sami's tuition, room, and board, the standard benefit for Saudi grad students abroad. The family didn't live lavishly. Sami drove a 1992 Pontiac Bonneville. He patronized a place called Mac Frugal's Bargains Closeouts, and his extravagances were few: expensive coffee from Starbucks and, for religious holidays, a live sheep procured from a local farmer to be slaughtered for the traditional Saudi-style feast.

Within a short time after arriving in Moscow, al-Hussayen became an influential member of the Idaho Muslim Students Association. The polite Saudi periodically accompanied Muslim students with visa problems to the university's international office. "He was obviously seen as the leader, a senior figure," Michael Whiteman, the director of the office, said. In 2001–02 al-Hussayen served as president for the MSA, which, like similar groups on other American campuses, helped run the local mosque. There was no full-time imam in Moscow, so al-Hussayen and other students often gave the sermon at Friday prayers.

After 9/11 the fifty or so members of the Idaho MSA—Saudis, Kuwaitis, Egyptians, and Pakistanis—turned reflexively to al-Hussayen. In addition to the press release condemning the attacks, which he issued on behalf of the mosque, he distributed a form letter on the MSA letterhead, thanking professors and administrators for "the support you provided to the members of our community and in advising against finger pointing." It continued, "We believe that the best way to combat terrorism and racism is to enlighten all of us about our shared believes [sic] and show our common desire in standing up against the perpetrators altogether."

One of the recipients of the letter, John Dickinson, was al-Hussayen's adviser on his doctoral thesis on the security of high-speed computer networks. The wiry white-haired professor thought of his student as competent but not brilliant. What made al-Hussayen stand out was his graciousness. After 9/11 Dickinson dropped in on the open house al-Hussayen and other Saudi students held to explain Islam. "There were posters of Mecca and rugs and pillows on the floor," Dickinson recalled. "I was invited to sit and eat dates and have coffee or tea." He sounded wistful. "I've thought about it many times," he said, "such a peaceful, friendly meeting."

FATWAS IN CYBERSPACE

While enrolled at Southern Methodist University in Dallas, al-Hussayen had met a fellow Saudi named Muhammad Alahmari, who headed a group called the Islamic Assembly of North America. The IANA was devoted to dawa. It sponsored religious conferences geared mostly to college and graduate students, operated English- and Arabic-language Web sites, and distributed translations of the Quran and other Islamic literature to prison inmates. It ran a "dial-a-fatwa" telephone line (1-800-95-FATWA) that offered quick rulings on questions of Islamic law.

As the Internet became more widely used and influential during the 1990s, IANA officials increasingly relied on al-Hussayen to launch and oversee the group's online activities. The graduate student felt drawn to the IANA's cause but sometimes resented the imposition. "Do not worry; I did not forget IANA," he wrote in one e-mail to a colleague who was nagging him about Web site administration. "I lost my studies for IANA. If they do not know that I am sure Allah knows."

Founded in 1993, the IANA sought to spread the stringent beliefs of Saudi Wahhabism in the United States and Canada. The home pages of the assembly's English-language Web sites don't reveal this orientation.

They point to such articles as "What Did Jesus Really Say?" and "Why Can't a Muslim Woman Marry a non-Muslim Man?" But when a user clicks deeper into the Web sites, it isn't hard to find the harsh tone of Wahhabism. "The creed of the Wahhabiyya," instructs one IANA English-language site aimed at university students, "is based upon witnessing that Muhammad is the Messenger of Allah and completely abandoning all innovations, superstitions, and whatever goes against the Shariah [Islamic law]." Disparaging "innovations" and "superstitions" is usually code language for disparaging Muslim sects and subgroups that don't toe the fundamentalist line. Anyone who disagrees with Wahhabism, the IANA site continues, "does not only lie but commits a great sin and claims what is totally unfounded. He will, no doubt, receive what Allah has promised to all the fabricators of lies."

The IANA, based in Ypsilanti, Michigan, rejected Western culture as decadent and ungodly. "A knowledgeable Muslim will find it hard to integrate into a non-Islamic society of the United States," Alahmari, the group's chairman, told *The New York Times* a month after 9/11. "We don't feel Wahhabism is something different" from other approaches to Islam, he added. "It is a purification of Islam." The IANA had about a dozen employees. It received roughly half its funding from the Saudi government and the rest from private donors, mostly Saudi.

If American society was so distasteful, why would the IANA's immigrant activists do their proselytizing here? Perhaps for the same sort of practical reasons that a Saudi grad student would seek his Ph.D. in Idaho. The United States may encourage mixing of the sexes and separation of religion and state, but it also boasts high-quality secular universities that dispense valuable doctorates. American Muslims offer a prosperous and growing target for fundamentalist missionaries. And Wahhabi proselytizers apparently enjoy some of the same American attractions that appeal to millions of other visitors. Before a family trip to the Pacific Northwest in spring 2002, Alahmari sent al-Hussayen an e-mail cheerfully seeking tourism tips: "Remember to tell us if there are beautiful parks or museums that deserve our seeing during our short visit."

The IANA sponsored an annual conference featuring speakers sounding a consistent theme of victimization. The Egyptian-American scholar Khaled Abou El Fadl, who was a graduate student in the United States in the 1990s, recalled that IANA conferences were well known for appeals that went something like this: "'Oh, brothers, they're after Islam. Save us. Help us save Islam.' There would be a lot of stories about the rapes of Muslim women [and] how Indian soldiers urinated on the Quran."

The IANA thus afforded al-Hussayen a means, beyond personal devotion, to express his dedication to defending and promoting Islam, even while far from home. It was a largely private means—online and at occasional conferences—off the radarscope of his American colleagues at the University of Idaho. Volunteering for the group and supporting it financially also fulfilled al-Hussayen's Islamic obligation of zakat, or charitable sacrifice.

At times he demonstrated amusement over locals who took a dim view of Islam. In a phone conversation with a friend in March 2002, he recounted attending a lecture by an evangelical Christian. The speaker's simplistic and irrelevant prescription for resolving strife between Israeli Jews and Arab Muslims struck al-Hussayen as "a comedy." The lecturer, he said, insisted that "the world needs Christianity to live in peace. So the solution for the Middle East crisis will be if everybody believed in Jesus, then everybody will reconcile as if nothing ever happened." Laughing, according to the transcript, al-Hussayen went on to say that the evangelical took a swipe at Wahhabis, saying that they prohibit women from driving or even riding in the front seat of cars. That's actually true of some Saudi Wahhabis. But Al-Hussayen challenged the speaker: "I said, 'For your information, I am Saudi, and my mother and wife ride next to me in the car.'"

Al-Hussayen, though devout, didn't adhere to all of Wahhabism's dictates. He had cordial professional dealings with non-Muslim professors and students—both women and men. In a letter written from jail in fall 2003, he praised the University of Idaho for its "very distinguished and high academic level on top of its kind and cooperative community and charming nature." His closest ties, though, were with fellow Saudis, and he obviously shared the IANA's aspiration to safeguard "correct" Islam against corruption or criticism. When communicating privately with like-minded Muslims, defensiveness about his religion, which he didn't display to most people at the University of Idaho, sometimes came to the surface. In an e-mail to an IANA colleague on September 17, 2001, he opposed posting on the group's English-language Web sites fatwas that condemned the attacks and said nothing more. Instead, he said, the IANA should explain "Islam as a whole." He added: "I'd rather be silent than being very weak and afraid and rush to show all the fatwas that show I am against [the attacks]." The IANA essentially followed his admonition, condemning 9/11 while insisting that Islam was not to blame.

The IANA's Arabic-language Web pages were more inflammatory than the English versions, a divergence that is common on fundamentalist Islamic sites. After the 9/11 attacks the IANA Web site Islamway.com—another one that al-Hussayen helped oversee—posted this statement in English: "We, the Islamic Assembly of North America, condemn the killing of innocent people as much as we condemn the false accusations against innocent people." Equating three thousand murders with "false accusations against innocent people" seems callous, but at least the first part of the statement has a conciliatory tone. Just two days *before* 9/11, however, the Arabic version of the same IANA site had carried a more sinister posting. Jihad is "the only means to eradicate all evil on a personal and general level," the author, who had fought the Soviets in Afghanistan, declared. "The only answer is to ignite and trigger an all-out war, a worldwide jihad."

Through his work with the IANA, al-Hussayen became involved in the online publication and broadcast of the writings of some of Saudi Arabia's best-known preachers, including Awakening Sheikh Safer al-Hawali, the author of the violently anti-Semitic and anti-American lecture "The Intifada and the New Tartars." On September 11, 2000, al-Hussayen had registered the IANA site Alasr.ws, an Arabic-language online magazine whose name means "The Age." In May 2001, Alasr.ws carried an article by a Saudi-trained Kuwaiti cleric entitled "The Rule on Suicide Bombing." Sheikh Hamed al-Ali parsed various ways that a mujahid may attack his enemy, knowing he will die in the process. A fighter may kill himself, the cleric asserted, "when he knows that this will lead to killing a great number of the enemy, and that he could not kill them without killing himself also, or to destroy a vital center of the enemy's leadership or his military power." Without identifying the enemy in question, the sheikh continued, "In modern times, this can be accomplished through the modern means of bombing or by bringing down an airplane on an important site that causes the enemy great losses." Some terrorism experts later speculated that this fatwa provided religious permission for the 9/11 attacks, although investigators didn't turn up evidence that the hijackers knew of Sheikh Ali's pronouncement.

UNDER SUSPICION

The heightened wariness that followed the 9/11 attacks reached all the way to the teller's desk at the Moscow, Idaho, branch of U.S. Bank. When an employee there became suspicious about foreign wire transfers of thousands of dollars into an account held by Sami Omar al-Hussayen, she contacted the FBI. (All told, al-Hussayen allegedly handled more than three hundred thousand dollars while in Idaho.) The information from the bank was turned over to the Inland Northwest Joint Terrorism Task Force. Formed in 1998 to investigate white supremacists, the FBI-led task force had seen a big part of its mission evaporate in 2000, when the main branch of the violent Aryan Nations movement collapsed after a series of arrests and convictions. The 9/11 attacks provided the task force with a new purpose.

U.S. Attorney General John Ashcroft, determined to arrest terrorists and project an aggressive profile in the wake of the FBI's failure to stop the worst attack ever on American soil, had instructed federal agents and prosecutors to employ a preemptive strategy that he compared with Robert F. Kennedy's pursuit of organized crime in the 1960s. In speeches, Ashcroft recalled that Kennedy's men weren't embarrassed to arrest mobsters for the equivalent of spitting on the sidewalk. "Let the terrorists among us be warned," Ashcroft proclaimed. "If you overstay your visa, even by one day, we will arrest you. If you violate a local law, you will be put in jail and kept in custody as long as possible. We will use every available statute. We will seek every available prosecutorial advantage."

At the Inland Northwest Joint Terrorism Task Force, the lead from the bank branch in Moscow landed on the desk of FBI Special Agent Michael Gneckow. Before joining the FBI in 1996, Gneckow had served for a decade with the Naval Criminal Investigative Service, focusing on terrorism threats against American military installations. His investigation of al-Hussayen's bank accounts grew into a broader probe of the IANA and its various arms. The FBI developed the theory that the IANA might have followed the example of other Muslim charities in the United States that sought donations for humanitarian causes but allegedly siphoned off funds for terrorist groups. In late 2001 and 2002, the federal government shut down several other Muslim nonprofits, although the charities denied wrongdoing. Would the IANA be next?

In its scrutiny of Muslim charities in the United States, the FBI suspected that wealthy Saudis had been laundering money meant for extremist causes by donating it first to Islamic nonprofits. It didn't escape Special Agent Gneckow's attention that al-Hussayen was a well-connected Saudi citizen. The agent learned that the grad student controlled six bank accounts and had been passing along money to the IANA, some of it flowing originally from Saudi Arabia. One donor the FBI became intensely interested in was al-Hussayen's uncle Saleh Abdel Rahman al-Hussayen. Uncle Saleh, who was in his early seventies, held the prestigious administrative post of president of the affairs of the Holy Mosque in Mecca and the Prophet's Mosque in Medina. He had sent his nephew about $135,000, in installments, which Sami allegedly then turned over to the IANA.

Saleh had a deeper history in the United States. He had been a director of the SAAR Foundation, a Muslim charitable organization in Northern Virginia that was the subject of a separate federal investigation. Neither Saleh nor SAAR was indicted, but the Northern Virginia probe did lead to the conviction of two men. One, Abdurahman Alamoudi, admitted he had been involved in a bizarre Libyan plot to assassinate the ruler of Saudi Arabia.

The more the FBI looked into Saleh's past, the more suspicious he seemed. In the summer of 2001 he and his wife had toured the United States and met with their nephew Sami and IANA officials in Michigan. Then, in the days before the terrorist attacks, Saleh and his wife stayed in a Marriott Residence Inn in Herndon, Virginia. Patronizing the Marriott at the same time were three of the hijackers of the plane that crashed into the Pentagon. Investigators thought there might be some very significant dots to be connected between the al-Hussayens and 9/11. As it turned out, no evidence surfaced linking Saleh to the suicide terrorism plot, and his hotel accommodations appear to have been a coincidence. The most likely explanation for his presence in Herndon was that he was visiting Northern Virginia friends from SAAR circles. By late 2001 Uncle Saleh was back in Saudi Arabia (and he declined my requests for an interview). But even without proof, the FBI never fully accepted that his presence in the United States in the summer of 2001 was innocent, according to people familiar with the probe.

Agents only got more excited as they received translations of the IANA's Arabic Web sites. If Sami had played a role in distributing discussions of holy war and suicide bombings, maybe he and the IANA were financing and encouraging terrorism. From the FBI's perspective, there had to be *something* illegal going on here.

Since 9/11 the Bush administration and Congress have rewritten laws to make it easier for investigators to pursue terrorism cases. Among the changes effected by the USA Patriot Act was the expansion of the prohibition of material support of terrorism. Already forbidden before 9/11 were such obvious sorts of aid as providing weapons or a safe house. Existing law also covered those who offered "training" or "financial services" to terrorists. The Patriot Act added "expert advice and assistance" to the list. The idea was to make it easier to prosecute, for example, a civil engineer who advised on how to blow up a building. But could the Patriot Act provision be used to target the webmaster for a group that allegedly used the Internet to encourage mass killings? The al-Hussayen case would be the Justice Department's first Internet terrorism prosecution. With Attorney

General Ashcroft's marching orders ringing in their ears, investigators were thinking expansively. They were also thinking that in the course of eavesdropping on al-Hussayen's every communication, they might find evidence connecting him in a more direct, old-fashioned way to the support or financing of terrorism.

For nearly a year, beginning in early 2002, the FBI exhaustively monitored al-Hussayen's phone calls and e-mail, in all, nearly thirty thousand communications to and from him. According to government officials, this surveillance was not part of the controversial National Security Agency electronic monitoring program that *The New York Times* brought to light in December 2005. The NSA eavesdropping sparked controversy because the Bush administration had ordered the monitoring of hundreds and possibly thousands of people without seeking warrants from the Foreign Intelligence Surveillance Court. In the al-Hussayen case, prosecutors said they did obtain permission from that court.

The foreign intelligence court was set up in the 1970s to oversee investigations of spies operating in the United States. After 9/11 the court, like the FBI, turned its attention to potential terrorists. More permissive than conventional federal courts in letting investigators poke through suspects' affairs, the foreign intelligence court issues warrants without demanding the usual showing of probable cause that a crime has been committed. Cases that come before the court remain secret, and evidence gathered with its warrants traditionally *wasn't* turned over to criminal prosecutors (thus the absence of the usual probable cause requirement). In the classic spy case, the evidence might be used to keep track of Soviet agents posing as diplomats. If the Justice Department decided to prosecute the target of such an investigation, a separate team of FBI agents would have to start a criminal investigation from scratch, seeking conventional warrants after showing probable cause and using none of the evidence gathered with a foreign intelligence warrant. After 9/11 a bipartisan majority in Congress concluded that segregating intelligence gathering from law enforcement had impeded the government's pursuit of terrorists, who were now more of a threat than old-fashioned spies. The Patriot Act—and related changes to Justice Department procedures—encouraged investigators to think more aggressively about using evidence collected with foreign intelligence warrants to build criminal terrorism cases. An appellate panel of the foreign intelligence court affirmed this change. The al-Hussayen case became one of the early demonstrations of how the new approach would work.

The FBI monitored the Saudi grad student month after month. There were thousands of hours of conversation and thousands of e-mails, mostly in Arabic. A half dozen FBI translators and analysts chipped away at this towering pile of communication; the government declined to say how much they ultimately rendered into English. Transcripts that surfaced at trial showed Al-Hussayen deeply involved in monitoring IANA Web sites and juggling balky server computers. He served on the IANA's board of trustees but also appeared to be the group's main troubleshooter and one-man human relations department. In an August 2002 phone call he told a colleague that he had arranged long distance to hire Saudi women in Riyadh to upload audiotapes of Islamic lectures to IANA sites. "The sisters are a really great resource," he explained. "You know how they are sitting at home, looking for jobs and money. But if Allah helps you get to them, their work is superb."

What the FBI didn't find in all its eavesdropping was any direct evidence that al-Hussayen had written a check to a terrorist group or designed a Web site for one. He helped oversee the IANA, but that group continued to operate as a legal, tax-exempt nonprofit organization. Prosecutors nevertheless followed Attorney General Ashcroft's spitting-on-the-sidewalk approach and decided to seek an indictment.

Over his years of travel between Saudi Arabia and the United States, al-Hussayen had certified on immigration forms that he had come to the United States "solely for the purpose of pursuing a full course of study." Focusing on the word "solely," the government concluded that he had lied, because he spent large amounts of time on his IANA chores. When asked to list all "professional, social, and charitable organizations" to which he had a connection, al-Hussayen provided the names of two computer associations but not the IANA. Prosecutors persuaded a federal grand jury in Boise, Idaho, to indict al-Hussayen on eleven overlapping counts of visa fraud and false statements. Terrorism charges could wait.

～

To announce the al-Hussayen indictment in February 2003, federal, state, and local officials put on a show the likes of which Moscow, Idaho, had never seen. Reporters and television cameras jammed the town's snug council chambers to hear from a posse of high-ranking investigators. "We're not at the end of the trail; we are at the beginning of the trail," Chip Burrus, a senior FBI agent, declared. Speaking off-camera and on condition of anonymity, ófficials told the *Seattle Post-Intelligencer* that the bureaucratic-sounding visa charges didn't reflect "the central role that investigators believe al-Hussayen has played in the flow of al Qaeda cash." The paper referred to al-Hussayen as a suspected "terrorist bagman."

The University of Idaho president Robert Hoover seconded the notion that al-Hussayen was guilty—of something. "I think all of us at the University of Idaho feel betrayed about how our institution was used," he told reporters. Idaho Governor Dirk Kempthorne also voiced dismay: "When this sort of thing happens in a state like Idaho, in a community like Moscow . . . where no one would ever expect activities like this would occur, then this network exists throughout the United States."

From jail al-Hussayen insisted on his innocence in statements conveyed by his lawyer. Despite being accused of betrayal by the head of the university where he had studied for nearly four years, al-Hussayen struck a magnanimous tone in an open letter addressed "Dear Beloved Students of the University of Idaho" and posted on an English-language Web site supporting him. Writing in fall 2003, al-Hussayen said, "With great respect, I greet my virtuous teachers, all the faculty members and my dear neighbors and colleagues on the occasion of the new academic year." The letter continued:

> I wish I were able to share with you the exciting feelings of being back to school together with my wife and three children, Muhanad, Tameem,

and Ziad, whom I have not seen them [*sic*] for more than 6 months, in other words, from the moment I was arrested and imprisoned. You can imagine how hard and painful it is to be forcibly separated from those whom you really love.

Finally, I abundantly and plentifully thank everyone who has supported and defended me in this terrible ordeal and defended the beliefs of justice and human rights that the American people believe in. Thanks a million to the faculty, the library staff, my colleagues, and neighbors who embody those believes [*sic*] that the American friends observe.

In a preliminary court hearing in March 2003, the legal team the Saudi Embassy had hired to defend al-Hussayen tried to counter the U.S. government's grim portrait of the grad student. The immediate goal was to show that al-Hussayen posed no danger or flight risk and could be released while awaiting trial. His older brother Abdul, a thirty-four-year-old cardiologist doing research at the University of Toronto, testified via videophone that the family had always taken a moderate approach to religion.

"Do you hate the West or the United States?" David Nevin, the lead defense attorney, asked.

"Not at all," Abdul answered. Referring to his affinity for Canada, he continued: "I've done my training here. I intend to work here, and why would I stay in a place that I hate?" His younger brother, he said, "always expresses how happy he is to stay and train in the United States. He has expressed how happy his kids were."

"Have you ever heard an expression of any kind from Sami in support of terrorism?"

"No, not at all."

Another defense witness was Marwan Mossaad, an undergraduate at the University of Idaho and a friend of al-Hussayen's. "He is the most cheerful guy," Mossaad testified. "He's never upset. He's never angry." One time Mossaad, a track star, hurt his foot and couldn't walk. Al-Hussayen brought groceries to his door. As for extremism, Mossaad testified, "He's the person that knows exactly what Islam is about and can see through the turbulence of the different extreme groups versus the true nature of the religion."

Mossaad shed light on Muslim student life and al-Hussayen's role in Moscow. In his mid-twenties, Mossaad, the son of professionals, grew up mostly in Egypt and Kuwait. He started college at Cairo University, but his success as a runner kindled an ambition to compete in America. The University of Idaho indicated the most interest, so that was where he decided to go. His clean-shaven face and light complexion didn't mark him as Arab, and he had no trouble blending in on campus. He married an American classmate who, he joked, showed no sign of converting.

Subconsciously 9/11 may have stirred something in him, Mossaad told me. About a year after the attacks he started going to the mosque in town. "It was time to get serious" about being a Muslim, he explained. That was when he became friends with al-Hussayen. Mossaad, an easygoing and charismatic young man, succeeded the Saudi as MSA president.

He insisted that he knew nothing about his friend's work with the IANA. "It is not our nature to ask each other about each other's business," he said a little testily. Al-Hussayen came from a well-to-do Saudi family, one that took seriously the Islamic obligation to give to charity every year, Mossaad noted. Al-Hussayen also knew a lot about computers. Mossaad couldn't see why the feds were surprised, therefore, by anything they had turned up. "Of course Sami's donating money" to promote Islam, he said. "Of course Sami's making a Web site." Mossaad thought the U.S. government was just trying to intimidate Muslim immigrants.

The federal magistrate who held the preliminary hearing ruled that al-Hussayen wasn't a danger or a flight risk and could be released pending trial. But the prosecutors didn't want him freed. They arranged for the defendant to be transferred to the custody of immigration officials. Apart from the criminal charges pending against him, Al-Hussayen was subject to deportation for his alleged visa violations. The deportation process provides fewer individual rights than the criminal system, and immigration officials often can hold potential deportees for indefinite periods. By engaging in the legal fiction that al-Hussayen was temporarily leaving the criminal system and entering the deportation pipeline, prosecutors could defy the federal magistrate's release order, and in practical terms, there wasn't anything for the defense to do about it.

"ROOTED IN AMERICA"

The loosening of U.S. immigration restrictions on non-Europeans in 1965 opened the door to Muslim students, thousands of whom arrived in the years that followed. They founded Muslim Students Association chapters that in turn gave birth to mosques and Islamic centers. Students formed the vanguard of a highly educated and prosperous segment of the American Muslim population. A tightening of visa policies in the wake of 9/11 has contributed to a drop in overseas applications to American graduate schools, but with a counterintuitive exception: applicants from the Middle East have *increased* in recent years—by 7 percent in 2005, compared with a 5 percent decline in foreign applications overall, according to the Council of Graduate Schools. The council didn't offer an explanation for the striking aberration. Admissions of graduate applicants from the Middle East rose 12 percent in 2005, compared with a 3 percent increase for all foreigners, showing that American universities remain relatively receptive to Muslims.

While Muslim students overall have served as a source of fresh perspectives, some have arrived with distinctly hostile views toward American government and society. Those views are sometimes reinforced at Muslim Students Association meetings and absorbed by some Muslim students born in the United States. MSA chapters across the country strongly condemn terrorism. Yet some members of these groups express respect for the religious and political arguments of Middle Eastern preachers who endorse the destruction of Israel, speak casually about snuffing out Jews in general, and spin dangerous fantasies about Western plots against Islam. Such apparent contradictions can make it difficult for outsiders to understand the true mind-sets of some young Muslims.

The immigrants who formed the national MSA in the 1960s were refugees from political repression in Egypt and other Muslim countries.

The members of this generation were heavily influenced by various strains of fundamentalism, especially that of the Muslim Brotherhood and Wahhabism. For decades the MSA had an unabashed fundamentalist orientation, fueled by Saudi money, according to Hamid Algar, who has taught Islamic studies at the University of California at Berkeley since 1965. By the 1980s fundamentalist fervor was moderating among most Muslims who had settled in the United States, started families, and built careers. But new waves of immigrant students continually renewed the flames of extremism, with ideological fuel and ready financing from Saudi-backed charities and wealthy individual Saudis. A number of U.S.-based Muslim groups worked in parallel with some MSA leaders to fan those flames. The Islamic Assembly of North America, whose followers were mostly college and graduate students, was one such group.

Altaf Husain, the national president of the MSA from 1997 through 2003, told me that most young Muslim immigrants and second-generation Muslim Americans interpret radical Islamic messages in an unthreatening way. He claimed that they screen out calls for martyrdom and violence and instead focus on demands for justice, whether in Palestine, Iraq, Chechnya, or the United States. "There was a fringe or minority type of group of either students or graduate students or outsiders that was espousing an anti-Western set of views pre–September eleven," he remarked. "We worked hard to put an end to that . . . I personally dealt with this to cut it off." Under his leadership, he added, the national MSA stopped accepting any funding from overseas. Husain, an earnest social worker born in India, said that MSA chapters "are much more mainstream in thinking and much more rooted in America" than they were in 1987, when he started college.

MSA chapters have branched out from proselytizing and Muslim-only religious activities. Often now headed by young people brought up in the United States, these groups do nonsectarian good works, such as feed the hungry campaigns timed to coincide with the Ramadan fasting period. Their political seminars and rallies tilt against U.S. foreign policy but are rarely more extreme than what is heard from secular leftist students. Some students, regardless of religion or cause, will test out radical rhetoric on campus that they later tone down or abandon. Sounding a note of reassurance, Husain said, "Young Muslims love the freedom of religion here."

For the most part, anti-American dissent among Muslims at the University of Idaho fell within the boundaries of campus political debate about U.S. foreign policy. Muslim students, including al-Hussayen, opposed U.S. military action in response to 9/11 and deplored the lack of American pressure on Israel to withdraw its settlements from the Palestinian territories. "I'm against occupying any land or country," al-Hussayen's friend Mossaad said. This didn't mean he hated Americans. "There is a separation between people and governments," he said. "When you live in this country and have so many friends, half agree with the government, and half are against the government. You can't say you are against America." In sermons and lectures at the Moscow mosque, al-Hussayen would sometimes "include some politics," criticizing Israel or U.S. policy toward Iraq, Mossaad said. "But it was more about religion itself and fasting and things like that."

One afternoon Mossaad and Ahmad al-Own, a personable twenty-year-old Idaho sophomore from Kuwait, sat down with me at a campus coffeehouse for some political discussion. Al-Own, another admirer of al-Hussayen's, wore an Adidas baseball cap and a jersey of black and gold, the colors of the University of Idaho Vandals. We discussed a couple of the radical sheikhs whose views al-Hussayen had helped circulate online.

Al-Own shrugged, not seeing the legal significance of al-Hussayen's actions. Many Muslim students, especially those from the Persian Gulf, admire the bold way fundamentalist preachers deride Israel and American support for the Jewish state. "It's not something hidden. They're not saying secrets," he said of the sheikhs. The fact that Osama bin Laden also admired the sheikhs—tapes of sermons given by one of them were found in a bin Laden residence in Afghanistan—didn't impress al-Own or Mossaad. "These are top scholars, brave men," al-Own said. They had served prison time in Saudi Arabia in the 1990s for criticizing the country's government.

Al-Own added that contacting controversial clerics isn't unusual, although he said he hadn't done so himself. "You can call to ask advice" on religious questions, he explained. "I don't find it shocking for Sami to have their phone numbers or that he sent them e-mail."

~⊃

Kim Lindquist, a veteran assistant United States attorney, wanted to make it clear that he had nothing against Muslims coming to this country for an education. "Muslim student organizations by and large are good, whole-some, and need to be there," Lindquist told me one morning at the federal prosecutor's office in a glassy modern building in downtown Boise. But, he added, immigrants "can make that transition fairly subtly and fairly quietly from appropriate student activities to a manifestation of things that are inappropriate, including advocacy of radical Islam." In most cases, this radicalization is "more a social phenomenon than a criminal phenomenon," Lindquist said. But al-Hussayen was different. "This was more than a computer science grad student," the prosecutor said. "There was something else going on."

Boise, three hundred miles from Moscow in southwest Idaho, has a population of two hundred thousand, making it the state's biggest city. In the mid-1800s it served as a supply and distribution center for gold and sil-ver miners. Today, in addition to being the state capital, it is the headquar-ters of an impressive array of big corporations, including the agribusiness J. R. Simplot and the forest products company Boise Cascade. Immigrants from a wide range of places have come to the city, which is at the base of the Rocky Mountain foothills. Basque sheepherders arrived in the 1930s, when their specialty was still a significant business in the area, and their descendants have blended into Boise's mainstream. More recently the tol-erant ambience and healthy economy have drawn Muslims—an estimated two thousand in all—including refugees from the Balkan wars of the 1990s.

Boise isn't New York or Washington, D.C. Residents don't think of themselves as vulnerable to international terrorism. Peering down from the wall of the conference room in the U.S. attorney's office where Kim Lindquist discussed the al-Hussayen case was a large stuffed elk head. It had been the victim of poachers federal prosecutors sent to prison. Traditionally, chasing fish and wildlife violators was a top priority in the office. Now there were daily conference calls with the Counterterrorism Section of the Department of Justice in Washington.

Perhaps because of the unlikelihood of Islamic terrorism in Idaho, officials in Washington at first regarded the al-Hussayen investigation with skepticism. Yes, Attorney General Ashcroft wanted federal authorities searching for sleeper cells, but a terrorism case based on Internet sites? In other material support of terrorism prosecutions, the government had gone after men who had set off for training camps in Afghanistan. Lindquist and his supervisor, Terry Derden, made several trips to Washington to sell their case to officials there. The Justice Department bosses asked each time whether al-Hussayen "was sending guns or bombs," Derden recalled. "We said what he's sending is more dangerous than bombs": expert advice on using the Internet to call holy warriors to battle.

Steeling the Boise prosecutors in their determination was a paid outside consultant named Rita Katz, who is fluent in Arabic and specializes in decoding extremist Islamic Web sites. Katz runs a small nonprofit research group called the SITE (Search for International Terrorist Entities) Institute, the location of which she asks be kept a secret. She explained to the Boise prosecutors how "jihadist" Web sites typically feature innocuous material in English, accompanied by terrorist propaganda in Arabic. With characteristic flair, she labeled the IANA "a glorified al Qaeda recruitment center." Katz, widely considered a leading authority in her field, isn't known for understatement.

Eventually her view won out, and the skeptics at the Justice Department gave Boise the green light. That meant additional manpower to prepare for trial: two more prosecutors to back up Lindquist and Derden; several FBI and INS agents; and a squad of intelligence analysts, translators, and document management specialists. The government would tie al-Hussayen to specific people who had been convicted in other terrorism cases, Derden predicted confidently. "There's a mountain of evidence," he told me before trial.

While the prosecutors got ready in Boise, the ranks of al-Hussayen's backers—Muslim and non-Muslim—grew steadily in Moscow. Some trekked to the Canyon County Jail near Boise, where al-Hussayen was held in a small isolation cell. Government officials said he was segregated from other inmates for his protection. Jailers kept him locked in his cell twenty-three hours a day. He was permitted a small shelf of books on computers and a laptop, but not a connection to the Internet.

John Dickinson, his doctoral adviser, continued to work with al-Hussayen on his dissertation on computer network security. The government's suspicion of the grad student had intensified when the FBI learned he knew a lot about how to protect, and therefore break into, computer systems. Papers al-Hussayen mailed to Dickinson from jail disappeared on several occasions, the professor said, perhaps intercepted by the government. Dickinson thought it was ludicrous to imagine that al-Hussayen intended any harm. "The government connected these dots: hijackers to Sami's uncle to Sami," Dickinson wrote in an e-mail to me. "In today's America, associating with a terrorist, such as having an uncle who stayed in the same hotel as a terrorist, is damning enough evidence" for an indictment.

Al-Hussayen's supporters used the Internet to publicize letters he wrote from jail. In one, addressed to an unspecified "Dear son," al-Hussayen appeared to direct his pained rhetorical questions to a broader audience. "Could a pen ever describe the ordeal of Jacob when he lost Joseph? Or could a poet or great writer ever portray how much they miss their baby?" Having alluded to the Old Testament and secular literature, al-Hussayen concluded, "Your hope in Allah the Almighty should reassure you and the thought of His great rewards should make you feel better. Your dad."

A local organization, the Latah County Human Rights Task Force, held a potluck dinner and gathered hundreds of names on a petition supporting al-Hussayen. The Saudi Student Association sponsored a dinner honoring him on Martin Luther King Day. The University of Idaho's law school organized a symposium on the Patriot Act at which Maha al-Hussayen haltingly read a statement asking President Bush to release her husband. On another day more than a hundred people came to a backyard barbecue and rally in Moscow. A burly farmer approached Maha and, in a breach of Saudi etiquette, threw his arms around her and said, "Honey, I just feel terrible for you." Maha laughed about it later.

S. M. Ghazanfar, the retired University of Idaho economics professor, attended some of these events and felt reassured by the presence of so many non-Muslims. "That's what America is all about," he said, "pluralism and multiculturalism."

Apparently seeking to set the stage for al-Hussayen's criminal trial in 2004, the government tried to deport his wife and children, arguing that Maha too was sympathetic to terrorism. In September 2003, seven months after her husband's arrest, she had a phone conversation (monitored by the FBI) in which she described to a friend the profusion of American flags on the second anniversary of 9/11. Maha said in Arabic, "As for me, I bought a sandal that has a flag, so the whole of America would be under my feet, and may the bountiful God increase their terror."

In an earlier conversation recorded by agents, Maha had discussed the October 2002 violent takeover of a Moscow theater by Chechen rebels, who seized hundreds of hostages. More than 150 people died in a botched rescue attempt. Repeatedly, as a woman named Latifa told her about the terrorist assault, Maha said, "Praise be to Allah."

Latifa then said, "Yes, praise be to Allah. But I do not love America." She asked Maha whether she loved America.

"No," Maha said, laughing. "Kraft cheese. I love Kraft cheese."

On the basis of this, the FBI labeled Maha a security risk and moved to have her expelled.

Lawyers representing Maha didn't have access to the original recordings but raised questions about whether her comments had been translated and interpreted correctly. For example, in Arabic, the phrase "praise be to Allah" doesn't necessarily signal approval. It can be the equivalent of "wow" or "oh, my God." Maha's odd-sounding remark about her sandals might have reflected little more than her anger over her husband's being prosecuted by the United States. "May the bountiful God increase their terror" sounds ominous, but it isn't clear how the comment threatened national security.

The interpretation issue was never resolved. Given her husband's situation, Maha was in no position to antagonize the government. She agreed to return to Saudi Arabia with her children before the trial began in April 2004.

ISLAM ON TRIAL

Days before Maha's departure a federal grand jury in Boise issued an expanded indictment of her husband. Attorney General Ashcroft himself announced the more severe charges in Washington, D.C. "Terrorists," he said, describing the al-Hussayen prosecution, "increasingly use the Internet to communicate their evil plans and to garner recruits, money and other material support for their violent activities. We will aggressively pursue and prosecute those who use their specialized computer skills to knowingly and intentionally support such terrorist conspiracies."

Supplementing the original eleven visa counts, the grand jury added three counts charging that from the late 1990s until he was arrested, al-Hussayen had provided "material support and resources to terrorists." He allegedly did this by running Web sites and an e-mail group that helped recruit fighters and collect funds "for violent jihad in Israel, Chechnya and other places." The indictment noted that one section of the Islamway.com site that al-Hussayen oversaw urged Muslims to contribute money to the Palestinian group Hamas to "assist their brothers in their honorable jihad against the dictatorial Zionist Jewish enemy." Islamway at one point included a link to the official Hamas Web site where such donations could be made.

The final indictment was silent about Osama bin Laden and 9/11. At the pretrial hearing in March 2003, the lead prosecutor, Kim Lindquist, had promised evidence "that the defendant has direct contact with indi-viduals directly associated with Mr. bin Laden and does espouse and sup-port Mr. bin Laden's beliefs and activities." But the FBI hadn't been able to connect al-Hussayen to al Qaeda in a direct way. Likewise, there was no mention in the expanded indictment of Uncle Saleh al-Hussayen.

Before and during their client's trial Sami's lawyers argued that the government was trying to punish the Saudi for his opinions. The legal standard on this issue comes from *Brandenburg v. Ohio*, a 1969 First Amend-ment ruling that reversed the conviction of a Ku Klux Klan leader in Ohio for advocating racial strife. The Supreme Court said the government may punish advocacy of illegal action, but only if the advocacy "is directed to inciting or producing imminent lawless action and is likely to incite or pro-duce such action."

Prosecutors in the al-Hussayen case conceded that people have a right to praise terrorist groups, but they said they were seeking to punish acts: the raising of funds for Hamas and the recruitment of terrorist troops. Al-Hussayen's expert advice, the government said, was comparable to "bomb-making instruction or piloting an aircraft." U.S. District Judge Ed-ward Lodge sided with prosecutors and declined to trim back the indict-ment. Still, the First Amendment was to resurface before the proceedings ended.

When the al-Hussayen trial began on April, 13, 2004, it seemed as if the government wanted to put the religion of Islam in the dock. Lead prose-cutor Lindquist in his opening argument declared that Islam encouraged jihad—and not the innocent kind. Ordinary jihad could mean "the struggle against evil, including against the influence of the infidel, the nonbeliever," he said. But there was also "the doctrine of extreme jihad, or terrorism." Jurors could read on an overhead screen that the "Doctrine of Extreme Ji-had" drew "authority from historical Islam" and tried to "replicate vio-lence of Medieval Islamic Empire," with the aim of making the "entire world Islamic by force if necessary." This was the sort of Islam the defen-dant was wrapped up with, the prosecutor said. "The evidence will show his dual persona, one face to the public and the other private face—the private face of extreme jihad."

When it was his turn, David Nevin, the lead defense lawyer, said al-Hussayen was innocent, of course: "He is not an angry Islamic fundamentalist bent on murder, maiming, kidnapping." But Nevin also came to the defense of the shadow second defendant, Islam itself. "Judaism, Christianity, and Islam share common roots," he said. In Muslim eyes, "Jews and Christians are 'People of the Book,' and they have special status." Muslims revere Jesus and Moses as prophets. Muslims attend mosques, as Christians go to church and Jews to synagogue. Islam is less foreign than you think, the lawyer told the jury. It puts "a heavy emphasis on hard work and industriousness, with hospitality and respect for elders." Gesturing toward the bearded young man at the defense table, Nevin said his client and his organization, the IANA, aimed at nothing more than "Muslim religious outreach." Al-Hussayen offered a tentative smile to the jury.

Look closely at all the phone calls and e-mail the government intercepted, his defense lawyer urged. You won't hear anything about "some conspiracy to fundraise or to recruit for violent jihad."

After the prosecutor had spoken, John Steger, listening from his front-row seat in the jury box, thought, "Holy God, this guy's going to jail for life." Then the jury heard from the defense, and Steger's thinking flipped; it sounded as if al-Hussayen had "done nothing wrong." They'd be lucky if they reached a verdict in six months, Steger thought.

The judge had dismissed a number of prospective jurors who said their religious or political views would make it tough for them to be fair. Of the twelve people selected to decide the case, few had had any substantive contact with Islam or Muslims. Steger, a retired civil engineer with the U.S. Forest Service who was in his late sixties, was raised Catholic, but he considered himself open-minded. He once had a disagreement with his wife about Muslim culture that led to a four-hour research session at the Boise State University library. Steger said he discovered that the Quran contains "all the sort of stuff any Bible has: love thy neighbor, be at peace, fight only to protect yourself; nothing about killing anybody, except in self-defense, nothing about stoning non-virgins."

Prosecutors had promised a case about terrorism and about a religion heavily focused on jihad. But for days jurors instead heard testimony about the corporate history of the IANA and the rules governing foreign student visas. The upshot of all this was that al-Hussayen had failed on immigration forms to disclose his involvement with the IANA. Did this amount to willful deception? As his lawyer pointed out during cross-examination of government witnesses, al-Hussayen used his own checks to send money to the IANA. He even registered as the group's official agent in Idaho. But it also seemed plausible that the Saudi grad student might have worried that if he had volunteered his IANA tie, immigration officials would have asked unwelcome questions.

During the second week of trial the government expanded on its case against Islam. Into the witness box stepped the Egyptian-born scholar Ahmed Subhy Mansour. Speaking with a thick Arabic accent, Mansour provided a pithy overview of the religion. Islam rested on the Quran, which observant Muslims view as God's literal word. Mansour described what he called intellectual jihad, a personal struggle toward a legitimate goal. "Physical jihad," he said, is the military defense of religion and nation. With prosecutor Lindquist's prompting, he narrated Islam's early history and then got to his punch line: that the vast military conquests that expanded the Islamic Empire from India and China in the east to North Africa and Spain in the west had been illegitimate under Islamic law.

"In violation of the limits of jihad, the defensive limits of jihad—is that correct?" Lindquist asked.

"Yes, it is true," said Mansour. "It was against Islam."

To justify violating the Quran's limits on jihad, the witness said, Muslim scholars manufactured sayings attributed to the Prophet Muhammad that supported taking over new lands. Mansour thus contradicted the conventional Muslim version of history that Islamic expansion had enjoyed divine sanction and occurred with little bloodshed or forced conversion. Mansour explained that Muslim conquerors gave vanquished populations three options: fight, convert, or keep their own religion and pay a special tax to live under Muslim protection.

Lindquist wanted to make a different point, one without nuances. "So the goal of these aggressive Muslims at the time," he said, "was to conquer the whole world and turn it into Islam?"

"Yes."

"The extremists today want to restore this political power, this reality?"

"Yes, sir," Mansour replied. The scholar explained that modern Muslim radicals, harking back to the glory days of the Islamic Empire, have distorted the Quran and relied on made-up sayings of the Prophet to justify war against infidels and apostates.

"Sheikh Mansour," Lindquist asked, "according to the doctrine of modern extreme jihad, is aggressive violence permitted?"

"Yes, sir."

Now ready to connect this historical colloquy to the case at hand, the prosecutor asked, "Does that include killing civilians by means of suicide actions?"

"Yes."

And where do the extreme jihadists get their religious authority?

"They have no argument from Quran, but they have fatwa," Mansour said. "That means the verdict issued by Muslim scholars."

Fatwas justifying "martyrdom operations" were what al-Hussayen had helped put on the Internet.

Claribel Ingraham readily admitted that she and her fellow jurors started out knowing little about Islam or Muslims. What had she learned? "Basically, the Muslim religion has to do with caring for people, for being kind to people, for being helpful to people," she told me. "There's one portion of it—the extreme jihadists—who believe in martyrdom and believe in violence. But that was just a portion of it."

Raised a Methodist, Ingraham, a semiretired nurse, liked the idea of religions mixing. "I don't have any problem with the Muslims being over here," she told me. "Basically, they're probably really nice people." But she worried that al-Hussayen might have been up to something. "My feeling was he knew he wasn't coming over here *solely* for educational purposes. He was practically running IANA and all of the Web sites." She thought it was suspicious that he failed to disclose his role with IANA. "I really had a problem with that."

As the proceedings entered a fourth week, the government began unveiling the troubling material al-Hussayen was charged with disseminating. An impassive FBI analyst read aloud portions of the violently anti-Jewish and anti-American intifada lecture that al-Hussayen had helped make available as an audio file on the Internet. "Expel this hated country [Israel] that consists of those unclean, defiled, the cursed," the witness read. He also read a poem entitled "A Martyr Under 20 Years of Age," which al-Hussayen had forwarded electronically to one of his brothers in January 2003. The poem was posted on Islamtoday.net, the Web site of Salman al-Ouda, another cleric known as an Awakening Sheikh for his radicalizing effect and someone al-Hussayen had advised on technical matters. The poet sang the praises of a young suicide bomber: "I kiss a hand that pours death upon the ugly faces of the infidels, ferocious animals with their Talmud." In an introduction, which al-Hussayen also forwarded to his brother, Sheikh al-Ouda praised the poem as a "wonderful contribution."

The hateful rhetoric kept coming. The government called a computer expert to the witness stand to explain how in the spring of 2001 al-Hussayen had uploaded onto the IANA's Alasr.ws Web site the fatwa on crashing passenger planes, as well as three similar edicts justifying suicide bombing. These jurisprudential works provided reasons why "martyrdom operations" weren't covered by the Islamic ban on suicide. In one, Sheikh al-Ouda opined with relative restraint that such attacks were legitimate only against "infidels who declared war against the Muslims."

In a more expansive fatwa, "Regarding the Suicide Operations Against the Jews," Suliman al-Alwan began with the premise that "the inferior Jews, the source of defects and shortcomings, and the source of evil and depravity, are the most severe enemy of Allah, Islam, and its followers." This led him to the conclusion that "the best treatment and effective medicine to treat the brothers of monkeys and pigs is to perform martyrdom operations."

The fatwas all cited precedents from Islamic history of heroes charging against hostile forces to certain death. Another technique approved by tradition, according to Sheikh Humood al-Shuaibi, was to allow the infidels to bed down for the night and then crush them. If this were done "for jihad intentions," he said, "the children and women of the infidels" could be killed too.

To put the fatwas in context, the prosecution called Reuven Paz to the witness stand. Paz had served for many years as a senior intelligence official with Israel's Shin Bet security service. Now he ran an independent research group on terrorism. He testified that since the late 1990s Muslim fundamentalist organizations, both violent and nonviolent, had used Web sites to foment violent resistance against Israel, America, and Russia (in the case of the Chechen rebellion). Easy access to the Internet provides extremists "the largest audience possible in order to spread their messages to recruit people" and raise money, Paz said, and the IANA followed this pattern precisely.

Prosecutor Lindquist showed Paz the fatwas from Alasr.ws, the poem praising the young "martyr," and similar material the government had tried to tie to al-Hussayen.

"This extreme jihad content," Paz said, "was placed on the Web site in order to promote the support for suicide operations and promote the legitimacy for suicide operations in either Palestine or in other places of conflict with non-Muslims." Paz came to the same conclusion about material that al-Hussayen had posted on a Yahoo! e-mail group where more than two thousand users could exchange information and exhortations about Chechnya. In February 2000, for example, al-Hussayen contributed a "cry and call" for opposition to Russian forces: "Oh, Muslims in the East and in the West, fight the polytheists with your money, your selves, your tongues, and your prayers."

On cross-examination, Paz made two interesting concessions. He acknowledged that calls for jihad were all over the Internet, not just on sites linked to al-Hussayen. And the ex-intelligence official conceded that those who preach violent jihad speak to a highly receptive audience, at least in the Middle East. "There is a kind of a consensus in the Arab world that suicide operations are permitted against Israel," he testified. The defense asked if that meant that all Muslims who held that view were bad. "I am not here in order to value people as good guys or bad guys," Paz answered.

David Nevin had experience defending clients whom the government portrayed as having repugnant beliefs. In 1993 he had represented Kevin Harris, a friend of the white separatist Randy Weaver's. The federal government prosecuted the pair after the death of a deputy U.S. marshal during the bloody eleven-day shootout and siege at Ruby Ridge in the Idaho Panhandle. Nevin won his client's acquittal, a victory that helped build his reputation as Idaho's sharpest criminal defense lawyer. On the losing side for the government in the Ruby Ridge case was the same Kim Lindquist who was prosecuting al-Hussayen. The judge in the Ruby Ridge case was Edward Lodge, the al-Hussayen judge. If Ruby Ridge taught any lessons, one was that many ordinary Idahoans distrust the federal government and especially federal law enforcement officials. Idaho is a conservative state, but it has a wide libertarian streak that colors local opinions of agencies like the FBI and the U.S. Attorney's Office.

Nevin faced a challenge in the al-Hussayen case similar to that in Ruby Ridge: chipping away at the huge edifice of evidence that federal prosecutors had amassed, in hopes of creating cracks of reasonable doubt. For the white separatists, that meant showing that a murky gunfight hadn't unfolded quite the way the FBI claimed. In the al-Hussayen case, it meant first trying to keep out as much damning material as possible by arguing that the government couldn't hang other people's statements around his client's neck. When that didn't work—Judge Lodge allowed in most of what the government offered—Nevin fell back on the First Amendment. Under *Brandenburg v. Ohio*, the 1969 Supreme Court decision concerning a KKK leader, it is legal to endorse terrorism, as long as one doesn't incite imminent violence.

Judge Lodge, a blunt former Golden Gloves boxing champion appointed to the federal bench by President George H. W. Bush, listened closely and then usually ruled for the government. "The charges against the defendant do not criminalize speech itself," the judge said. He agreed with the prosecution that posting material on the Internet is more like action than expression. The question for the jury was whether al-Hussayen's actions amounted to aiding terrorism.

Taking a different tack, Nevin appealed to a grim strain of relativism. Al-Hussayen, he said, was merely amplifying opinions that are commonplace in the Middle East. Prosecution witness Reuven Paz had said as much. "Americans don't typically talk about this stuff around our dinner table, but I guarantee you, if the Israeli-Palestinian conflict were being played out in northern Arizona, let's say, this stuff would be on our minds all the time, and it is on the minds of people in the Middle East all the time," Nevin told the judge. "It is discussed in the press, discussed in media. This stuff is passed around all the time."

That didn't work either. In came more evidence, leaving Nevin with no option other than to show in cross-examination that in some cases the government was offering jurors only the worst parts of various articles and exhortations. The defense lawyer pointed to sections that focused more on prayer and diplomacy than on guns and bombs. But there wasn't much to nitpick about when the material in question urged the wholesale slaughter of Jews, referring to them as "the brothers of monkeys and pigs."

One critical bit of context that never surfaced at the trial was the vast universe of radical Islamic Web sites that carry information far more useful to potential terrorists than anything the government found on the IANA–al-Hussayen sites. After 9/11, al Qaeda and its offshoots began building what amounts to an online encyclopedia of mayhem, with information on how to build bombs, mix poisons, and attack American soldiers. *Al-Battar*, an online magazine associated with al Qaeda, provides advice on using weapons and conducting surveillance. In July 2005, the Egyptian Tawhid Wal Jihad Group went online to take credit for bombings in that country that killed ninety, as part of their "daring war against the Jews and Christians in the Land of Peace." Another site, Abu al-Bukhary, has urged attacks against American and Israeli targets and carried offerings such as "The Art of Kidnapping" and "Military Instructions to the Mujahedeen." According to some estimates, there are more than four thousand terrorist-related Web sites operating from computers around the world.

The prosecutors in Boise didn't want jurors to think about other Web sites because to do so risked making the IANA–al-Hussayen sites seem tame by comparison. The sites at issue in the trial could be said to recruit terrorists in only the most general sense: by applauding jihad and suicide bombing. For his part, David Nevin wouldn't risk jurors' seeing the more explicit terrorist sites and confusing them with the work of his client. The defense lawyer didn't want jurors to view al-Hussayen as part of the larger world of online Islamic fanatics.

The government had promised to introduce the jury to "living, breathing proof" that al-Hussayen's activities drew people to terrorism. Prosecutors considered candidates from three groups of Muslims who had been convicted in the United States since 9/11 on terrorism-related charges and who were thought to have been fans of fundamentalist Web sites: The so-called Portland Seven tried but failed to travel to Afghanistan to fight American troops. Six Yemeni-Americans from Lackawanna, New York, made it to an al Qaeda training camp in Afghanistan but came home without seeing combat. A third group of twelve men, some of whom planned to fight in Afghanistan or Kashmir, practiced paramilitary tactics with recreational paintball guns in the Virginia woods. All these plots had a bumbling quality, but terrorists, like common criminals, don't have to possess genius to do great harm. Most of the participants received long prison terms, and their objectives provide a reminder that a small portion of the Muslim population in the United States is susceptible to the call of jihad.

After much out-of-court vetting by prosecutors and in-court legal wrangling, Judge Lodge permitted only one man to testify. Khwaja Hasan, twenty-eight, had been part of the Virginia paintball crew. An immigrant from Pakistan, he spent time in the United States as a child and moved here permanently in the early 1990s. He attended high school in northern Virginia and earned a college biology degree in 1995. Hasan, who wore a thick beard and a yellow prison jumpsuit, spoke without evident emotion as he narrated the unusual direction his life took in 2000. He began participating in drills using paintball guns—air rifles that fire small pigment-filled spheres—with a group of other young Muslims. At least one member of the group had already fought overseas with mujahideen in Bosnia and Kashmir, Hasan said. He had read about jihad online and, in particular, had watched a gruesome video titled *Russian Hell 2000*, in which a Muslim rebel leader in Chechnya is shown shooting a wounded Russian soldier.

"What effect did it have?" he was asked.

"I felt it was something that a Muslim should do," Hasan said, "that he should train himself, prepare himself for jihad."

The connection between the witness Hasan and the defendant al-Hussayen was slight. Prosecutors had noted that the Chechnya-oriented Web site on which Hasan watched the *Russian Hell 2000* video was touted by a separate site that al-Hussayen helped oversee. The Chechnya-oriented site in turn had links to similar videos of battle scenes on an IANA site.

Hasan said that he decided to go to Afghanistan after learning that Mullah Omar, the Taliban ruler, had issued a call to Muslims to protect that country against the expected American invasion after 9/11. "My in-

tention was to go and go for jihad, but I had to go for training first," Hasan
said. Using aliases, he and three others from the Virginia paintball group
traveled to Pakistan. There, Hasan said, he learned to use an AK-47 and a
rocket-propelled grenade launcher. But before seeing action, he changed
his mind. "I mean it was kind of obvious that this was not something I
should have done," he said, as if describing a poorly thought-out career
move. Eventually, back in the United States, he was arrested. As part of a
plea bargain, he was sentenced to serve eleven years and three months in
prison.

On cross-examination, defense lawyer Nevin elicited from Hasan that
a Muslim cleric in northern Virginian had instructed him to obey Mullah
Omar's call for all Muslims to fight the Americans. Had anything else happened to precipitate this discussion of jihad?

"Yes."

"What?"

"Nine-eleven, I mean the buildings."

Hasan's reduction of the murder of three thousand people to that
bland formulation—"the buildings"—captured his moral vacuity. But
Nevin's point was that 9/11, not a Web site, had precipitated the instruction
from Hasan's local imam to heed Mullah Omar's call. Then the lawyer
added, "Your personal relationship with the cleric—that was why you decided to go to Afghanistan, isn't that true?"

"Yes, that is correct," Hasan said.

Pro-jihad imagery on the Internet may have helped shape Hasan's
opinions, but it didn't spur his abortive attempt to fight the United States.

After Hasan's testimony, the government rested. David Nevin now offered
a different theory of how violent fanatics get their inspiration. He called
to the stand Frank Anderson, a former American spy with ramrod posture and thick white hair. Anderson said that during his twenty-seven
years with the CIA, he had become acquainted with a number of Middle
Eastern terrorists. "I've ducked terrorists who tried to kill me," he testified. "They killed my friends and colleagues." Anderson disputed the gov-

ernment's central claim: that terrorists can be recruited via the Internet. Strong personal persuasion is needed to motivate someone to murder innocent victims, he said, adding, "People are not inclined to kill women and children."

The government, in its cross-examination, pointed out that Anderson had done his terrorist spy recruiting in the 1970s, long before the Internet became an essential means of communication. But he countered by reiterating earlier testimony in the trial that the Internet was littered with the sort of alarming fatwas the government tied to al-Hussayen. Anderson eagerly echoed the defense line that at worst, al-Hussayen had spread ideas the U.S. government didn't like. "I lived for thirteen years in countries where you could be put in jail for what you write or say—" Anderson declared, before a prosecution objection cut him off.

Nevin caught almost everyone by surprise when he then announced that the defense would rest after just one witness. The attorney gambled that without any more help from him, the jury would see fissures in the government's case. Putting on defense witnesses would only give the prosecution opportunities to ask those people whether they were familiar with the fatwas, drumming the odious rants into the jurors' heads. Nevin took his chances that the jurors would follow the judge's instructions that the government has to prove guilt to a near certainty. The defense, in theory, doesn't have to prove anything at all.

Lindquist stepped up to the lectern to summarize the government's case. He sprinted through the fatwas and the Web sites, repeatedly asking, "Is this scholarly analysis? Is this just news? Or is this stuff meant for recruitment and funding to get people to go out there and blow themselves up or to send money to those groups that send people out to blow themselves up?" Al-Hussayen felt a "passion" for Islam, Lindquist said, returning to the tactic of putting the faith on trial. "That religion," he said, "includes extreme jihad and suicide, and we are not just talking about scholarly analysis. We are talking about getting people to do those things—those terrorist acts and the funding for those terrorist acts." Al-

Hussayen had lied on immigration forms, revealing malign motives, the prosecutor said. "Hold him accountable for why he came to this country," Lindquist concluded, "and how it related to terrorism outside this country."

"Terrorism takes everything and changes it," Nevin responded in his closing argument. "There is an irresistible impulse at times like this . . . to strike out at people who are not like us." But the government had failed to show a connection between the fatwas and even a single specific act of terrorism. Having combed through all those thousands of private communications, the FBI apparently didn't find one example of al-Hussayen himself endorsing terrorism. "If, as the government sees it, there is this grand plan, this grand conspiracy to further the murder, maiming, and kidnapping occurring overseas," Nevin said, surely at some point al-Hussayen would have asked, "How is the fund-raising going? What has the turnout been like at the camps?" The jurors never heard such evidence. From the start, the defense lawyer said, this case amounted to a suspicion in search of an actual crime.

When the twelve jurors assembled to begin deliberations—the first time they were permitted to discuss the case—there was reluctance about immediately addressing the first three counts in the indictment, those laying out the allegations of material support of terrorism. Jurors knew those counts were "the main act," as one put it, but for that very reason, it seemed easier and preferable to deal first with the side show, the eleven counts on visa fraud and false statements.

About half the jurors said that they thought al-Hussayen had been deceptive in failing to acknowledge his role with the IANA. There was debate about the meaning of the word "solely," in connection with his certification that he would come to the United States solely to study. The jurors, moving carefully, didn't resolve these questions.

Instead after several days the panel turned to the question of whether al-Hussayen had had anything to hide regarding terrorism. To their collective surprise, the jurors found they had individually come to very similar conclusions on counts one through three. David Nevin's gamble had paid off: the jurors scrupulously focused on whether the prosecution had met its burden of proving guilt beyond a reasonable doubt. They all agreed it had not.

Edward Hiddleson, a thirty-four-year-old banker who served as foreman, said later that he respected what the government had tried to do. "I was impressed with the depth the prosecution went into," he told me. While listening to evidence, he felt reassured that the FBI was hunting for terrorism in the heartland. But "after climbing to the top of the mountain of all this evidence," he added, "you got there, and there was nothing there to put your finger on." Al-Hussayen channeled money to the IANA, but the IANA remained a legal charity. He posted other people's objectionable ideas on the Internet, but the government hadn't proved that he agreed with those messages. "It would have been nice to have that silver bullet that would take you to terrorism," Hiddleson said. "It wasn't there."

Claribel Ingraham, the veteran nurse, thought al-Hussayen violated the visa and false statement laws on at least some of the secondary counts. But the terrorism charges left her baffled. "The fatwas, some of them, did promote martyrdom—in essence, terrorism," she told me. But "Sami didn't write any of them. He did put them on his Web site. If he didn't write them, did he approve of them just by putting them on the Web site? We couldn't say that he did."

John Steger, the retired Forest Service engineer, said jurors never got sidetracked on debating the nature of Islam, as the prosecution seemed to encourage them to do. As for the material support of terrorism counts, he said, "I thought we would get pounded with smoking gun evidence." But "day after day it wasn't coming forth." Steger took eighty pages of notes during the trial. When he went back to read them, he found skeptical annotations next to most of the prosecution evidence, comments such as "No significance" and "I don't get what this is." The key for Steger was that the government hadn't found any communication in which al-Hussayen explicitly supported terrorism. Yes, prosecutors showed that one of the

IANA Web sites at one point included a link to a Hamas site, but that link later disappeared, and there was no evidence that al-Hussayen himself raised money for Hamas.

One thing Steger said he found eye-opening was the degree to which the First Amendment protects dissemination of dangerous views. The judge had instructed the jury that the government could legally punish only communication aimed at provoking immediate violence. "You can pass along very killing-type information, as long as it doesn't produce actions which are imminent," Steger said, sounding astonished. But in the end, he said, the First Amendment hadn't proved all that relevant because the jurors never concluded that al-Hussayen definitely supported terrorism, let alone incited any.

The discussion of the terrorism counts took less than a day. The unanimous vote: not guilty. In the end the jurors also acquitted al-Hussayen of three of the immigration counts pertaining to his earlier years in the United States, when his IANA involvement seemed less time-consuming. On the other eight immigration counts, a majority favoring conviction couldn't dislodge holdouts who wanted to exonerate al-Hussayen across the board. After the jury had deliberated for seven days, Judge Lodge pronounced the defendant not guilty of material support of terrorism and declared a mistrial on the eight unresolved immigration charges. That meant that the government had the option of retrying al-Hussayen on just those eight counts.

Ed Hiddleson worried that friends in Boise might disapprove of the terrorism acquittal, that people would assume there must have been something to justify the government's alarm. Surely the prosecutors were correct that there was some connection among Arabs, Islam, and terrorism. But Idahoans' libertarian instinct apparently prevailed. In an editorial, Boise's newspaper, *The Idaho Statesman*, applauded the verdict, and Hiddleson never heard much criticism. "The majority understands the verdict and understands the evidence just wasn't there," the foreman said.

After several weeks of indecision, prosecutors offered al-Hussayen a deal: they would drop the eight unresolved immigration counts, in exchange for his agreeing to immediate deportation. The defense accepted.

On July, 21, 2004, al-Hussayen was taken from custody and put on a plane to Riyadh, his wife and sons having preceded him by four months. A joyful crowd of friends and family met him at the airport. He had spent seventeen months in jail in Idaho. He never spoke to journalists seeking interviews, including me.

SIFTING THE WRECKAGE

Hunkered down in the U.S. attorney's office in downtown Boise, the al-Hussayen prosecution team sifted the wreckage of the government's first Internet terrorism case. Supervisor Terry Derden recalled that Attorney General Ashcroft had ordered the disruption of those supporting terrorism. The al-Hussayen investigation, Derden figured, had disrupted the IANA Web sites. But even Derden seemed to acknowledge the slenderness of that claim when he joked that he was glad his office windows didn't open; there were moments he considered jumping.

The Justice Department wasn't backing off, however. "We're just figuring out the Internet and terrorism," Derden said. "This is not going to be the last case like this, I can assure you of that."

Less than four months after the al-Hussayen acquittal, IslamToday.net, the Web site of Salman al-Ouda, one of the Saudi sheikhs al-Hussayen had occasionally assisted, carried an "open message" encouraging Muslims to attack U.S. forces in Iraq. "Jihad against the occupation is a duty," the message declared. It was signed by twenty-six Saudi scholars, including al-Ouda and Safer al-Hawali, the two Awakening Sheikhs whose views al-Hussayen helped disseminate. There was no indication that al-Hussayen had anything to do with the open letter, but prosecutors doubtless would have tried to make use of it had the trial in Boise unfolded later.

True to Terry Derden's word, the FBI continued to patrol the Internet. At about the time the Saudi Awakening Sheikhs were posting their call to arms, a federal grand jury in Hartford, Connecticut, indicted Babar Ahmad, a British computer specialist of Pakistani descent, on allegations that he used U.S.-based Web sites to recruit al Qaeda, Taliban, and Chechen fighters and raise money for terrorism. Ahmad's sites allegedly carried such material as Osama bin Laden's 1996 declaration of war against the United States and instruction manuals on weapons. As of this writing he is fighting extradition from Britain.

In a more conventional, person-to-person recruitment case, the Justice Department won a conviction of the imam in northern Virginia who exhorted his followers, the paintball enthusiasts, to go to Afghanistan and fight with the Taliban. One of those followers was Khwaja Hasan, who testified for the prosecution in the al-Hussayen trial. Lawyers for the Virginia imam, Ali al-Timimi, protested that his religious and free speech rights had been violated. But a jury in Alexandria, Virginia, convicted al-Timimi in April 2005 of counseling others to wage war against the United States. Rather than have to speculate about whether Web sites spark jihad, the prosecutors in Virginia could place their defendant in the same room with the men he was accused of recruiting. Al-Timimi was sentenced to life in prison. All told, eleven people were convicted in the Virginia investigation; two were acquitted.

Attorney General Ashcroft announced in November 2004 that he would not serve in the second Bush administration. "Securing the safety of Americans from crime and terror has been achieved," he declared, and then opened a Washington lobbying firm.

Had Ashcroft "achieved" safety from terrorism on his watch? As of mid-2005, the Bush administration said that since 9/11, four hundred people had been charged with crimes stemming from terrorism investigations. Two hundred so far had been convicted, most on guilty pleas. Most of the convictions and still-pending charges, however, were for visa or document fraud or other relatively minor infractions, according to *The Washington Post*. Thirty-nine were related to supporting terrorism or threatening national security. Among the thirty-nine were 9/11 plotter Zacarias Moussaui and Richard Reid, the foiled "shoe bomber," who tried to bring down a passenger jet over the Atlantic. There were also the Virginia paintball crew and the groups from Lackawanna, New York, and Portland, Oregon, who sought training in Afghanistan. An Ohio truck driver born in Pakistan was sentenced to twenty years after admitting he had met with al Qaeda members to discuss an unlikely plan to destroy the Brooklyn Bridge. A Lebanese native received what amounted to a life sentence for organizing a cigarette-smuggling ring in North Carolina that diverted profits to the Lebanese terrorist group Hezbollah.

These defendants took specific actions—or conspired to do so—aimed at helping the cause of Islamic extremism. They unquestionably deserved attention from the authorities, and their punishment may help deter others from starting down the same dark path. But these were not terrorist masterminds, and their convictions didn't achieve any sort of victory over the patient architects of mass destruction.

Sami Omar al-Hussayen also merited scrutiny from the FBI. Jury foreman Ed Hiddleson was correct that the government ought to be on the lookout, whether in New York or Idaho, for people financing or otherwise supporting terrorism. Learning that a Saudi national on a student visa had passed along large amounts of money to an organization that endorsed suicide bombing, the FBI sensibly decided to investigate. But after more than a year with access to their suspect's every electronic utterance, federal agents could not tie al-Hussayen to terrorism. At that point the agents should have put their information into a computer file, indexed it in the event that al-Hussayen ever came up in another investigation, and moved on to other suspects. Instead investigators and prosecutors overly eager to find a terrorism case in their obscure jurisdiction proceeded to a trial that cost taxpayers millions of dollars and diverted the energies of a small army of federal employees. Jurors, unimpressed, came back with a verdict that ought to be seen as a colossal embarrassment to the government.

The cost of the al-Hussayen fiasco exceeded wasted dollars and courtroom exertion. Justified prosecutions may deter future crime. Unjustified prosecutions undermine popular resolve to root out real threats. Unjustified prosecutions can also disillusion critical segments of the law-abiding public—in this case, American Muslims—and make them less eager to help the government identify dubious characters in their midst. Finally, unjustified prosecutions are simply unjust. They undercut the basic values of our legal system.

In this regard, the al-Hussayen case wasn't unique. In 2004 a federal judge in Detroit threw out the convictions of two Arab-American men accused of being members of a "sleeper cell" after the Justice Department had admitted withholding relevant evidence. The same year the government dropped all charges against Captain James Yee, a Muslim military chaplain accused of mishandling classified information while working at the Guantánamo Bay detention camp. These were cases—and sadly, there were others like them—in which government incompetence or vindictiveness cast a cloud of confusion over the genuine need to investigate potential terrorism threats.

What of the spitting-on-the-sidewalk strategy? It did appear that al-Hussayen violated immigration law when he failed to disclose his affiliation with the IANA. Why not prosecute him for that?

Here is why not: when the government has gone after big-time gangsters on tax charges or the like, the assumption is that there is certainty that the targets are responsible, as well, for serious violent crime. In the al-Hussayen case, the charges of material support of terrorism were always shot through with doubt. A case like this had never been brought under the new Patriot Act language on "expert advice and assistance" to terrorists. For that very reason, officials at Justice Department headquarters were cautious at first about seeking an indictment. Without a rock-solid underlying case related to terrorism, the paperwork violation that al-Hussayen committed was too peripheral to be worth a criminal prosecution. When the terrorism case failed to come together, the government should have switched gears. Investigators should have summoned al-Hussayen for questioning about his IANA work and explored whether he knew anyone who really *was* recruiting terrorists or sending them money.

The al-Hussayen case quickly became part of a broader debate over free speech and individual liberties during a "war on terrorism." Liberal critics of the Patriot Act cited al-Hussayen as a victim of what they saw as the law's overreaching. Most of the act didn't apply to the al-Hussayen case, but the prosecution in Idaho did illustrate one weakness of the law as well as its broader benefit.

One of the Patriot Act's main purposes was to eliminate legal and administrative barriers between intelligence gathering and law enforcement in situations in which terrorism is suspected. Those barriers helped impede investigations of some of the 9/11 hijackers who were identified as threats as early as 2000. FBI counterterrorism agents need wide latitude to follow leads even where there isn't (yet) probable cause to believe that a specific crime has occurred. What if al-Hussayen really had been signing up suicide bombers? This kind of potential danger goes beyond that of ordinary crime. If terrorism suspicions prove true, then relevant evidence should be available to criminal prosecutors. The al-Hussayen case doesn't suggest the need for greater constraints on investigation. We need a *more* agile and aggressive FBI, one with the language and analytical skills to sort through reams of evidence and identify genuine threats. Once threats have been stopped, the government should still be in a position to prosecute. In the al-Hussayen case, the main error occurred after the evidence was piled up on the conference room table. That is when prosecutors and investigators failed to realize, or admit, that they hadn't identified either a real threat or a significant crime.

The al-Hussayen case does point to a possible weakness in the Patriot Act, however. That is the language about "expert advice and assistance" to terrorists. Making communication itself a crime seems like an invitation to First Amendment snarls. The right to hold and express ideas the government considers dangerous lies at the core of the First Amendment. Incitement that leads directly to violence is another matter—and something that Supreme Court precedent leaves open to prosecution. Before the al-Hussayen trial even began, federal judges in other jurisdictions had questioned whether the expert advice provision was constitutional. One federal judge pointed out that it would appear to criminalize efforts to advise extremist groups to lay down their arms. If the Patriot Act would prohibit negotiations with militants who might be talked into engaging in conventional politics, then that part of the law needs to be amended.

Sami Omar al-Hussayen is the sort of controversial speaker we ought to protect from criminal punishment. In time he will find his way into the footnotes of American constitutional law books. But that shouldn't turn him into a free speech hero, and neither should his good manners or unquestioned love for his wife and sons. The appalling venom he spread on the Internet might have earned him a jail sentence in such countries as Germany, which prohibit speech larded with ethnic hatred. The Bill of Rights and a conscientious jury spared him formal conviction in the United States, while the Ashcroft Doctrine caused his incarceration and deportation, a species of rough justice often seen in troubled times.

SEVEN

The Activist

ustafa Saied learned of my interest in American Muslims
from articles I had written in *The Wall Street Journal*. He introduced himself by e-mail. "I am now fully aware of the difficulties and problems orthodox Islam presents our American society, let
alone the extremist Wahhabi kind. I used to adhere to it, but I now reject
it," he wrote in October 2003. "My approach to Islam now would be classified by most Muslims as heretical, but the more I think about it and delve
into it, my interpretation makes so much more sense and is so much more
accepting of other religions and people."

In an electronic exchange that unfolded over several days, Saied explained that he had come to America from his native India to obtain an engineering degree. It was only when he reached the American heartland
that he got mixed up with fundamentalism. He hinted warily that he had
joined an extremist group but had since recovered his senses and quit.

We met on an overcast day at a hotel restaurant in Miami, near where
he now lives. Saied, in his early thirties, wore a T-shirt and jeans. He asked
if we could talk over dinner. It was Ramadan, and he had been fasting
since dawn. His main mission in life, apart from supporting his young

family, he said, was to spread what he called progressive Islam. It was Saied who first pointed me to such scholars as Khaled Abou El Fadl and books and Web sites that fall under that loosely defined heading.

He said that he wanted to make amends for his earlier attachments and activities. (He told me he hadn't done anything illegal.) Saied wanted Americans, Muslim and non-Muslim, to know more about the realities of Islam in this country—the good and the bad. Sometimes the collision between the two can be seen within one person.

HOW TO GO TO AMERICA

His roots were anything but radical. On the plane from India to America in 1990, Saied, eighteen, made a to-do list: learn to skateboard and bungee-jump, go on road trips, and hang out with girls. Although this would be his first time in the United States, he already spoke fluent English, learned from rebroadcasts of *Sesame Street* and *Starsky & Hutch*. As a teenager he had read and reread a guidebook titled *How to Go to America*. He selected the University of Tennessee because its catalog was in the library of the American consulate in his home state of Chennai and happened to include an application. There was a color photo of a quaint red-brick clock tower that reminded him of the clock tower in a favorite American movie import, *Back to the Future*, the 1985 Michael J. Fox comedy about time travel and teen romance.

In Knoxville he roomed with another outgoing engineering major who, like Saied, came from a highly educated Indian family. "We had many hobbies in common: basketball, football, movies, especially music," the roommate, Rajesh Juriasingani, recalled. Pop singers George Michael and Paula Abdul were favorites. Religion didn't come up much, said Juriasingani, a Hindu.

When the Walt Disney Company recruited on campus for a work-study program, Saied leaped at the chance to spend a semester in an entry-level job at DisneyWorld, taking evening classes on the company's approach to business. "It was like a dream come true for me," he said. He left Orlando in 1993 with a "Ducktorate" degree and a formal photograph of himself, in a suit and tie, shaking hands with Mickey Mouse.

Back in Knoxville, he decided on impulse one afternoon to drop by the inconspicuous mosque near campus, even though it wasn't a Friday. "I don't know what it was; I just wanted to go there," he recalled. In the sparsely furnished one-story mosque, he found a small group of students sitting on the floor, discussing verses from the Quran. Never shy, Saied offered a few opinions—showing off, really. His listeners praised his insight and his Arabic pronunciation. They invited him back.

He was deeply flattered. "I knew a couple of things, and they were so impressed," he said. It wasn't a deeply spiritual experience. Instead he felt as if he had been invited into an elite club, a semisecret fraternity. Displays of piousness, rather than drinking prowess, established one's credentials. He decided on the spot to grow a full beard and begin praying five times a day.

Such transformations, if usually not quite so abrupt, aren't rare on university campuses: the relatively secular young Muslim who tilts toward religious orthodoxy while in a strange environment heavy on beer, dating, and casual sex. In many cases, Islam becomes a shelter from the unfamiliar, an identity taken to extremes as a cure for loneliness. But Saied didn't fit the model precisely. He had gone to parties and mingled easily with non-Muslims, and when he suddenly got caught up in his faith, he went a big step beyond praying regularly and attending mosque.

He had received a religious education growing up. But his father, a petroleum plant supervisor, and his mother, an electrical engineer who stayed home to raise Mustafa and his older sister, taught their children that as Muslims they weren't better than their Hindu neighbors, just different. He attended a Hindu school and accompanied friends to Hindu celebrations. As a boy he spent two years with his family in Saudi Arabia, where his father worked for the oil industry. His parents shielded the children from Saudi fundamentalism, leaving young Mustafa with the sense that it was something foreign. He once saw a public beheading from a car window, but his stronger memories were of a shiny American-style shop-

ping mall and the green, well-watered lawns of the gated residential com-
pounds for oil executives.

Now, spurred on by his new friends in Knoxville, he reshaped his
worldview according to a handful of passages from the Quran. He and
other Muslim immigrant students were drawn to verses that, when interpreted literally, seemed to encourage intolerance, such as the one stating,
"Whomsoever follows a religion other than Islam, this will not be accepted from him, and in the Hereafter he will be among the losers" (3:85).
He loved the admiration his new friends showed for his skill at flinging
bits of scripture. "It polished up my ego," he told me. He blithely adopted
an outlook—Muslims are superior to all others—that was sharply at odds
with what he had learned as a child. Americans, with their mysterious rituals—children dressed as devils on Halloween, the anthropomorphic
bunny on Easter—are no better than pagans. Jews secretly scheme to take
over the world. "You're sitting there, ready to be brainwashed," Saied recalled years later. "You want to be accepted, so you say, 'Oh, yeah, you're
right.' You accept it."

Within a few months of his first visit to the Muslim Community of
Knoxville, as the mosque is known, Saied was asked to deliver the sermon
during a Friday prayer service attended by about three hundred students
and other Muslims. Speaking from the minbar, or pulpit, he excoriated
Americans who indulged in alcohol, premarital sex, and "false" holidays.
He continued periodically to give sermons, peppering them with condemnations of Jews and Israel. Anti-Semitism provided the glue connecting claims of Muslim persecution worldwide. "Our view was that suicide
bombings were fine," he recalled. "Israel is the oppressor; Israel does not
have the right to exist. It must be destroyed." After such talks a few worshipers sometimes would scold him, but there were no other negative
consequences. Saied and his circle of a dozen or so Muslim immigrant
friends laughed off any critics as ignorant or corrupt.

As he gained confidence in his new persona, he tried it out in more
open settings. When a visiting religion scholar gave a talk on campus expressing skepticism of Muslim fundamentalists, "Mustafa stood up, glared
around at people, and announced, 'I'm a Muslim fundamentalist, and

there is only one true Islam,'" remembered Rosalind Gwynne, the long-time faculty adviser of the University of Tennessee chapter of the Muslim Students Association. "You see this among some of the immigrant students from time to time, trying to live in this country in a box, hermetically sealed," she said. Saied began wearing a kaffiyeh headdress similar to that favored by the late Palestinian leader Yasser Arafat. His freshman roommate, Rajesh Juriasingani, listened in dismay as Saied declared he was through with pop music, movies, and dating. Saied eventually dropped all his non-Muslim friends, including Juriasingani.

Like many activist Muslim students, Saied joined a small Islamic study group. His often focused on the writings of Youssef al-Qaradawi, the Egyptian cleric based in Qatar who is a leading figure in the Muslim Brotherhood movement. Al-Qaradawi gained fame in the 1960s by publishing *The Lawful and the Prohibited in Islam*, a book that presents Islam as a compendium of rules for all aspects of life. Considered by many Muslims to be a moderate on relations with the West, al-Qaradawi endorses "martyrdom operations" against Israel and Jews. For months in 1994 Saied sensed that members of his study group were testing his allegiance to fundamentalism. He steadfastly expressed enthusiasm for al-Qaradawi's views.

One afternoon an older member of the study group who came from the United Arab Emirates summoned Saied to a nearly empty campus cafeteria. The two settled into a quiet corner, and Saied's friend invited him to join the Muslim Brotherhood. "Everything I had learned pointed to the Muslim Brotherhood being an awesome thing, the elite movement," Saied said of his initiation. "I cannot tell you the feeling that I felt; it was like awesome power . . . Needless to say, I said yes."

WHAT THE STONE AND THE TREE WILL SAY

Saied began meeting weekly with a subset of fundamentalists who were deemed hard core enough for admission to the Brotherhood. Over tea and baklava, they discussed how to convert Americans to Islam and promote a way of life entirely shaped by the Quran and Islamic law. "Islamicizing" society has been the Brotherhood's goal since its formation in

Egypt in the 1920s, and it has traditionally organized itself in networks of small prayer groups. The Knoxville members compared various methods of recruitment and talked of the need for secrecy. The leader of the group, the graduate student who recruited Saied and who has since returned to the United Arab Emirates, recounted with admiration how the Brotherhood functioned as a wellspring of fundamentalist factions around the world. Omar Abdel-Rahman, the blind Egyptian cleric, was a Brotherhood member who helped form a terrorist organization called the Islamic Group, which tried to stir revolution in Egypt. In 1995 he was convicted in New York and sentenced to life in prison for inspiring the plot to bomb the United Nations and other landmarks in that city. The Knoxville Brotherhood circle talked about the use of violence in the United States, but the consensus was that "we don't do that here, unless necessary," Saied recalled. The trigger would be "the Muslim population being in danger, as it is in Palestine."

In addition to his secret Brotherhood gatherings in Knoxville, Saied attended conferences hosted by Brotherhood-influenced organizations, such as the Muslim Arab Youth Association (not to be confused with the Idaho grad student Sami Omar al-Hussayen's Saudi-dominated Islamic Assembly of North America). MAYA sponsored conventions attended by thousands of university students from around the country. The programs consisted of lectures, communal meals, and worship in makeshift prayer areas, usually a portion of a large banquet room with sheets spread on the floor to mark a sanctified zone.

In December 1995 Saied attended a MAYA gathering at a hotel in Toledo, Ohio. Sheikh al-Qaradawi, the Brotherhood cleric, gave a speech predicting that Islam would "overcome all the religions" and dominate the world, according to a transcript made by the Investigative Project, an antiterrorism research group. Addressing an audience of several hundred people, al-Qaradawi quoted the same Islamic text invoked by one of the Saudi sheikhs whose rantings al-Hussayen helped disseminate on the Internet. "You shall continue to fight the Jews," al-Qaradawi said, "and they will fight you, until the Muslims will kill them. And the Jew will hide behind the stone and the tree, and the stone and the tree will say, 'Oh, servant of Allah, Oh, Muslim, this is a Jew behind me. Come and kill him!' The resurrection will not come before this happens."

None of this dismayed Saied at the time. During the weekend in Toledo he ran into al-Qaradawi as the luminary emerged from a crowded hotel elevator. Conference attendees flocked around the sheikh, trying to kiss his hand. Saied greeted al-Qaradawi, and they talked briefly. "I was awestruck because he was the biggest Muslim Brotherhood figure in the world, and I had met him," Saied said. (As a result of his Brotherhood ties and support for Palestinian terrorists, al-Qaradawi was banned from visiting the United States in 1999.)

At a MAYA conference in Chicago a year earlier, one session in a packed hotel ballroom included a moment when the overhead lights suddenly went dark. Spotlights shone only on the stage, where several speakers sat. Suddenly, Saied recalled, six or seven young men dressed as masked Hamas militants ran down the aisles, waving the organization's green flag and shouting, "Idhbaahal Yahood!" (Slaughter the Jews!).

"There were people who were ecstatic over the display, shouting in response, 'Allahu akbar!' And there were also people who were simply shocked that something like this was going on," Saied said. His own reaction: "Cool."

During this period Saied said he raised thousands of dollars after Friday prayers at the Knoxville mosque to buy supplies for needy Muslims in Bosnia and Chechnya. Once he stood up and asked the congregation for enough money to buy a hundred tents at sixty dollars each. By the next day the full six thousand dollars had been donated. He contacted the Benevolence International Foundation, a nonprofit with an office in Chicago that sent money to Muslims overseas. A foundation representative began periodically visiting Knoxville to pick up contributions. Saied said he assumed the money was going to civilians. He claimed that he immediately stopped raising funds when, in 1995, the foundation emissary acknowledged that some of the money was channeled to Muslim fighters. There was no way to verify this, but Saied's claim seems plausible; on a student visa he didn't want trouble with American authorities.

Eight years later, in 2003, Benevolence International's chief executive pleaded guilty to illegally buying boots and uniforms for Muslim fighters in Bosnia and Chechnya. It was only after 9/11 that American law enforcement began systematically investigating Muslim charities and businesses suspected of links to the Brotherhood, the Palestinian group Hamas, and other extremist organizations. The government has shut down the American branches of several charities, including Benevolence International.

Saied left the University of Tennessee in 1996, several credits shy of graduating. He moved to Florida with his new wife, Sadaf, whom he had met at a Muslim student conference in Baltimore. Devoutly religious, Sadaf Saied was born in the United States and is of Pakistani descent. She told me she had been dismayed by the arguments her husband and his Arab-immigrant friends made in favor of suicide bombing. "That was a foreign thing to me," she said. As an undergraduate at the University of Miami she had helped start a moderate Muslim group on campus as an alternative to the one dominated by Arab students whose views were similar to her husband's. But she didn't try to talk him out of his opinions.

Saied continued his activism, keeping an eye out for potential Muslim Brotherhood recruits and preaching his view of Islam at a camp for Muslim teenagers in South Florida. In 1997 he brought Yasir Billoo, one of his former campers, to a meeting of about thirty men in an Orlando hotel conference room. Billoo, then eighteen, came to the United States from Pakistan as a child. "Leadership was the topic: how to organize and get people to follow Muslim Brotherhood members," Billoo recalled. Afterward he was invited to join the Brotherhood. Scared by the experience, he declined. "It was way too secretive for me," he said. The chilling part, in retrospect, Saied said, was that it was never clear when one or another small group of Muslim Brothers would deem it appropriate to take matters into their own hands and commit acts of violence.

AN INTERVENTION

A year later, after attending yet one more Muslim conference, Saied joined a group discussion in the book-lined basement of another attendee's family in Chicago. He was about to have another life-changing experience.

Over tea and fresh fruit, Saied launched into a tirade against non-Muslims and Americans. Assim Mohammed, who was hosting the gathering at his parents' home, had encountered the same attitudes in Muslim circles as a student at the University of Illinois. Mohammed said he and another young man fired back, arguing that "the basic foundations of American values are very Islamic—freedom of religion, freedom of speech, toleration." The verbal battle raged for four hours, as several other people listened avidly.

Saied said he and his friend Yasir Billoo, who had accompanied him, were hearing "answers that we had never heard before." Mohammed and his ally deployed Quranic verses that suggest an embrace of pluralism. One he quoted states, "Oh humankind, God has created you from male and female and made you into diverse nations and tribes so that you may come to know each other" (49:13). To his surprise, Saied said, a thought bubbled up from the back of his mind: "Wait a minute, this is what I *used* to do"—that is, engage in freewheeling conversations during which he listened to his opponents' opinions.

Late that night Saied and Billoo realized they "were out of arguments." Mentally exhausted, Saied thought, "Oh, my God, what have we been doing?" The effect was similar to that of an intervention with an alcoholic or drug addict. Billoo described it as a deprogramming.

In the following months Saied gravitated back toward the more moderate values he had learned growing up. He felt as if he had awakened from a bad dream. "We had lived in our own world," he said. The self-righteousness, the anti-Semitism: "the whole thing lost its aura." The critical factor galvanizing this change of heart was the pressure of more mature and open-minded Muslims, people who were determined to remind Saied that Islam did not command insularity and resentment of non-Muslims.

Pressed to explain his transformation, he could identify only one other reason: his clash with other Muslim activists over money. As he rose in the activist ranks, he saw more and more petty divisiveness over fund-raising. He had quarreled with colleagues who raised money from Saudi Arabia but declined to account for how much they received or from whom. The fundamentalist cause began to look less pure to Saied. Even before the fateful evening in Chicago, the thought had crossed his mind: "There's nothing special about these people, and in fact there may be nothing special about me." This slight doubt, he said, may have made him more receptive to arguments for dropping out of the Brotherhood.

By the time I met him in late 2003 Saied no longer wore a kaffiyeh or any other head covering. He had trimmed his beard short. He was again listening to music, both American pop and traditional Indian. He helped run an environmental testing firm in Hialeah, Florida, owned by his wife's family. Later he left the family business to start a firm that produces artful portraits on canvas of American sports heroes. His best friend, Yasir Billoo, launched a successful legal career.

Sadaf Saied said with a laugh that she and her husband have reversed positions on the spectrum of Islamic practice: She prays more often, dresses more conservatively, and wants her four daughters to cover their hair when they reach adolescence. Mustafa would prefer that the girls not set themselves apart. He confessed to me that he wishes his wife didn't wear hijab, either, but insists, "It's no big deal." He and Sadaf have agreed to let their daughters decide for themselves. The parents also concur that in time the girls may date—but only young men who are serious marriage prospects. Any suitor of a Saied daughter will get a close inspection. Mustafa has big dreams for the girls beyond marriage. He envisions one going into business, one the arts, one professional sports, and one politics. But as with wearing hijab, he will let them choose.

He still feels guilty about his years of extremism, a remorse exacerbated by 9/11. For months after the attacks he could think of little else. He stirred controversy within Muslim circles by writing opinion pieces for *USA Today* and *The Christian Science Monitor* that called on American Muslims to raise their voices in support of religious moderation. Participants in Islamic Internet chat rooms called him a heretic, a label he adopted for a time as his online moniker. He demanded in sometimes fiery exchanges that Muslims take responsibility for the presence of extremism within their ranks.

He showed the most regret for the anti-Semitism he had regurgitated years earlier without any thought beyond impressing his fundamentalist cadre. "I must admit that I was caught in this anti-Jewish web that is so popular in Islamic circles and therefore didn't respect you," he said in a lengthy e-mail apology to his college MSA adviser, Rosalind Gwynne. She forgave him. She also told him that she isn't Jewish, contrary to what he and other Muslim students believed.

In the wake of 9/11 much of the kind of militant networking and fundraising Saied once engaged in was tamped down in the United States. The Muslim Arab Youth Association appears to have stopped functioning, at least publicly. The apparent cessation in this country of pro-Hamas rallies and overt fund-raising for militant causes constitutes progress, but it isn't a guarantee that all is well. Having been on the inside, Saied was in a position to know that "anti-American sentiment is usually reserved for closed-door discussions or expressed in languages that most Americans don't understand. While such rhetoric has been drastically reduced since 9/11, it is still prevalent enough to be a cause for concern." The Muslim Brotherhood hasn't evaporated in the United States. There could be thousands of members here, he explained. Some he knows for a fact are active in other U.S.-based Islamic organizations. But "let's say there are only five hundred" men in the United States who consider themselves active Brotherhood members, he said. "Let's say that ten out of those five hundred could be influenced toward a terrorist act. That's scary."

In May 2002 Saied opened his morning newspaper to see the enlarged mug shot of someone he recognized. Within seconds it came to him: the quiet young Hispanic man, a convert to Islam he knew from his extremist days in Florida. They had mutual acquaintances and once played touch football on a field next to a mosque. The newspaper identified the man as Jose Padilla, a former Chicago gang member who became a Muslim while behind bars. After being arrested that May, Padilla was held for more than three years in a military prison, accused of involvement in an al Qaeda plot to smuggle a radioactive "dirty" bomb into the United States. In November 2005 he was finally indicted on charges related to his alleged membership in a North American "terrorist support cell"; the indictment didn't refer to a radioactive bomb.

Years earlier Padilla had seemed notably modest and respectful, Saied recalled. What is worrisome, he added, is that the people who taught Padilla about Islam are probably now teaching others, in jails or on the street.

In a country that protects religious freedom, opportunities inevitably will arise for impressionable young people to be exposed to radical ideology. That can happen in a prison cell or a college cafeteria. The ideas shouldn't be banned, and as a practical matter, they can't be entirely eliminated. But they can be brought to light, cross-examined, and replaced by better ideas. Saied's story shows that the force of argument and goodwill can turn people around. Are those arguments being made? How often?

A former extremist, Saied believes a moderate Muslim majority eventually will make its presence more noticeable in the United States. One salutary response to extremism is open debate. In online Islamic forums he argues for separation of religion from politics and against reflexive anti-Americanism. As he now sees it, "religion is a very personal thing. I understand it. I practice it, and I answer to God.

"There needs to be adaptation," he said. Christianity and Judaism have evolved—and continue to adapt, he added. Why not Islam?

The Way Ahead

ntolerance versus broad-mindedness: Sami Omar al-Hussayen versus the UCLA law professor Khaled Abou El Fadl. Reform versus reaction: Asra Nomani versus her foes in Morgantown, West Virginia. Moderation versus militancy: Sufi Sheikh Muhammad Hisham Kabbani versus African-American Imam Siraj Wahhaj. Integration with American society versus retreat into foreign antagonisms: the Dearborn publisher Osama Siblani versus . . . himself.

Muslims face critical choices as they struggle for the soul of their faith in the United States. It is impossible to predict which attitudes and ideas will prevail. Much depends on unknowable variables—not least, events in the volatile Middle East and the possibility of more terrorist attacks in Europe and the United States. As long as there is a realistic fear of terrorism in America, there will be heightened government scrutiny of Muslims. That will lead to resentment when people are questioned, detained, deported, or imprisoned. Those disposed to exacerbate tensions—extremist imams, right-wing media personalities, vituperative Christian preachers—will doubtless exploit the situation. Mistakes or abuses by the authorities, high and low, will make matters worse.

Conflict in the Middle East and America's actions there will probably continue to provoke Muslim anger, especially the U.S. presence in Iraq and support of Israel. Even as there is progress in this country, as second- and third-generation American Muslims take their places in our diverse society, some immigrants from the Middle East and South Asia will continue to import the fundamentalism common in those regions. It bears repeating that not all fundamentalists endorse violence, let alone commit violence themselves. But an influx of those holding, and able to spread, immoderate views will retard assimilation and create pockets of extreme ideology. Within those pockets dangerous ideas can take root.

In the United States, after years of defensiveness and denial, some Muslim organizations are beginning to find their voices on the topic of terrorism committed in the name of Islam. These groups were shocked by the July 7, 2005, bombings in London, committed by Muslims born in Britain and relatively assimilated to life there yet willing to slaughter their neighbors. This undeniable evidence of Islamic fanaticism launched not from the distant Middle East or South Asia but from within the West caused some American Muslim groups to reassess their past tendency to deflect and evade questions about what mainstream Muslims are doing to address terrorism. Noticeably toned down were the arguments that Muslims aren't the only ones who commit violence, that Islam is a religion of peace, and that what needs to change is American foreign policy (though when raised in the proper context, each of those contentions contains important truth).

By mid-July 2005 such organizations as the Islamic Society of North America (ISNA), based in Plainfield, Indiana, had crafted a new, more direct message, that American Muslims must reject anyone promoting extremism and violence as religiously justified. The ISNA condemned "any such tendencies in the Muslim community in this country and in the world." Kareem Irfan, chairman of an ISNA committee that produced a new antiterrorism brochure distributed at the group's annual convention in Chicago over the Labor Day weekend in 2005, said the goal is to promote "balanced Islam." While most American Muslims already opposed terrorism, he candidly acknowledged that there remain "inklings of doubt" among others.

This new bluntness is of course welcome. Whether it will erase the inklings of doubt remains to be seen. At the Islamic convention a controversial African-American cleric from New York, Warith Deen Umar, dismissed the antiterrorism brochure, saying, according to *The New York Times*, "A lot of this is phony." He added, "Their intentions are good, but most of these are immigrant Muslims who want to be accepted in America."

Which message will imams and local lay leaders convey to their flocks? Will they be swayed by the likes of Umar, who for decades preached to prison inmates and served as the top Muslim chaplain in the New York Department of Correctional Services?

That it took the ISNA and other national organizations until mid-2005 to clarify their antiterrorism stance, sifting out distracting qualifications, is a disappointing reminder of the lack of bold Muslim leadership on the national level. Whether the issue has been women in the mosque or responses to extremism, the dearth of moderate Muslim leaders possessing charisma and eloquence has been striking. Perhaps now that is changing. But Islam in America is so divided by ethnicity and outlook that it is difficult to imagine a single leader having a decisive effect. What Muslims may need is a battery of talented people to guide and inspire disparate communities.

The promising, if still embryonic, movement of progressive Muslims may be too provocative to lead a majority, but it is seeking to become a front line for change. People like Khaled Abou El Fadl, the reform-minded UCLA law professor, and Asra Nomani, the feminist from Morgantown, West Virginia, are writing books, contributing to Web sites, and appealing to younger activists. Coming from a more spiritual perspective, Sheikh Muhammad Hisham Kabbani and other Sufis promote patriotism and ecumenical beliefs. There is, however, a risk of reactionary backlash when someone like Nomani defies deep-seated custom without a broad constituency behind her, demanding, for example, not just space for women in the mosque but that women lead communal prayer. Kabbani engenders a similar risk when he uses hyperbolic language to describe the breadth of Muslim extremism in the United States.

Some members of the aspiring vanguard argue that a moderate "silent majority" of American Muslims will make itself known in coming years. Opinion surveys support the assertion that such a majority exists. The Pew Research Center summarized the results of its comprehensive poll of American Muslims in 2007 by saying that as a group they are "largely assimilated, happy with their lives, and moderate with respect to many of the issues that have divided Muslims and Westerners around the world. ... [T]hey are decidedly American in their outlook, values, and attitudes." While Muslims aren't as upbeat about their circumstances as Americans generally, the differences aren't large, and Muslims overall told Pew that they are satisfied with life in the United States. Seventy-eight percent said they are "very happy" or "pretty happy" with their lives, compared to 87 percent of Americans generally. More than seven in ten Muslims rated their immediate community as "excellent" or "good," only slightly less than the comparable overall figure. Muslims are *more* likely than members of the general public to say that Americans can get ahead with hard work: 71 percent versus 64 percent.

Asked about terrorism, 83 percent of American Muslims said that suicide bombing of civilians is never or rarely justified, even if intended "to defend Islam." But 8 percent believe this form of terrorism at least sometimes can be justified in religious terms. The Pew Center interprets this split optimistically, noting that "higher percentages of Muslims in Great Britain, France, and Spain said that suicide bombings in the defence of Islam are often or sometimes justified." But terrorism is a game of small numbers, and one can reasonably worry about the 8 percent who would countenance terrible destruction. What is beyond dispute is that moderate Muslims must speak up and act forcefully to protect America—and American Islam—from a tiny minority capable of doing harm.

The choices American Muslims make don't occur in a vacuum. Put another way, the entire burden doesn't rest on Muslims. There are important things American government and society should do to help the forces of moderation prevail.

First, and most generally, the rest of us need to recognize the pressure American Muslims have lived under since 9/11. Even advocates of tough domestic security policies—in fact, *especially* those advocates—should acknowledge the unavoidable human costs of the war on terrorism. Fear of undeserved punishment haunts many law-abiding Muslims, particularly those who don't have citizenship. Most Muslims I have met, even if they don't fear for themselves, live with a daily sense of humiliation and frustration that their religion has been associated with so much barbarity. Publicly acknowledging this psychic burden and showing some empathy would improve relationships with Muslims of all stripes and begin to counter accusations that Americans seek to persecute followers of Islam.

At a rhetorical level, many American leaders, including President Bush, have made a decent effort to distinguish Islam and Muslims generally from the targets of the antiterrorism campaign. But we need to do more than simply say we respect Islam and empathize with law-abiding Muslims. Behavior has to change. Some of what follows may be wishful thinking, but progress on these fronts could help determine Islam's future in America.

President Bush and other national politicians should speak out against Islam-hating Christian fundamentalists. Public officials who demean Islam and Muslims should be removed. Lt. Gen. William Boykin, the senior Pentagon official who spoke of battling Islam "in the name of Jesus," comes immediately to mind. Religious leaders such as Pat Robertson (Muhammad was "an absolute wild-eyed fanatic"), Jerry Vines (the Prophet was "a demon-possessed pedophile"), and Franklin Graham (Islam is "a very evil and wicked religion") deserve public condemnation. Just a few signals of this sort from top political leaders would send an invaluable message to Muslims looking for reasons to be more enthusiastic about their country. In the summer of 2005 Muslim activists pressured WMAL, a radio station in Washington, D.C., to fire conservative talk show host Michael Graham for making bigoted remarks ("Islam is a terrorist organization"). When Graham was shown the door, Muslims responded with unabashed gratitude and a sense of accomplishment.

In the Middle East, the recent bloodshed in Lebanon and Gaza has heightened Muslim hostility toward Israel's benefactor, the United States. Without abandoning Israel or the principle that a sovereign nation must protect its people, the U.S. will have to persuade its ally to make sacrifices in exchange for peace. Compromise, even with hated and distrusted adversaries, is the only way to achieve normality for the Israelis, Palestinians, and Lebanese. Pushing compromise isn't solely a Republican responsibility. Most Democrats as well as Republicans who have national political aspirations, and nearly all politicians representing New York and California, reflexively defer to Israel and big American Jewish organizations. Both political parties will have to show courage and convince Israel to fortify its moral position by pulling back from more of the areas it conquered in 1967.

The United States also has a right and duty to protect its citizens. But as federal agents continue the laborious search for terrorists, the Justice Department must seriously upgrade its performance. Prosecutors have called too many press conferences to trumpet peripheral arrests, and they have taken some shoddy cases to court. These empty gestures demoralize moderate Muslims and provide fodder for the propagandists and extremists. If someone seems like an imminent threat, finding an excuse to get him off the street temporarily makes sense—but only until the FBI has time to confirm if the threat is real. Pushing for convictions based on spit-on-the-sidewalk charges, when there is no larger underlying crime, comes at a significant cost, the appearance of government vengefulness.

The Bush administration also erred in its arrogant decision to ignore established legal procedures and authorize the National Security Agency to eavesdrop on American citizens and others communicating with people overseas. Few Americans would object to surveillance of suspected terrorists, at home or abroad. But the administration's eagerness to circumvent the requirement of obtaining warrants—even from the secret and highly cooperative Foreign Intelligence Surveillance Court—inevitably provokes suspicion that officials have nefarious agendas. If investigators need new legal procedures to keep up with an evolving terrorist threat, Congress must approve those changes. Lawless government monitoring starts us down an ominous path.

Even more important, when the United States is holding Muslim suspects or convicts—whether they face questioning, deportation, or prison time—our jailers and interrogators must cease the appalling physical abuse that has shamed the nation. The Justice Department's inspector general found numerous instances of discriminatory and abusive treatment of Muslim inmates held in domestic lockups after 9/11. FBI agents working at the Guantánamo Bay detention center in Cuba have objected to rough treatment of inmates there, according to FBI e-mail correspondence disclosed in civil litigation. The sadism photographed at the Abu Ghraib prison in Iraq has given America's enemies grounds for arguing that we are no more principled or humane than they are. This isn't the place for a discussion of how to interrogate purported terrorists. Many who have been mistreated in American custody, including most of those arrested for immigration violations after 9/11, were never serious terrorism suspects in the first place. Most prisoners held in Cuba and Iraq were quickly determined to be, at worst, foot soldiers, not masterminds with access to future terrorist plans. Some U.S. military interrogators, including navy experts at Guantánamo, have raised questions about whether tough tactics ever produce reliable intelligence. But however the debate on interrogation techniques is resolved, it is clear that there have been excesses that only confirm Muslim suspicions that religious animus fuels American antiterrorism efforts.

At home we have to distinguish between extremist words and acts. The former deserve condemnation but not necessarily criminal punishment. For one thing, people evolve. Siraj Wahhaj, the African-American imam from Brooklyn, has shelved some of his more radical diatribes since 9/11—an opportunistic adjustment, yes, but one for the better nonetheless. Some young people are prone to testing out extreme language and ideas in the same way that classmates experiment with illicit drugs. One shouldn't trivialize hateful speech or ideology. The allure of fashionable extremism among young Muslims warrants close attention, and correction, from peers and elders. If there are hints of dangerous activities beyond speechifying, the authorities ought to investigate. But as Mustafa Saied's story illustrates, essentially decent young people who don the cloak of radicalism, for whatever reason, are not necessarily lost causes. Troubling ideology isn't hard wired. If skillfully challenged, it can sometimes be defused.

It is worth remembering that the promising trajectory on which we now find the Saied family is a common one within the varied and at times tension-ridden ranks of American Islam.

Afterword

In the eight months since *American Islam* initially appeared, attention to the role of Muslims in the United States has intensified for both positive and negative reasons. Muslims in small groups and individually continued to demonstrate that the American dream applies to them. The Pew Research Center's significant survey reinforced one of this book's central themes: that as a group Muslims are integrating successfully in American society. In academia and on op-ed pages, more voices than ever, from within and without the Muslim community, discussed Muslims' relations with other Americans.

While such discussion is both healthy and necessary, it is understandably shadowed by fear of violence. From Glasgow to Gaza, from Baghdad to Islamabad, bulletins of carnage or the threat of it multiply. A National Intelligence Estimate released by the Bush administration in July 2007 warns that Al Qaeda has regained strength in the badlands of Pakistan and is more determined than ever to strike the United States. And at home, news of criminal conspiracies starring Muslims lends some credence to that warning.

In May the FBI arrested six Muslim men from southern New Jersey and Philadelphia, Albanian, Jordanian, and Turkish immigrants who were charged with plotting to kill soldiers at the Fort Dix military base in New Jersey. Members of the group allegedly tried to buy high-powered weapons from a government informant who had infiltrated their circle. Several weeks later, four other Muslim men, including a onetime airport cargo handler from Guyana, were charged with planning to blow up fuel tanks and terminal buildings at Kennedy International Airport in New York. The scheme allegedly included contacts with an extremist Muslim group in Trinidad. The internationally tinted discontent simmering in these cases illustrated that the variety within American Islam extends from its healthier mainstream to an agitated fringe.

Like a number of the other domestic terrorism investigations since 9/11, the indictments in mid-2007 revealed suspects who seemed more skilled at mouthing radical-sounding slogans than actually perpetrating violence. The Fort Dix Six allegedly took target practice, but the government's account of their plot implicitly conceded that the FBI informant had to goad the defendants toward action. In the Kennedy airport case, the sixty-three-year-old retired baggage worker who confided in another government informant about destroying his former place of employment seemed singularly ill-equipped to carry out his daydream. These plots joined a list of thwarted post-9/11 plans—most more accurately described as overheated fantasies—that included one Muslim Pakistani American's musing about bringing down the Brooklyn Bridge and another's talk of bombing the New York subway system.

The authors of the subway and bridge schemes received long prison sentences, as will, in all likelihood, the participants in the Fort Dix and JFK airport cases, if they are convicted. After 9/11, no one living in America should feel free to toss around plans for blowing up buildings. Stiff punishment seems appropriate to deter other wannabe terrorists, even if the defendants in these cases seem more like sad buffoons than real threats.

But set to one side for a moment the severity of prison terms and the question of whether particular plots would ever have been carried out. What one is still left with are snapshots of Muslims in America brooding about how to murder fellow Americans in the name of Islam. In late June 2007, the would-be car bombers in London and Glasgow—a group including physicians and other professionals, according to the British authorities—only served to underscore what appears to be a spreading danger in the West of homegrown Islamic terrorism.

How, then, do these events affect an assessment of American Islam?

First, the trans-Atlantic comparison serves as a reminder that Europe has a more acute problem with Muslim extremism than does the United States. Filled with nails, gasoline, and gas canisters, the car bombs in the United Kingdom were delivered to their target destinations, where they could have caused tremendous carnage. Thankfully they failed to detonate, though a vehicle in Glasgow burst into flames. Only days after these attempts, four other Muslim men were sentenced to life in prison for their botched attack on London's transit system in July 2005. News reports noted that more than one hundred people were awaiting trial in Britain on charges arising from several other conspiracies following the July 7, 2005, suicide bombings that killed fifty-two commuters in London.

The post-9/11 conspiracies uncovered in the United States haven't progressed as far as the British plots. That may be in part because the FBI has become more alert since 9/11 and has intervened before conspiracies become reality. But it's also likely that there are far fewer American Muslims, as compared to British, planning mayhem. Those Americans who are indulging in violent rumination appear less serious about following through.

The 9/11 Commission made the important observation that the nineteen hijackers had little contact with American Muslims and apparently received no support from them. The FBI's hundreds of investigations since the 9/11 attacks so far have not detected a terrorist menace that threatens this country from within. Certainly future attacks on the United States are possible, perhaps even probable. But they are more likely to come, again, from abroad.

What the Fort Dix and Kennedy airport cases remind us of is the eight percent of Muslims who told the Pew Research Center in its 2007 poll that terrorism—specifically, suicide bombing of civilians—can at least sometimes be justified to defend Islam. The poll didn't ask respondents whether they themselves would consider violent action. It's a fair guess that few would. More likely, American Muslims endorsing suicide bombing have in mind attacks on Israelis by Hamas or Hezbollah or sectarian bloodshed between Iraqi Sunnis and Shiites. But as the chapter on Dearborn, Michigan, notes, there are Muslims in the United States who justify violence against American troops in Iraq. And the Fort Dix and Kennedy airport cases illustrate that in certain Muslim circles bloodshed at home is seen as defensible, even laudable.

The Pew poll and my reporting suggest that the Muslim-American advocates of terrorist violence are a very small minority. But they should be a source of anxiety to their neighbors, especially their Muslim neighbors, who have the most to lose if evil thoughts explode into deeds.

ↄ

Today these concerns are very much on the minds of several of the subjects of this book.

Not long after the spring 2007 arrests in the United States and the failed car bombings in the United Kingdom, Mustafa Saied received an anxious phone call from his friend Yasir Billoo. Saied, "the activist" of Chapter Seven, belonged to a secretive cell of the notorious Muslim Brotherhood in the 1990's and at one point tried to recruit his friend into the organization. Billoo backed away, and both men, who live in Florida, long ago abandoned any interest in extremism. Billoo, a successful attorney, called to ask whether Saied had thought about what he would do if "a couple of crazy guys"—Muslims, he meant—drove a car bomb into an American airport and killed a lot of people.

Saied said he would expect a government security crackdown far more severe than what happened after 9/11, as well as a backlash from angry non-Muslim citizens. All Muslims would become targets, Saied speculated.

"The first thing I would do if we stayed would be to change my name," Saied later told me. "My wife would stop wearing the hijab. We would avoid any identification with the religion for our own safety." But that seemed unacceptable. Saied didn't want to abandon his identity as an

Indian-born Muslim, and he wouldn't expose his four young daughters to physical danger. Instead, he said he probably would take his wife, Sadaf, and the girls somewhere safer to live. "It's scary. Where would we go?" he wondered. "It's possible for a few guys to make the place we love, America, something we cannot live in."

Although distracted by these worries, Saied hasn't lost his enthusiasm for the popular culture of his adopted homeland. In fact, his gusto for all things American has inspired him to leave his job with a family-owned engineering firm. First he started a sports memorabilia business selling oil-on-canvas paintings of professional football and basketball stars. From there he pursued perhaps the most American of dreams: making it big in the movie business. His first project, a film called *The Camel Wars,* is based on a story he wrote about the American invasion and occupation of Iraq. The title refers to a famous seventh-century Muslim clash, also in what is now Iraq, and the sectarian hostility that has persisted ever since. Saied has recruited a director and is securing financing. He hopes to start production in 2008. He has moved his family from Hialeah to Orlando, where he rents space for his three-person production company on the back lot of Universal Studios. "This is what I always wanted to do," he told me. "This is why we love America—whatever is possible, you can give it a try."

Asra Nomani, the Muslim feminist in Morgantown, West Virginia, dismisses the latest terrorist investigations in the United States as "bogus stings." The FBI, she told me, is "making busts while Muslims here lie low," by which she meant they are stepping back from mainstream life out of fear.

American authorities have indeed overstated the gravity of some of the arrests they've made in post-9/11 terrorist investigations. The case of Sami Omar al-Hussayen, the Saudi computer-science graduate student and Webmaster, provides one illustration. But there is a difference between al-Hussayen, who was prosecuted for disseminating vicious anti-American and anti-Semitic pronouncements by others, and defendants who are accused themselves of plotting mass violence. Stings aimed at the latter group are not bogus, even if the targets turn out to be less than terrorist masterminds.

Nomani's frustrated remark that Muslims are lying low also seems subject to question. Muslim student associations have never been more active on campus. Muslim conferences and conventions of all sorts crowd the calendar. For the most part, Muslims are carrying on normal lives, as Nomani's own routine demonstrates. She takes her young son, Shibli, to McDonald's and Tae Kwon Do classes. She even coaches his T-ball team, the Citizens Bank Dinosaurs. In addition to her freelance writing, she has begun teaching a journalism course at Georgetown University in Washington.

The controversy Nomani sparked over the place of women within Islam has continued to stir debate in mosques across America. At home in Morgantown, however, her campaign has had mixed results. She won tacit permission to pray in the main hall of the local mosque, but few women have followed her example. When they attend communal prayer, the Muslim women of Morgantown are content to worship unseen, from the removed balcony built to isolate them. Nomani and her family, meanwhile, remain pariahs, ostracized because of Asra's demand for better treatment.

Strife in the Middle East haunts the successful American life of Osama Siblani, but, as he readily admits, it's also good for business. The publisher of *The Arab American News* in Dearborn, Michigan, has seen his weekly paper's circulation rise by 60 percent, to 36,000, in just a year. The increase, he says, reflects his readers' growing anxiety over bloodshed in Iraq, Afghanistan, Gaza, and Lebanon. More advertisers have come with more readers, and among employers buying space in the paper is the U.S. Department of Homeland Security, which desperately needs Arabic linguists. Siblani, who hasn't backed off from his fierce criticism of America's foreign policy, acknowledges the irony of his profiting from the U.S. security establishment. "It seems like the niche we have is working for us," he deadpans.

But more is at work here than one Lebanese immigrant entrepreneur's instinct for profits. Agree or disagree with the views expressed in Siblani's unabashedly partisan tabloid, one must recognize its persistent subtext that Arab Americans should put down roots here. *The Arab American News* of July 7, 2007, for example, carried articles lacerating Israel for occupying the West Bank and the United States for occupying Iraq. But it also bore the prominent advertising image of Sgt. Hassan Tirgui, a handsome, uniformed, and evidently Arab-American recruiter for the Michigan National Guard. Tirgui offered Siblani's readers a twenty thousand dollar enlistment bonus, college tuition assistance, and low-cost life insurance. If pictures communicate more powerfully than words, this ad sent a clear message that young Americans of Arab descent ought to consider joining the U.S. military.

In local news, Siblani reported on the accomplishments of two friends: the first was Imad Hamad, whom immigration authorities attempted to deport in the 1990s because of his alleged (and unproven) involvement with extremist Palestinians. Hamad, since honored for his work as an intermediary between federal authorities and Arab Americans, had been appointed to the Michigan arm of the U.S. Commission on Civil Rights. Another article reported on the conviction of a local real estate fraud artist. The victorious prosecutor in that case was Abed Hammoud, an intense Lebanese immigrant whom Siblani is promoting as a candidate to be Dearborn's mayor.

Ancient animosities persist in Detroit's Arab-American suburbs, but they compete for attention with the great American parade of outsiders becoming insiders, pushing for political influence and demanding respect.

Khaled Abou El Fadl, the Islamic jurisprudence scholar at UCLA and proponent of a modern, humane Islam, has continued to face hostility from fellow Muslims angered by his critique of what he calls puritanical forms of his religion. "The only way that Muslims can remain true to the moral message of their religion and at the same time discharge their covenant with God is through introspective self-criticism and reform," he writes in his latest book, *The Great Theft: Wrestling Islam From the Extremists.*

In early 2006, Arabic-language newspapers in Egypt and the United

States (though not *The Arab American News*) reported falsely that Abou El Fadl had advised President George W. Bush to support Israeli attacks in Lebanon against Hezbollah. Then in April of that year, someone fired a round into Abou El Fadl's suburban Los Angeles home. The bullet lodged in a book, and no one was hurt. An attacker hasn't been caught, and it's possible the bullet was a stray. But Abou El Fadl, who lives nowhere near the slums of South Central Los Angeles, believes the shooting was linked to the reports portraying him as a Bush lacky. "This was a response to a solicitation for murder," he said. He has faced death threats before and has no plans to stop writing or speaking in public. "If they scare me into silence," he says, "they will have succeeded. I cannot give in."

Siraj Wahhaj offers his followers a very different interpretation of Islam from that of Abou El Fadl, but one that also reflects an attempt to make the religion relevant to American worshipers. In 2007, the prominent African-American imam sought to broaden his appeal among black Muslims nationally by inviting members of the racially separatist Nation of Islam to align itself with more conventional Muslims.

Wahhaj, a Nation of Islam minister before his turn decades ago to orthodox Islam, delivered a widely noted sermon in February to a national gathering in Detroit of the elite of what remains of the declining Nation of Islam. Urging unity among Muslims, Wahhaj, whose home mosque is in Brooklyn, New York, implicitly offered himself as a spiritual guide to those who have followed Louis Farrakhan, the physically ailing leader of the Nation. Farrakhan, seventy-three, billed the event as the occasion for his final public address, heightening the attention paid to Wahhaj's appearance.

The fragmented ranks of black Muslims will prove difficult to organize, even for someone with the charisma, intelligence, and street credibility that Wahhaj possesses. He has made impressive progress in bridging the gap between black Muslims and the many immigrants who still believe that African-Americans don't appreciate "real" Islam. But a final obstacle to his desire for national influence will be his past expressions of sympathy for certain radical Islamic figures. Those affections will make it difficult for him to win the trust of many non-Muslims. One hopes it will give Muslims pause as well.

↝

Abdul Kabir Krambo, who offers himself as neither a leader of Muslims nor a scholar of Islam, is nonetheless one of the most thoughtful and perceptive people I met during my reporting for this book. The white convert, who hews to the spiritual Sufi path, mourns the headlines and broadcasts about terrorist plots, but without looking away from the unsettling realities they represent. Political polarization at home and the morass in Iraq have left him in a pessimistic frame of mind. But he told me he's "optimistic about individual people and the opportunities we have to change the world." His grown children have followed him in his faith and married other Muslims.

His mosque in rural Northern California receives hostile e-mail from born-again Christians, "who tell us Islam is the work of the devil," and from puritanical Muslims who disapprove of Sufi beliefs. But when a Muslim friend gave a talk recently at a local bookstore about the Sufi poet Rumi, forty people turned out and listened appreciatively. An electrical contractor by trade, Krambo not long ago helped renovate a Sufi-influenced mosque in Oakland, where he sometimes visits for communal meditation.

"You follow the teachings of the religion, the teachings of the Prophet, peace be unto him, and you try to live an exemplary life," Krambo said. "You leave the rest to God. What else can I tell you?"

↝

Despite the lack of hard census data, we know that the Muslim segment of American society, in all its diversity, is growing swiftly. High birth rates and continuing immigration drive the increase. Given that growth and the turmoil around the world involving Muslims, the role of Muslims in America deserves more attention and intelligent debate. This book is meant as a starting point.

—Paul M. Barrett
August, 2007

Selected Bibliography

An accessible translation of the Quran, together with illuminating commentary, is found in Muhammad Asad's *The Message of the Quran*. Gibraltar: Dar Al-Andalus, 1980.

I benefited from reading these books:

Abou El Fadl, Khaled. *Conference of the Books: The Search for Beauty in Islam*. Lanham, Md.: University Press of America, 2001.

———. *Speaking in God's Name: Islamic Law, Authority, and Women*. Oxford: Oneworld Publications, 2001.

———. *The Place of Tolerance in Islam*. Boston: Beacon Press, 2002.

Algar, Hamid. *Wahhabism: A Critical Essay*. Oneonta, N.Y.: Islamic Publications International, 2002.

Armstrong, Karen, *Islam: A Short History*. New York: Modern Library Chronicles, 2000.

Aslan, Reza. *No god but God: The Origins, Evolution, and Future of Islam*. New York: Random House, 2005.

Carson, Clayborne. *Malcolm X: The FBI File*. New York: Carroll & Graf Publishers, 1991.

Dannin, Robert. *Black Pilgrimage to Islam*. Oxford: Oxford University Press, 2002.

Eck, Diana L. *A New Religious America: How a "Christian Country" Has Become the World's Most Religiously Diverse Nation*. New York: HarperCollins, 2001.

Esposito, John L., ed. *The Oxford Encyclopedia of the Modern Islamic World*. Oxford: Oxford University Press, 1995.

Hadad, Yvonne Yazbeck, and Jane Idleman Smith, eds. *Muslim Communities in North America*. Albany: State University of New York Press, 1994.

Haley, Alex. *The Autobiography of Malcolm X*. New York: Grove Press, 1965.

Herberg, Will. *Protestant—Catholic—Jew*. New York: Anchor Books, 1955.

Kabbani, Sheikh Muhammad Hisham. *Classical Islam and the Naqshbandi Sufi Tradition*. Washington, D.C.: Islamic Supreme Council of America, 2004.

Kahf, Mohja. *E-mails from Scheherazad*. Gainesville: University Press of Florida, 2003.

Leonard, Karen Isaksen. *Muslims in the United States: The State of Research*. New York: Russell Sage Foundation, 2003.

Lewis, Bernard. *The Crisis of Islam: Holy War and Unholy Terror*. New York: Modern Library, 2003.

Lincoln, C. Eric. *The Black Muslims in America*. Boston: Beacon Press, 1961.

Nomani, Asra Q. *Tantrika: Traveling the Road of Divine Love*. San Francisco: HarperSanFrancisco, 2003.

Poston, Larry. *Islamic Da'wah in the West: Muslim Missionary Activity and the Dynamics of Conversion to Islam*. Oxford: Oxford University Press, 1992.

Rauf, Imam Feisal Abdul. *What's Right with Islam: A New Vision for Muslims and the West*. San Francisco: HarperSanFrancisco, 2004.

Safi, Omid, ed. *Progressive Muslims: On Justice, Gender, and Pluralism*. Oxford: Oneworld Publications, 2003.

Wolfe, Michael, ed. *Taking Back Islam: American Muslims Reclaim Their Faith*. New York: Rodale, 2002.

Acknowledgments

Many of the people named in this book gave generously of their time; I am deeply grateful to them. There are others I would like to acknowledge: Mitch Horowitz, a thoughtful friend, urged me to write the book in the first place. My agent, Stuart Krichevsky, helped sharpen the proposal and has provided wise counsel every step of the way. John Glusman, formerly of Farrar, Straus and Giroux, got things launched there. Paul Elie, who took over as my editor at FSG, asked astute questions and offered excellent suggestions on structure and tone. My tireless in-house editing staff of Laurence Barrett and Julie Cohen improved early drafts. Betsy Russell and Ashley McGovern helped with research, and copy editor Pearl Hanig saved me from many errors.

Several chapters stem from reporting I did while at *The Wall Street Journal*, where Mike Miller and Ellen Pollock offered valuable guidance. My longtime *Journal* colleague (and current *BusinessWeek* boss) Stephen Adler backed the book from the start.

Once again, my beautiful and talented wife, Julie Cohen, untangled the knots—journalistic and psychological—and never wavered in her love. I don't know where I'd be without her.

Index